MIDLOTHIAN PUBLIC LIBRARY

3 1614 00187 19

P9-CCG-950

DUCT TAPE CREATIONS

Jane Yates

WINDMILL BOOKS

MIDLOTHIAN PUBLIC LIBRARY
14701 S. KENTON AVENUF
MIDLOTHIAN, IL 60445

Published in 2017 by Windmill Books, an Imprint of Rosen Publishing
29 East 21st Street, New York, NY 10010

Copyright © 2017 Windmill Books

All rights reserved. No part of this book may be reproduced in any form
without permission in writing from the publisher, except by a reviewer.

Developed and produced for Rosen by BlueAppleWorks Inc.
Creative Director: Melissa McClellan
Managing Editor for BlueAppleWorks: Melissa McClellan
Designer: T.J. Choleva
Photo Research: Jane Reid
Editor: Kelly Spence
Craft Artisans: Eva Challen (p. 8, 9, 12, 14, 20, 24, 28); Jane Yates (p. 10, 16, 18, 22, 26, 30)

Photo Credits: cover left Mahathir Mohd Yasin/Shutterstock; cover right Siberia Video and Photo/Shutterstock; title page, page
tops, p. 4, 6–31 Austen Photography; TOC background Madlen/Shutterstock; p. 4 top right Gerald Bernard/Shutterstock; p. 4
bottom left antpkr/Thinkstock; p. 4 bottom right Samantha Roberts/Shutterstock; p. 5 left to right and top to bottom: kontur-
vid/Shutterstock; Odua Images/Shutterstock; Austen Photography; oksana2010/Shutterstock; Austen Photography; Coprid/
Shutterstock; Everything/Shutterstock; Austen Photography

Cataloging-in-Publication Data

Names: Yates, Jane.
Title: Duct tape creations / Jane Yates.
Description: New York : Windmill Books, 2017. | Series: Cool crafts for kids | Includes index.
Identifiers: ISBN 9781499482294 (pbk.) | ISBN 9781499482300 (library bound) | ISBN 9781508192800 (6 pack)
Subjects: LCSH: Duct tape--Juvenile literature. | Tape craft--Juvenile literature. | Handicraft--Juvenile literature.
Classification: LCC TS198.3.A3 Y38 2017 | DDC 745.5--dc23

Manufactured in the United States of America
CPSIA Compliance Information: Batch #BW17PK: For Further Information contact Rosen Publishing, New York, New York at 1-800-237-9932

CONTENTS

GETTING STARTED

You don't need a lot of materials for duct tape projects. Duct tape, also known as duck tape, is a strong, sticky **adhesive** made with cloth. Most duct tape is silver, but you can buy different kinds. Some rolls have colorful patterns, and you can write on others!

You can purchase all of the materials you need at a craft store or hardware store. Organize your supplies in boxes or plastic bins. Then, you can pull them out whenever you want to create duct tape projects!

PATTERNED
DUCT TAPE

DRY-ERASE
DUCT TAPE

COLORED
DUCT TAPE

SCISSORS

PENCIL

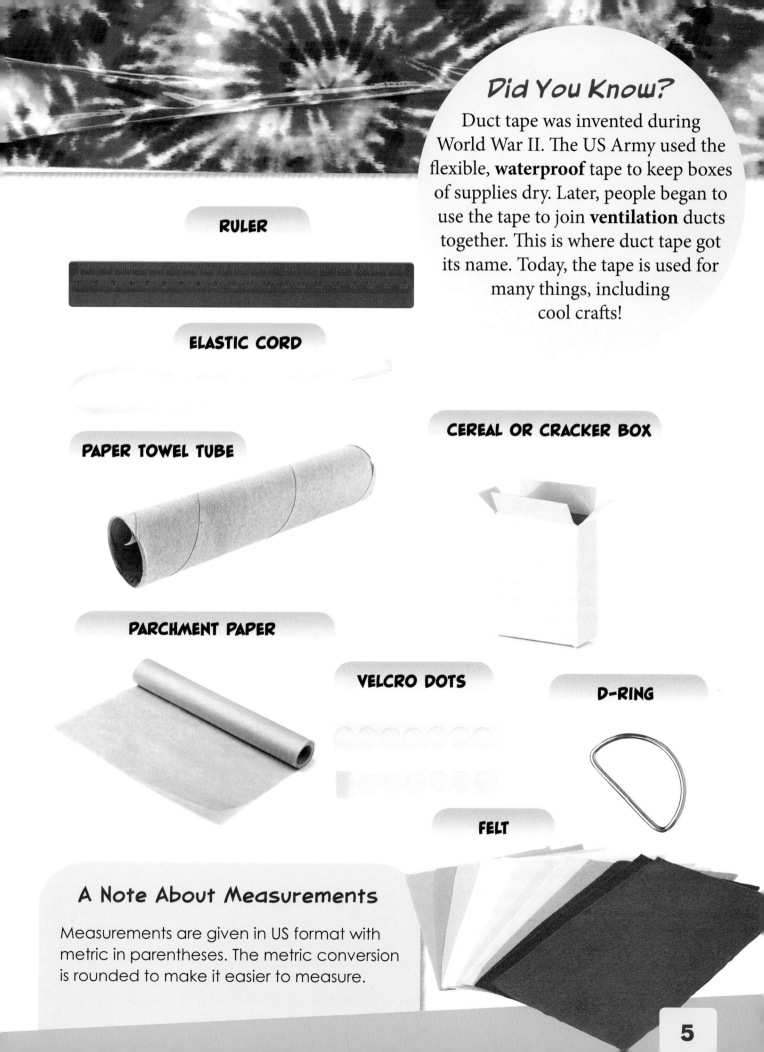

RULER

ELASTIC CORD

PAPER TOWEL TUBE

CEREAL OR CRACKER BOX

PARCHMENT PAPER

VELCRO DOTS

D-RING

FELT

Did You Know?

Duct tape was invented during World War II. The US Army used the flexible, **waterproof** tape to keep boxes of supplies dry. Later, people began to use the tape to join **ventilation** ducts together. This is where duct tape got its name. Today, the tape is used for many things, including cool crafts!

A Note About Measurements

Measurements are given in US format with metric in parentheses. The metric conversion is rounded to make it easier to measure.

TECHNIQUES

Have fun while making your duct tape projects! Your projects do not have to look just like the ones in this book. Choose the colors and patterns you like the best. Be creative and have fun!

Use the following techniques to create your duct tape crafts.

DOUBLE-SIDE FABRIC STRIPS

Cut one piece of tape. Lay it sticky side up, then cover it with another piece of tape.

DUCT TAPE RIBBON

Cut one piece of tape. Fold one side lengthwise toward the middle, then press it down. Repeat this step with the other side.

SINGLE-SIDE DUCT TAPE SHEET

Cut a piece of parchment paper. Cut several strips of tape that are about the same length as the paper. Place the strips on the paper. Each strip needs to slightly overlap the next. Continue until the sheet is covered. Use scissors to trim any extra tape that hangs off the edge. Then, peel the parchment paper off.

DOUBLE-SIDE DUCT TAPE SHEET

Make a single-sided sheet. Then, flip it over and cover the sticky side with overlapping strips of tape.

Tip

You can tear duct tape by holding each side and pulling in opposite directions. Wherever it says cut in the book, you can tear instead. (The edges are not quite as neat as when cut with scissors).

3-STRAND BRAID

To make a braid, start with three ribbons of tape. Tape the ends of each ribbon to a table. While you are braiding, don't pull the ribbons too tightly. Press down to keep them flat as you go.

1 Pull the yellow strand under the green strand.

2 Pull the patterned strand over the green strand.

3 Pull the yellow strand over the patterned strand.

4 Pull the green strand over the yellow strand.

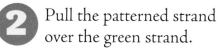

5 Pull the patterned strand over the green strand. Continue pulling strands over each other in this pattern. Try to make the braid as tight as possible.

BE PREPARED
- Read through the instructions and make sure you have all the materials you need.
- Clean up when you are finished and put away your materials for next time.

BE SAFE
- Ask for help when you need it.
- Ask for permission to borrow tools.
- Be careful when using scissors.

WRIST BAND

You'll Need:

✔ A cardboard toilet paper roll
✔ Small paper coffee cup
✔ Duct tape
✔ Scissors

1 Cut the toilet paper roll in half. Cut a space about 1 inch (2 cm) wide so the bracelet can fit around your wrist.

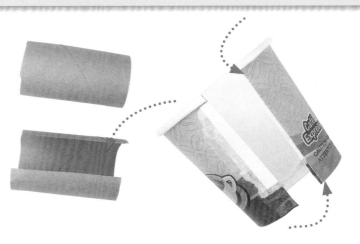

2 Measure a piece of tape that is slightly longer than the bracelet. Wrap it around the cardboard. Fold the tape over the edges to completely cover the bracelet.

Tip

Use a paper cup instead of a toilet paper roll. Make a cut across the side of the cup and remove the bottom.

3 To decorate your bracelet, cut squares, strips, and triangles out of different colors of tape. To make a border, fold narrow strips around the edges.

8

BASIC BELT

You'll Need:

✔ Two rolls of duct tape
✔ Two D-rings
✔ Scissors

1 Measure and cut two strips of tape. They need to be long enough to wrap around your waist. Press the sticky sides of the pieces together to make a double-sided strip.

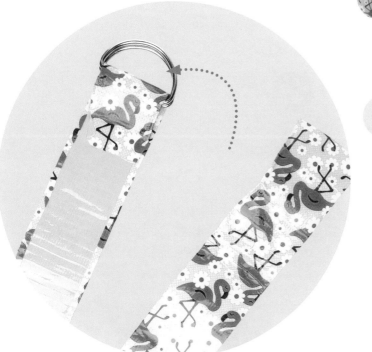

2 Lay the two D-rings at one end. Slide the strip through the rings, then fold it over as shown.

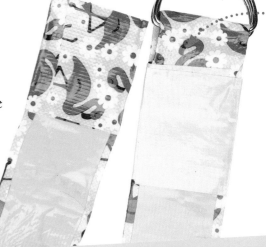

3 Use a small piece of tape to hold the folded end in place. Wrap a second piece of tape around the other end.

Tip

Use one of your own belts to measure the length needed for your duct tape belt!

9

BEADED JEWELRY

You'll Need:

- ✔ Two rolls of duct tape
- ✔ Drinking straws
- ✔ Elastic cord
- ✔ Scissors

NECKLACE

1 Cut a long strip of tape in half. Divide and cut it into 2-inch (5 cm) pieces.

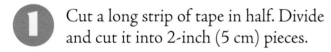

2 Wrap each strip around a straw.

3 To make each bead, cut the straw at the edges of the tape. Repeat Steps 1–3 until you have 24 beads.

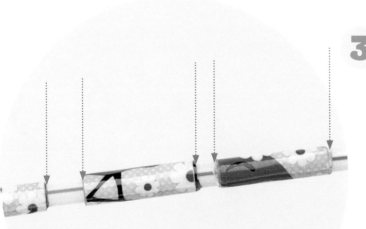

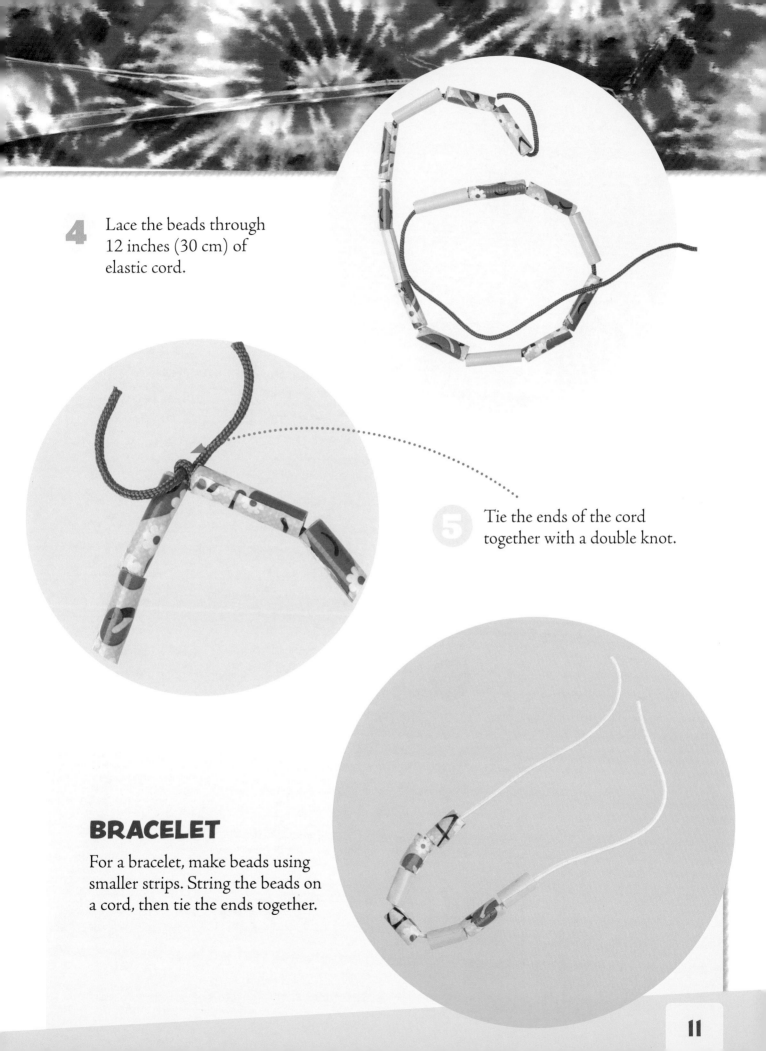

4 Lace the beads through 12 inches (30 cm) of elastic cord.

5 Tie the ends of the cord together with a double knot.

BRACELET

For a bracelet, make beads using smaller strips. String the beads on a cord, then tie the ends together.

FLOWER PENCIL

You'll Need:

- ✔ Four rolls of duct tape
- ✔ Pencil
- ✔ Scissors

1 To make the stem, cut a piece of green tape. It should be as long as the pencil. Tightly wrap the tape around the pencil. Make sure the tape is smooth and there are no ripples.

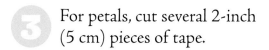

2 Wrap a small piece of orange tape around the eraser. This will be the center of the flower.

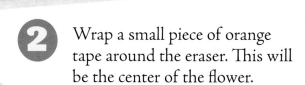

3 For petals, cut several 2-inch (5 cm) pieces of tape.

Tip

Try making different kinds of flowers with colored tape and by cutting the petals into different shapes.

4 Fold one end to make a triangle. Leave some of the sticky side showing at the other end. Repeat this step to make more petals.

5 Stick a petal onto the pencil just below the orange center. Continue attaching petals all the way around the pencil. Move down as you work. Add as many petals as you like to make a beautiful blossom.

SHAPED PETALS

6 For shaped petals, cut several 3-inch (8 cm) pieces of tape. To make a shaped petal, fold the piece almost in half, leaving a sticky strip at the bottom. Use scissors to shape the folded end into a petal shape.

BOW TIE

You'll Need:

- ✔ Two rolls of duct tape
- ✔ Elastic cord
- ✔ Scissors

1 Make an 8-inch (20 cm) double-sided strip.

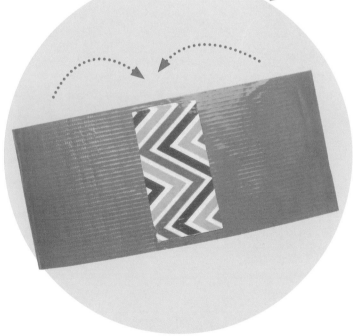

2 Fold each end toward the center. Use a small piece of tape to join the two ends together.

3 Cut a 4¼-inch (11 cm) piece of tape. Cut it in half lengthwise. Fold one half into a ribbon.

4 Hold the orange bow in the middle and pinch it to create folds.

5 Wrap the small ribbon around the center of the orange bow. Tape it in place.

6 Cut a piece of elastic long enough to fit comfortably around your neck. Tape the ends together, then the bow tie to it.

Tip
Tape the bow to a barrette to make a cool hair accessory!

STICKER HAT

You'll Need:

✔ Baseball cap
✔ Two rolls of duct tape
✔ Parchment paper
✔ Pencil
✔ Scissors

1 Cut several strips of tape that are slightly longer than the bill of the hat.

2 Cover the bill with the tape. Make sure you tuck the end of each strip under the bill.

3 Use a small strip to cover the band at the back of the hat.

4 Cut several long strips of tape. Cut one end into a point as shown. Cover the hat by lining up the points at the center. Tuck all the ends under the rim. Cut out a circle and place it on the top of the hat.

ADD STICKERS

5 To make stickers, you will need parchment paper. Draw shapes like hearts, stars, and circles. Then cover the other side of the paper with tape.

6 Cut out the shapes. Peel the paper away and decorate the hat with the stickers.

DRY-ERASE BOARD

You'll Need:

✔ Foam board
✔ One roll of dry-erase duct tape
✔ Two rolls of duct tape
✔ Scissors

1 Cut a 9-inch (23 cm) by 12-inch (30 cm) rectangle out of the foam board.

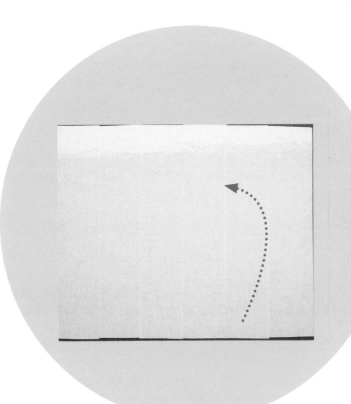

2 Cut six pieces of dry-erase duct tape. They should be about the length of the board. Remove the backing from the tape and stick each strip to the board. The edges should slightly overlap.

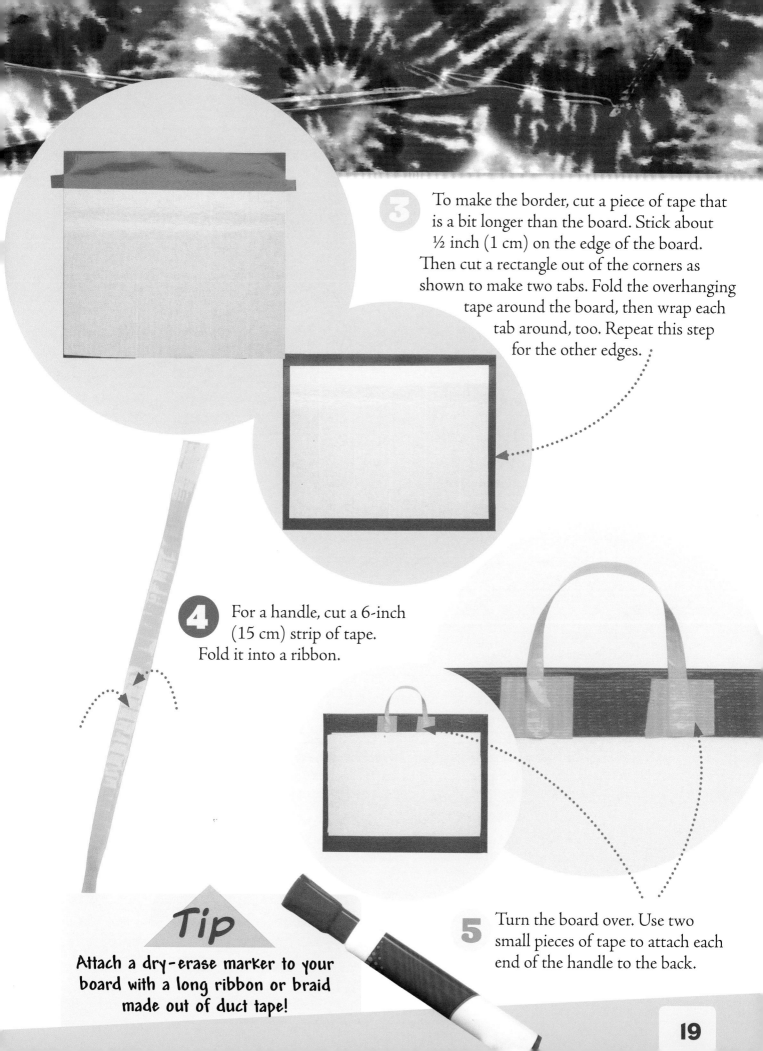

3 To make the border, cut a piece of tape that is a bit longer than the board. Stick about ½ inch (1 cm) on the edge of the board. Then cut a rectangle out of the corners as shown to make two tabs. Fold the overhanging tape around the board, then wrap each tab around, too. Repeat this step for the other edges.

4 For a handle, cut a 6-inch (15 cm) strip of tape. Fold it into a ribbon.

5 Turn the board over. Use two small pieces of tape to attach each end of the handle to the back.

Tip

Attach a dry-erase marker to your board with a long ribbon or braid made out of duct tape!

ADVENTURE BAG

You'll Need:

✔ A thin cardboard box
✔ Five rolls of duct tape
✔ Scissors

1 Find an empty cardboard box to use for your bag. A cereal box or cracker box works well. Cut off the top.

2 Cut long strips of tape. Use the strips to cover the front and back of the bag. Overlap the strips so there are no gaps.

3 After covering both sides, use red tape to add strips that cover the sides and bottom.

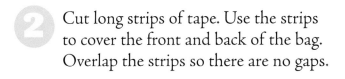

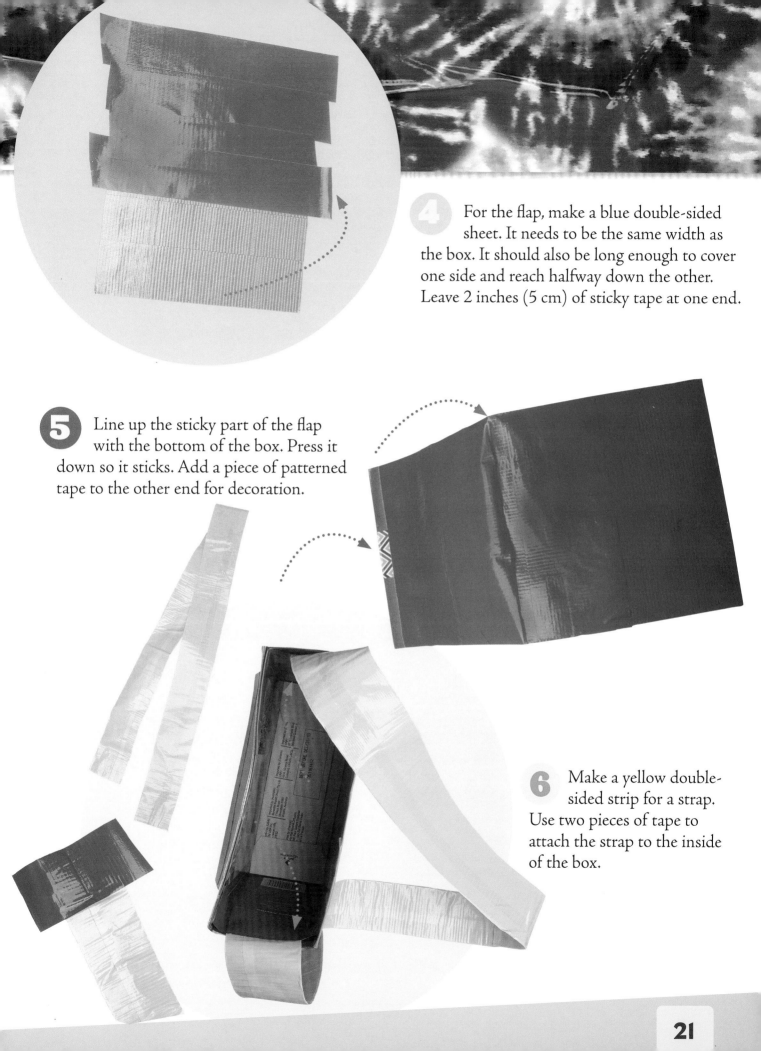

4 For the flap, make a blue double-sided sheet. It needs to be the same width as the box. It should also be long enough to cover one side and reach halfway down the other. Leave 2 inches (5 cm) of sticky tape at one end.

5 Line up the sticky part of the flap with the bottom of the box. Press it down so it sticks. Add a piece of patterned tape to the other end for decoration.

6 Make a yellow double-sided strip for a strap. Use two pieces of tape to attach the strap to the inside of the box.

DUCT TAPE SNEAKERS

You'll Need:

- ✔ A pair of sneakers
- ✔ One roll of patterned duct tape
- ✔ Scissors

1 Cut a piece of tape, then trim one side to made a half circle. Use it to cover the back of the shoe.

2 Cut more tape and cover the toe and tongue of the shoe. Smooth out any creases. Tuck the ends underneath the tongue.

Tip

If you have a ripple in your duct tape, pull it off and stick it back on. Rub your hand over it to remove any bumps.

3 Continue covering the sides. Tuck the ends inside the shoe.

4 Cut a long strip to cover the edge of the sole. Press the tape down, then smooth it out.

5 To make a slip-on shoe, cover the laces. For a lace-up shoe, poke holes through the tape on the eyelets, then feed shoelaces through.

TIE-DYE TIE

You'll Need:
✔ One roll of duct tape
✔ Scissors
✔ Elastic cord

1 Make a double-sided sheet that measures 3½ inches (9 cm) by 15½ inches (40 cm).

2 Cut the end into a point. Trim the sides so they taper toward the top as shown.

3 Make a double-sided sheet that measures 5½ inches (14 cm) by 2 inches (5 cm). Cut two corners off as shown.

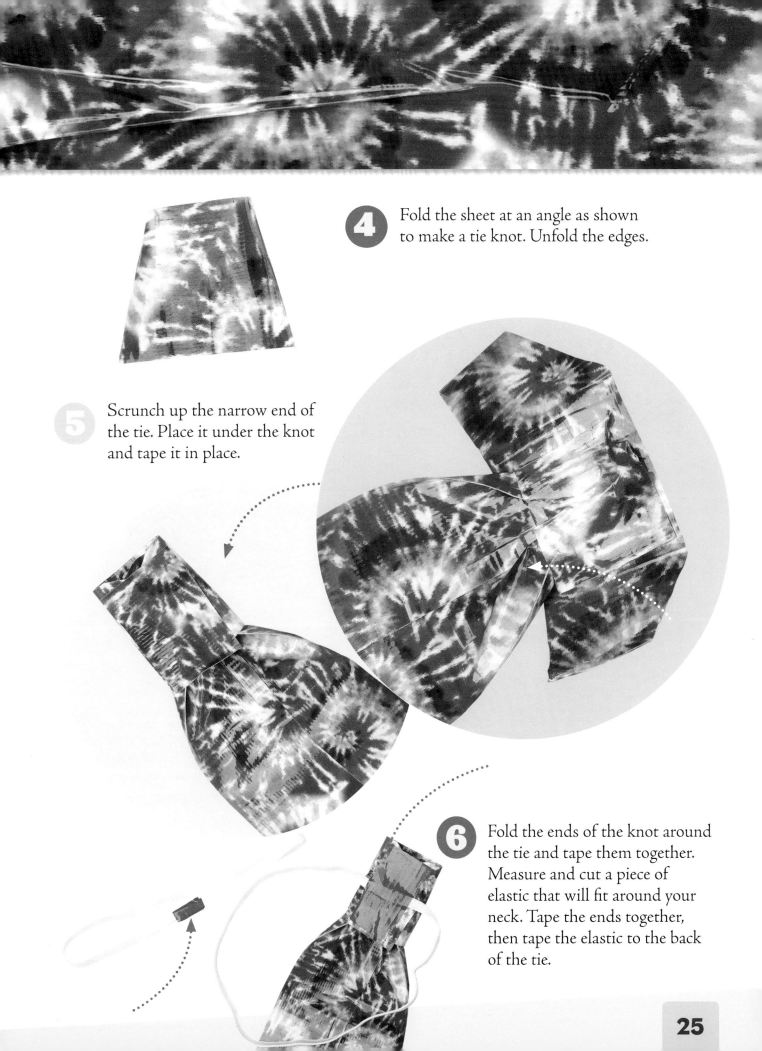

4 Fold the sheet at an angle as shown to make a tie knot. Unfold the edges.

5 Scrunch up the narrow end of the tie. Place it under the knot and tape it in place.

6 Fold the ends of the knot around the tie and tape them together. Measure and cut a piece of elastic that will fit around your neck. Tape the ends together, then tape the elastic to the back of the tie.

FLAG WALLET

You'll Need:

✔ Two rolls of patterned duct tape
✔ Ruler
✔ Scissors

1 Make two double-sided sheets that measure 8 inches (20 cm) by 3½ inches (9 cm).

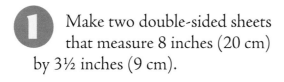

2 Line up the two sheets, then tape them together along the bottom. This will be the billfold.

3 To make two pockets, make another double-sided sheet. It needs to measure 7 inches (18 cm) by 3 inches (7 cm). Cut the sheet in half.

4 Cut three 3-inch (8 cm) strips of tape, then cut each strip in half lengthwise. Set four strips aside. Then, place one strip along the bottom of each pocket. Leave half of the strip overhanging the edge as shown.

5 Line up each pocket with the bottom of the billfold and at either end. Fold the sticky tape around the billfold to attach each pocket. Then, tape the top of each pocket to the inside edge of the billfold with two more strips of tape.

6 Use the last two strips to close the sides of the wallet as shown.

TABLET COVER

You'll Need:

- ✔ Three rolls of duct tape
- ✔ Felt
- ✔ Parchment paper
- ✔ Scissors
- ✔ Velcro dot

1 Trace an outline of the tablet on parchment paper. Cut it out. This will be your **template.**

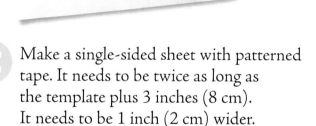

2 Make a single-sided sheet with patterned tape. It needs to be twice as long as the template plus 3 inches (8 cm). It needs to be 1 inch (2 cm) wider.

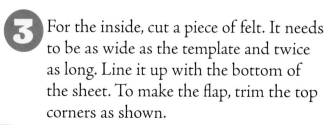

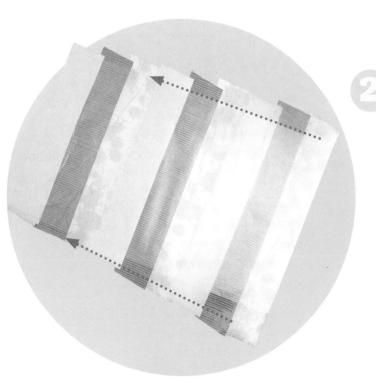

3 For the inside, cut a piece of felt. It needs to be as wide as the template and twice as long. Line it up with the bottom of the sheet. To make the flap, trim the top corners as shown.

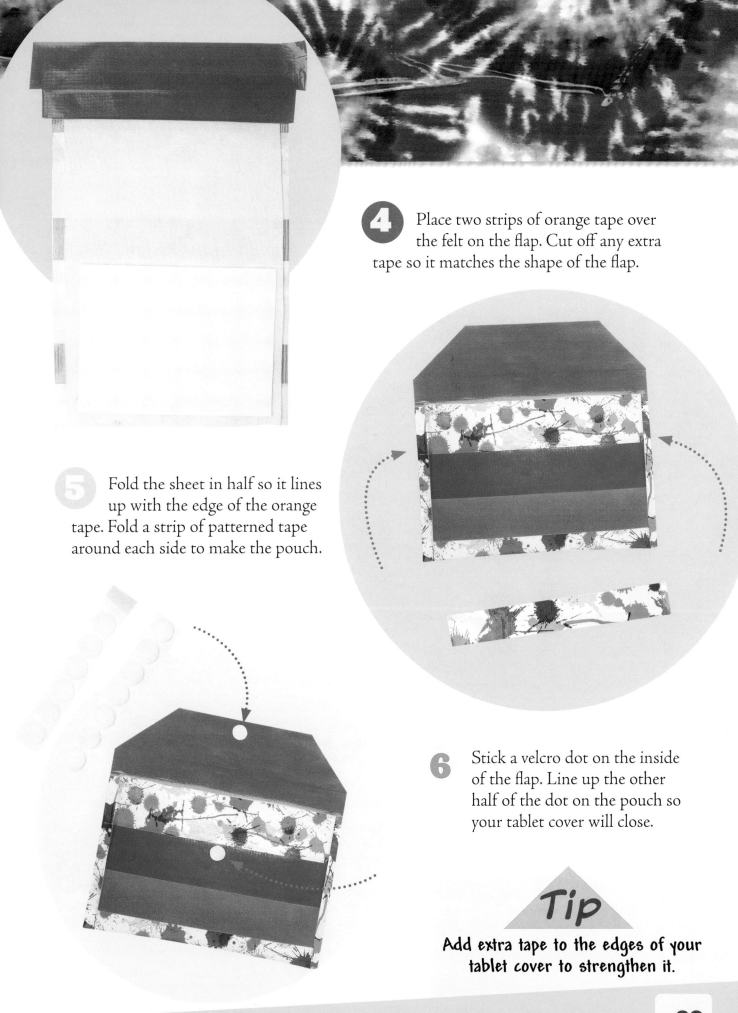

4 Place two strips of orange tape over the felt on the flap. Cut off any extra tape so it matches the shape of the flap.

5 Fold the sheet in half so it lines up with the edge of the orange tape. Fold a strip of patterned tape around each side to make the pouch.

6 Stick a velcro dot on the inside of the flap. Line up the other half of the dot on the pouch so your tablet cover will close.

Tip

Add extra tape to the edges of your tablet cover to strengthen it.

BRAIDED BRACELET

You'll Need:

✔ Three rolls of duct tape
✔ Scissors

1 Cut three strips of tape using different colors. Each strip needs to be 8 inches (20 cm) long. Cut each strip in half. Then, fold each strip into a ribbon.

2 Cut a small piece of tape and wrap it around the three ribbons at one end.

3 Tape the end to a flat surface. Braid the ribbon. (See page 7.)

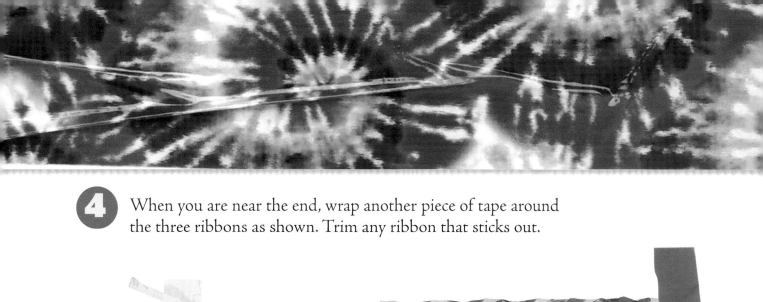

4 When you are near the end, wrap another piece of tape around the three ribbons as shown. Trim any ribbon that sticks out.

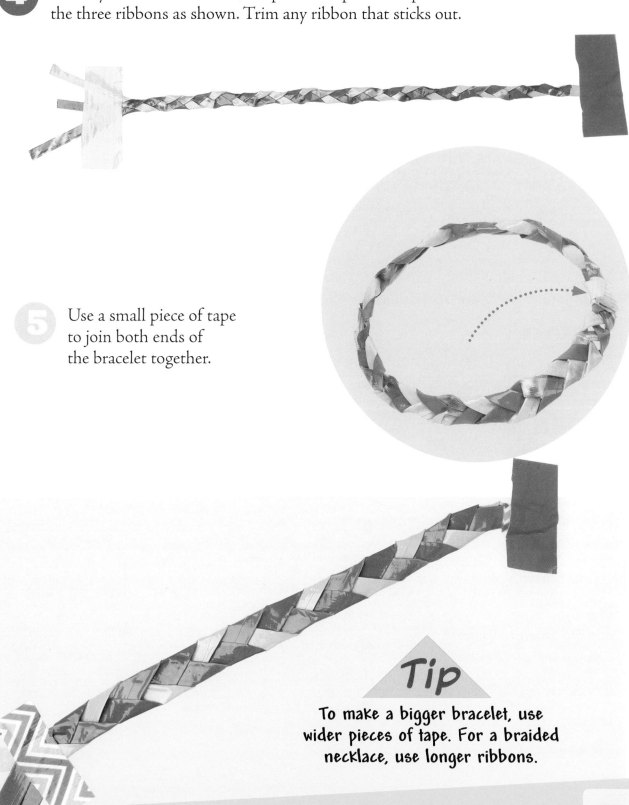

5 Use a small piece of tape to join both ends of the bracelet together.

Tip

To make a bigger bracelet, use wider pieces of tape. For a braided necklace, use longer ribbons.

GLOSSARY

adhesive Something that sticks to something else.

template A pattern or outline that is used as a guide.

ventilation A system through which air flows.

waterproof Describing a material that keeps water away.

FOR MORE INFORMATION

Further Reading

Formaro, Amanda. *Duct Tape Mania.*
White Plains, NY: Studio Fun International, 2014.

Knight, Choly. *Awesome Duct Tape Projects.*
East Petersburg, PA: Fox Chapel Publishing, 2014.

Morgan, Richela Fabian. *Tape It & Wear It.*
Hauppauge, NY: Barron's Educational Series, 2014.

WEBSITES

For web resources related to the subject of this book, go to:
www.windmillbooks.com/weblinks and select this book's title.

INDEX

W9-CII-023

Advance praise for

Plan Now or Pay Later

Judge Jane's No-Nonsense Guide to Estate Planning

by Jane B. Lucal

"It's common knowledge that you can't rule from beyond the grave. However, your will and your estate planning are your last conversation with your family. **This eye-opening book will help you** frame that conversation."

JUDITH A. SHINE, CFP
President, Shine Investment Advisory Services, Inc.

"An exciting and quick read …. **I wish all my clients would read Judge Lucal's book** prior to coming in for their first estate planning meeting."

RONALD CAPPUCCIO, J.D.
Tax and Estate Planning Attorney, Cherry Hill, NJ

"This book gives the average person all that's needed to plan and organize an estate. **It's like having a consult with an experienced estate attorney.** The judge's real-life case anecdotes illustrate why planning now truly does avoid paying later."

ROBERT CLOFINE
Certified Elder Law Attorney

"In my years of financial planning, I've found that death is a subject most people want to ignore. Procrastinate no more. Judge Jane's straightforward step-by-step approach to estate planning **makes it easy for anyone to take control**."

GINITA WALL, CPA, CFP
Financial Guidance, Forensic Accounting
Women's Institute for Financial Education

"**A clear, concise, and comprehensive look at estate planning**, this book not only gives the reader real-life examples of the consequences of not having an estate plan and not planning correctly, but also has an action guide to get the reader on the road to proper estate planning practices. **A must-read for anyone who is concerned about their assets and providing for their loved ones.** I highly recommend this book for anyone who is concerned about protecting their estate during their lifetime and at their death."

    KETRA A. MYTICH, J.D.
    Attorney and Counselor at Law, Peoria, IL

"I was impressed with the balance between lifetime planning and death planning. Judge Jane shows the importance of having your whole professional team involved in the process and proves that it's not really about documents—**it's about the results that are achieved for you and your family.**"

    DANIEL P. STUENZI, ATTORNEY AT LAW
    Coauthor of *Legacy: Plan, Protect, and Preserve Your Estate*
    National Network of Estate Planning Attorneys

"This is **a practical and fun book** to read. Readers especially learn a lot from the real-life stories."

    VIRGINIA L. WEBER
    Counselor at Law, San Diego, CA

PLAN NOW *or* PAY LATER

*Judge Jane's
No-Nonsense Guide to
Estate Planning*

Also available from
BLOOMBERG PRESS

Investing 101
by Kathy Kristof

Don't Die Broke:
Taking Money Out of Your IRA, 401(k),
or Other Savings Plan—and Creating
Lasting Retirement Income
by Margaret A. Malaspina

A Commonsense Guide to Your 401(k)
by Mary Rowland

The New Commonsense Guide
To Mutual Funds
by Mary Rowland

A complete list of our titles is available at
www.bloomberg.com/books

ATTENTION CORPORATIONS

Bloomberg Press books are available at quantity discounts with bulk purchase for sales-promotional use and for corporate education or other business uses. Special editions or book excerpts can also be created. For information, please call 609-279-4670 or write to: Special Sales Dept., Bloomberg Press, P.O. Box 888, Princeton, NJ 08542.

PLAN NOW *or* PAY LATER

*Judge Jane's
No-Nonsense Guide to
Estate Planning*

JANE B. LUCAL

BLOOMBERG PRESS

PRINCETON

© 2001 by Jane B. Lucal. All rights reserved. Protected under the Berne Convention. Printed in the United States of America. No part of this book may be reproduced, stored in a retrieval system, or transmitted, in any form or by any means, electronic, mechanical, photocopying, recording, or otherwise, without the prior written permission of the publisher except in the case of brief quotations embodied in critical articles and reviews. For information, please write to: Permissions Department, Bloomberg Press, 100 Business Park Drive, P.O. Box 888, Princeton, NJ 08542-0888 U.S.A.

Books are available for bulk purchases at special discounts. Special editions or book excerpts can also be created to specifications. For information, please write to: Special Markets Department, Bloomberg Press.

BLOOMBERG, BLOOMBERG NEWS, BLOOMBERG FINANCIAL MARKETS, OPEN BLOOMBERG, BLOOMBERG PERSONAL FINANCE, THE BLOOMBERG FORUM, COMPANY CONNECTION, COMPANY CONNEX, BLOOMBERG PRESS, BLOOMBERG PROFESSIONAL LIBRARY, BLOOMBERG PERSONAL BOOKSHELF, and BLOOMBERG SMALL BUSINESS are trademarks and service marks of Bloomberg L.P. All rights reserved.

This publication contains the author's opinions and is designed to provide accurate and authoritative information. It is sold with the understanding that the author, publisher, and Bloomberg L.P. are not engaged in rendering legal, accounting, investment-planning, or other professional advice. The reader should seek the services of a qualified professional for such advice; the author, publisher, and Bloomberg L.P. cannot be held responsible for any loss incurred as a result of specific investments or planning decisions made by the reader.

First edition published 2001

1 3 5 7 9 10 8 6 4 2

Library of Congress Cataloging-in-Publication Data

Lucal, Jane B.
     Plan now or pay later : Judge Jane's no-nonsense guide to estate planning / Jane B. Lucal.-- 1st ed.
         p. cm.
     Includes index.
     ISBN 1-57660-079-3 (alk. paper)
         1. Estate planning--United States--Popular works. I. Title.

KF750.Z9 L634 2001
346.7305'2--dc21

2001025318

Acquired by KATHLEEN A. PETERSON

Edited by RHONA FERLING

Book Design by LAURIE LOHNE / DESIGN IT COMMUNICATIONS

To Dean, who encouraged me to
keep writing this book when I wanted to stop;
To Jenny, who wanted me to finish the
book so she could read it.
To them—best friends—I dedicate this book.

Contents

P a r t   T w o

Estate Planning Tools

P a r t   T h r e e

Six Months to a Solid Estate Plan

A c k n o w l e d g m e n t s

I WISH TO THANK THE FOLLOWING people for their expertise, assistance, and willingness to provide valuable support and information.

— Barbara J. Lamb

— Carl McGookey

— Sarah S. Tintor

— Bea Van Meter

Special appreciation to Dean S. Lucal and the editorial staff of Bloomberg Press, in particular Rhona Ferling.

Part One

The Basic Concepts

Chapter One

Why You Need Estate Planning

WE AMERICANS PRIDE OURSELVES on taking care of our financial affairs—our checkbooks, savings accounts, investments, and company retirement benefits. In fact, we are willing to go to great lengths to obtain some measure of financial security for ourselves and those we love.

But we have a dangerous blind spot: we consistently fail to do the proper estate planning for ourselves, our families, and our estates. We are not aware of or do not understand how to shield our assets and our families in the event of an unexpected illness or disability. Even more important, we do not recognize that it is necessary, and essential, to safeguard our own interests, our assets, and our families at the time of our death or disability.

Do you care about who will make decisions for you if you get sick or disabled? Do you care who will receive your assets when you die? Do you care how your assets will be managed if you have a stroke or an automobile accident or are afflicted by Alzheimer's?

Do you want to control the decision making that is crucial if you become disabled? Do you want to avoid chaotic family decision making in the event of an unexpected illness or accident? Do you want to avoid crisis management and costly legal delays at the time of your disability or death?

If any or all of this matters to you, you need to do estate planning for yourself and your family—right now. This is the only way to protect yourself and your family and to secure your assets for the future.

What Is Estate Planning?

YOU MIGHT THINK ESTATE PLANNING is as simple as creating a will, something that one out of three adults has. If I have a will, you might reason, haven't I done my job? Haven't I protected myself and my family? Many people tell me, "This is what my Dad did, and everything went OK when he passed away."

This is how most people tend to think about estate planning, and they couldn't possibly do themselves a greater disservice. If you have a will, you have done only 10 percent of the estate planning you need to do, and not necessarily the most important 10 percent.

So what is estate planning, exactly? Some of its most important facets include:

➤ managing your resources to provide for your family before and after your death;

➤ determining how your possessions will be distributed to your heirs;

➤ arranging your assets so that they will escape probate and minimize estate taxes;

➤ financial planning to maximize the wealth you leave to your heirs.

Although there are probably as many definitions for estate planning as there are lawyers, you might think of it as a huge ball with strings attached in all directions, contained neatly and precisely in a box. The ball is your family. The strings are parents, grandparents, sisters, brothers, aunts, uncles, and children. Along the way, each has a different life: One gets married; one doesn't; one is poor; one is unemployed; one lives with Mom; one dies young. Some acquire a few dollars, some don't. Some plan, most don't. The box represents estate planning. It's like the shoe box on your back shelf that contains treasures, important papers, and pictures of the family. Like that shoe box, estate planning encompasses everything that is important to you and allows you to help the people you love get through life.

Estate planning is far more than a bunch of old legal documents. It is the way you look at life, and it reveals what you think is important. It is the unique way you contemplate and plan for the future, whatever it may hold. It gives you the once-in-a-lifetime opportunity to make decisions and plans that will safeguard you, your family, and your estate.

What Happens If You Don't Create an Estate Plan?

HERE'S A SAMPLING OF THE POTENTIAL CONSEQUENCES:

➤ You and your family members could be excluded from control of decision making during your lifetime and at your death.

➤ Your family and you could be denied access to your assets, during your life and at your death.

➤ The preservation of your assets could be limited at best.

➤ You may not have the fiscal management over your assets that you might have wanted.

➤ You and your family may have to expend time and funds to make or provide for the health care decisions that you failed to anticipate when you were able.

➤ The whole issue of income, state and federal taxes could be left to someone else to decide.

➤ Your estate taxes could be vastly increased.

➤ The cost of legal fees and administrative expenses could skyrocket because you failed to plan for yourself and your needs.

➤ You might add to the pain your family members will suffer if you become ill or disabled or die without making basic decisions to help them in their greatest time of need and of loss.

➤ Avoiding probate could be impossible if you don't plan properly.

Estate planning is a puzzle, one that you solve with your decisions. Planning for life is one half of the puzzle; planning for death is the other half. Both parts must be put together to make one comprehensive estate plan. Planning is critical to preserve your assets at the time of death, but it is just as important to manage life-and-death issues that may arise during your lifetime.

If you think about it, planning is involved in every aspect of your life. Your typical errands might be to go shopping at the grocery store, fill the car with gas, visit the library, stop by the bank, or go to the post office. You make plans to do these things because you want to accomplish something.

The only difference between the casual kind of planning you do on a day-to-day basis and estate planning is that estate planning deals with all of your assets, not just the check you write for groceries or clothing. Estate planning involves literally everything you own—cash, stocks, bonds, cars, house—and everything you owe, including your mortgage, loans, and debts. It is the combination of the two, superimposed over the events in your life and wrapped over, around, and through your life and that of your family.

To demonstrate how thoroughly estate planning considerations are entwined in our lives, assume that I am a married woman who works and contributes to the financial security of my family. What happens to me, to my family, and to the economic stability of my family if: (1) I become ill, (2) I become disabled, or (3) I die?

What happens if I must be cared for in a nursing home? What happens to my family's financial picture? Have I signed all of the documents to make certain that my family will make the medical decisions for me? That I will be taken care of with the least stress to my family? That my family will be financially protected under these new circumstances?

None of us wants to think we will become disabled—the victim of a stroke, brain disease, or car accident—but, of course, some of us will experience disability. Actually, the fact is that most of us will experience some disability at some time in our lives. No one is immune from some degree of disability, and this is true regardless of age, gender, or the nature of our employment.

Statistics indicate that 8.6 percent of the total U.S. adult population are work-disabled. Of those workers between the ages of fifty-five and sixty-four, 22 percent are work-disabled. Thus, those of us who are actively working today have a one-in-five chance of becoming disabled at some point in our lives.

In addition, we are living much longer than did our grandparents, and even our parents. An individual born in 1900 could expect to reach the age of forty. In 1950, that individual at birth was expected to live to age sixty-four. A person born in 1975 could expect to live to age seventy-two, in contrast to a person born in 1990, who can expect to live to age seventy-five.

With the advent of greater longevity comes the greater possibility of injury or disability. When the unexpected occurs, as it most assuredly will, you should have plans in place to make certain that you and those you love will have both the legal and the financial ability to continue to function. You need good planning for disability during your lifetime, because nothing is as important to individuals' long-term well-being as the planning necessary to care for a loved one incapacitated by illness, aging, or disability.

Upon your death, you want to make sure that your planning protects and preserves your assets for the benefit of your family. This is why you cannot afford to believe that a last will and testament is all you need for estate planning. A will may take care of a few things at the time of death, but it certainly does not address every estate planning issue, and takes care of nothing whatsoever during your lifetime.

As you can see, no other area of the law governs our personal well-being, our assets, and the financial well-being of our families as does that of estate planning. This is why estate planning is the most dynamic and, certainly for many people, the most important area of the law in this country today. No other area of the law touches as many people and their families as that of estate planning.

Who Needs Estate Planning?

EVERY ADULT WHO OWNS ANYTHING OR who has a family needs estate planning. Because you don't have a crystal ball to determine your future, you have to decide what might conceivably take place and plan for possibilities.

Planning may include looking for a better job, seeking medical benefits, or searching for the best investments for your money. It is not merely arranging your legal documents. It is integrating your daily life, your financial planning, your own special needs, and your family's needs into one comprehensive estate plan. Good estate planning also means spotting and creating opportunities to maximize assets and minimize risks, as well as integrating opportunities and assets into a plan for yourself or your family in order to meet future contingencies.

No planning is simple. In fact, even with a plan, it is possible that your estate will not be managed as smoothly as you hope. However, with solid advice from legal and financial advisers, you can develop a successful plan that will work for you and meet your future needs.

Unfortunately, through the years, both as an attorney and as a probate judge, I have witnessed cases that serve as prime examples of either poor or incomplete planning.

The Case of the Two Wills

IN 1967, MISS MARY KELLY died at age eighty-two, leaving a beautiful-ly handwritten will. In fact, she left two wills, each a masterpiece of the old-fashioned cursive writing that she learned as a child. In each will, she carefully listed each and every person she wanted to remember at her death, naming more than two dozen friends and leaving gifts to each one of $20 or $30. These gifts were not large by today's standards, but to a single woman who lived a frugal life working as a seamstress, the bequests represented substantial and meaningful gifts.

Perhaps the most unique thing about these wills was that Miss Kelly tried to achieve what most of us would like to do: she tried to remember, by each small gift, every person who had ever done her a kindness. Each name of a friend was listed with care, an amazing effort in itself.

Her first will was not admitted to the probate court because although she had signed it, there were no witnesses to her signature. Thus, by law, the document failed to be entered into the court's records. None of the individuals Miss Kelly had so carefully named ever knew of this will or of the gift of remembrance she intended to make.

Her other will, dated earlier in her life, was not admitted to the probate court because although her witnesses had signed it, she had not. Again, this will was not admitted, and again, none of the individuals named ever knew of Miss Kelly's wish to remember them.

What happened to her estate? All of her possessions were liquidated. Even her few family heirlooms, such as an antique train set that had been in the family for years, an antique marble table, and a small, beautiful old lamp, were sold.

After the sale, a legal proceeding followed that lasted approximately three years. It was called a "determination of heirship proceeding," in which the court determined that 32 of the approximately 133 distant relatives (whom Miss Kelly had never seen) qualified to receive fractional interests from her estate. The largest distributive share, $606.64, went to an individual who had never heard of Miss Kelly. Her friends received nothing and never heard about her two wills.

Since her intentions were so strong, why didn't Miss Kelly see a lawyer? Probably for the same reason one of my clients was reluctant to have a lawyer draft her will. She told me, "It's the last thing that people will read of mine and the last statement of my philosophy I can leave, and I simply want to make sure it reflects who I am, and not some lawyer's wording." This is not unusual. More people write their own wills than is commonly known. Often those wills are fine and continue smoothly through the court system. Unfortunately, Miss Kelly's will was not one of those.

As with all wills that fail to be admitted in the probate court, the real tragedy of this story is that Miss Kelly's friends never knew of her attempts to remember them. But courts work by concrete standards established by legislative process. One of the most stringent is the law that a will must be in writing, signed, and witnessed. This is known as the "threshold" issue: If you want to gain access or a threshold to the court, so that your wishes are followed and your property distributed, then you must comply with this law.

The moral of the story is that if you are serious about having your wishes followed after you die, get legal advice and follow it.

The Case of the Man Who Forgot

ATTORNEY JAMES J. WHITE was one of the brightest attorneys in the field of estate planning in his community. He represented hundreds of individuals and families and was legal counsel to large multimillion-dollar corporations. He was a "lawyer's lawyer" who was highly respected.

Years before trusts became popular, Jim created a trust for the management of his assets. His thinking was that if he became disabled, he and his wife would be protected because his trustee, who was some years younger than he, could manage his investments and continue to provide income for his and his wife's care.

In fact, Jim did become disabled in his eighties from age-related infirmities. All went well. His trustee continued to manage his assets and forwarded monthly checks to his home.

But then more important problems arose. Jim gradually entered into the early states of dementia. At the same time, his wife became very ill and could not make any decisions other than taking care of herself from day to day.

The trustee continued to manage the funds, and caretakers continued to look after the couple and their daily needs. But finally the day came when it was no longer feasible to care for Jim at home. The wife's caretakers could handle her, but Jim was a physically big man and needed more and more specialized help. But by this time, his wife was in the middle stages of Alzheimer's disease and could no longer make decisions.

Although the trustee could make investment decisions under the terms of the trust, no one had the authority to make day-to-day health care decisions for Jim. His wife and family were not authorized to act for Jim, as he had not given them the power to do so. Nor did anyone have the authority to act for Jim's wife. No one could deal with the doctors and the lawyers at a time in their lives when important decisions had to be made.

Eventually, the court appointed as guardian Jim's secretary of many years, who had handled a great deal of his banking for him. She served as Jim's guardian for a few years, until he died, and then served for seven years longer as his widow lingered on in dementia. As Jim's guardian, she had to deal with medical treatment issues and, eventually, with "do not resuscitate" orders and orders prohibiting the use of feeding tubes and ventilators, in accordance with Jim's wishes. But because the court had appointed the secretary and not some well-meaning cousins, conflict overshadowed the last years of Jim's life—the very thing he had tried to prevent.

As a lawyer, Jim did exactly the right things: he established a living trust, funded it, and put a professional investment counselor in charge of the funds and distribution of the income to himself and his wife. He could well foresee the time when he would no longer be astute enough to manage his business affairs. But he simply could not fathom that one day he would not be able to manage his own day-to-day needs. This is not unusual, because even intelligent and realistic planners have a difficult time planning for a future that may include dementia and senility. However, that possibility makes it all the more essential that we plan ahead for our own well-being.

The tragedy? Although his trustee could make investment decisions for Jim during his lifetime, no one was authorized to make health care decisions for him. A court-appointed guardian had to be appointed to deal with medical treatment issues and, eventually, with "do not resuscitate" orders and orders prohibiting the use of feeding tubes and ventilators, in accordance with Jim's wishes. But during the last days of his life, his loved ones were burdened with uncertainty. It was a sad legacy.

These are real cases and real people—two people who tried to plan but failed. Miss Kelly wanted to remember each friend but did not understand the legal requirements necessary to carry out her wishes. Jim used his considerable legal talents to authorize a trustee to manage his assets in the event of his disability, but he failed to take the simple precautions necessary to guide health care decisions for him and his wife when he could no longer make those decisions for himself.

Estate Planning Reduces Taxes, Fees, and Frustration

YOU MAY HAVE HEARD STORIES ABOUT HOW some wealthy man failed to do proper estate planning and his estate ended up paying millions of dollars to state and federal taxing authorities. The Howard Hughes estate is one such prime example. Hughes, an eccentric, reclusive billionaire who was said to have been the richest man in America, died aboard a small private plane en route from Mexico to the United States.

Three states—Texas, California, and Nevada—claimed Hughes as a resident, and his estate was subject to millions of dollars in state estate taxes. The IRS claimed that the document known as his "will" was an invalid instrument. As a result of these arguments and the resulting litigation in a number of state and federal courts and before various agencies, the Hughes estate paid millions in taxes to both federal and state taxing authorities.

But how does estate planning save money for the average person who is not a Howard Hughes? First, if you plan in advance, taxes payable at death may be diminished or completely eliminated. Second, proper planning can either reduce or eradicate both court costs and legal fees.

With that said, there are some instances in which you may need a court to oversee your estate, especially if you anticipate problems among family members. In such cases, a probate process may be essential, and the fees may be acceptable expenses.

Typical candidates for court intervention include cases of conflicting interests among family members or cases that involve a family farm or business. For example, a man who runs his own business may say in his will, "I want all of my assets divided equally among my four children." But a bank or trust company may have a difficult time deciding how best to do that when one child wants to run the business and the other children need the money and want to sell it.

This is not to say that arguments cannot be settled in other ways, but they seldom are. Parents often avoid direct discussion with their children about serious financial differences in the family and therefore usually do not resolve problems while they are alive. The real-life case that follows perfectly illustrates the consequences of this type of avoidance and underscores the need for careful estate planning.

The 1945 Open Case

ONE SUNNY DAY IN THE SPRING of 1986, a young woman came into my court to ask when her grandmother's estate would be settled. When I asked her the date of her grandmother's death, she replied, "Nineteen forty-five." Upon hearing that, I insisted that the case must be closed because "courts do not keep estate matters open that long." The young woman was equally adamant that it was not closed. After examining the file, I was amazed to find the case was still open. Furthermore, the estate still contained assets valued in excess of $100,000 that had never been distributed.

Apparently, the young woman's aunt, whom the court appointed in 1946 to be the estate administrator, lived in a house that was part of the estate property. This woman, a daughter of the original owner, thought that as long as she lived, she would control everything. As it turned out, she did. Her sisters and brothers—the owner's other children—probably did not intervene because they loved her and didn't want to undergo embarrassing litigation. They also believed that she was entitled to live in the house for the rest of her life.

The matter resurfaced upon the death of this estate administrator. When the owner's will was reexamined, the truth was that the property should have been distributed to the owner's children in equal shares! Unfortunately, because forty years had passed, some beneficiaries (the owner's children and grandchildren) had died without ever receiving their rightful inheritance, since no distribution from the estate had been made while the estate was in the court system.

In the end, a proper distribution was made of all of the assets in the estate so that each beneficiary (or their beneficiaries) finally received the proper share according to the wishes of the deceased, although it took forty years from the time the estate was first filed in the court.

How can this sort of thing happen? The answer is, much more easily than you would think. Before computers, much of a court's case tracking was done on paper. When estates moved through the courts to conclusion, all was well. However, when some cases got stuck in the process and there was no one to file a motion or in any other way bring the matter to the judge's attention, then the case could languish in dusty file cabinets for years and years, unresolved and forgotten.

This is why judges today are mandated by strict guidelines to expedite estate cases. Those who fail to advance cases on their dockets may be held accountable by the supreme court of their state, through sanctions, fines, and other penalties. These new rules, together with computerization of the probate process, helps ensure that every case that comes into the system is tracked, moved along, and finished. Still, there may be other old, forgotten cases, just like this one—waiting for someone to walk into a court and tell the judge that they are still unresolved.

Deciding Who's in Charge

OF COURSE, NOT EVERY ESTATE THAT is involved with the court system gets enmeshed for so many years. It is safe to say, however, that when a case enters the probate system, it remains in the system between nine months and two years. During that time, things remain unsettled, and often the fiduciary (the court-appointed person in charge of the estate) cannot make any distribution of assets to family members during the probate administration. This may create significant hardship for a family or a family member who has real financial needs that must wait for a distributive share.

A sad truth is that whenever an individual becomes disabled or dies, a whole series of events takes place, but the primary question driving all of those events is: Who is now in charge? The issues of decision making and control in disability and death situations are the two central questions that emerge in estate planning. Evaluating who should be in charge of making decisions, under what circumstances, when, and for how long is a continuous process that underlies all estate planning. This can encompass choosing which stocks to buy, naming an individual to make health care decisions in the event of your disability, targeting the proper legal documents to put in place, and deciding how someone will administer your assets if you are unable to do so.

No other goal is as important today as making sure that you will be taken care of during your lifetime if you become unable to care for yourself. You want to make sure that you have enough assets to pay for your care and that your family will be financially secure even if you become ill or disabled.

Although you may not know right now how you will ultimately handle all of these issues, you will begin, as you work through your estate plan, to address and resolve your estate planning concerns. You will make decisions for yourself, and you will choose who will address health care, investment, and family matters for you, if and when you cannot do so.

Six Common Myths About Estate Planning

ONE OF THE MAJOR REASONS PEOPLE fail to do effective estate planning is that they make false assumptions about a number of legal issues. Many people have acquired the following ideas:

➤ Avoiding probate is always a good idea.
➤ Taking the full marital deduction is a given.

➤ Making lifetime gifts to your children helps them.

➤ Assigning ownership of a life insurance policy to your spouse is a smart move.

➤ Jointly owning property is the easiest and best way to transfer property on death.

➤ You should put property in trust for your spouse so that he or she won't have to be concerned with handling financial matters after your death.

In fact, each one of these statements is fundamentally wrong, and each reflects a common misunderstanding of legal reality. First, circumventing the probate process is not always the best idea. The truth is that completing the probate process may be the most efficient way to handle a problem estate. Courts determine conflicts through a clear and concise process. Each person has the right to legal counsel, and each has the right to assert a claim or defense. Such a process can be helpful when a family consists of several different spouses, children of different marriages and different ages, inherited property, and alimony and child support issues. In these complicated situations, courts are more ideally suited to resolve conflicts because they have the authority to impose either settlement or resolution and, ultimately, to issue a court order that imposes finality on the dispute.

You may be wondering why you should not take a full marital tax deduction, which is a dollar-for-dollar tax deduction given for property passing to a surviving spouse upon the other spouse's death. The reason is that using the full deduction may prove to be extreme costly when both spouses are gone. By not taking the full marital deduction at the time of the first spouse's death, you will be able to increase, up to a maximum of 200 percent, the total amount of property flowing to the ultimate beneficiaries free of federal estate taxes. This is the underlying purpose of a marital deduction trust—to increase the total amount the beneficiaries of a married couple can leave to their beneficiaries, who are often their children and grandchildren.

The treatment of tax issues upon the death of the first spouse must be carefully determined by calculations and consultation with a tax expert to make the correct decision for the deceased spouse's estate as well as for the surviving spouse. There are no easy answers, because each situation is unique.

On the issue of lifetime gifts to children, making such gifts may put them in higher tax brackets and may actually cost them more money in taxes now or later than you are giving them today. As for assigning ownership of your life insurance policy to your spouse, you are gambling that your spouse will outlive you; if that doesn't turn out to be the case, you have just increased the taxability of his or her estate significantly.

Finally, if you put funds in trust so that your spouse will not have to be concerned about financial matters, consider this: your spouse may have no say whatsoever in how the funds are invested, managed, or distributed to him or her. Do you really want to deprive your spouse of any control whatsoever of those funds that may be crucial to his or her day-to-day lifestyle?

Start Setting Your Goals Now

LATER CHAPTERS WILL DISCUSS each of these issues in more depth. For now, just remember not to be swayed by bits and pieces of things that you read or other people tell you. Set your own goals, seek professional guidance, and then make your decisions based on sound advice. Here are some examples to jump-start your thinking.

Goals of Estate Planning
➤ Maximize lifetime assets and make sound health care decisions
➤ Preserve your assets
➤ Save time and money
➤ Efficient distribution of assets
➤ Minimize taxes
➤ Provide for control of assets and health care decisions at times of disability and death
➤ Protect your business interests
➤ Integrate your financial picture into your legal plans … for life and for death
➤ Pull together all of the financial, legal, and personal strands of your life into a single unified plan to serve you over the course of many years

With good planning, many of these questions and concerns can be managed. With no planning, calamity is likely to occur. You or your family will pay, not only in dollars and in time but also in frustration, stress, and anxiety. If you fail to plan, your family members will be required to participate in a legal procedure with which they are completely unfamiliar. They will be enmeshed in a system that is extremely frustrating to them at a time in their lives when they are least able to deal with it: when there is a death or a serious disability.

So now is the time to begin your estate plan. With some knowledge of basic estate planning concepts, a bit of patience, and good common sense, your plan will not only protect your family, it will protect you now, during your lifetime, when an estate plan is the most important protection you will ever need.

Chapter Two

Your Estate Today

S IMPLY STATED, YOU SHOULD BUILD an estate, preserve it, use it wisely during your lifetime, and, at death, pass it on to your family or others, ideally without first having it go through the IRS or the courthouse doors.

In order to understand and plan, however, you must first put yourself "in the picture." Understand that you are unique. No other person in the universe has exactly the same situation as you. Whether you are a single person or a married person, you have a real concern that your interests will be protected by good planning, especially during your lifetime.

And not only are you concerned about your own well-being, but you also have concerns about other family members, such as your spouse or children, and perhaps elderly parents, a handicapped child, or a close friend who is facing hardship. Therefore, if your estate plan is to succeed, you need first and foremost to focus on the particulars of your situation so that your estate plan will reflect your present and future concerns.

Identify Your Planning Goals

FIRST DECIDE WHAT YOU WANT to achieve with estate planning. Of course, you want to preserve your assets, but there are other goals that you may want to consider:

➤ Do you want to manage your assets all of your life?

➤ Do you want to share that responsibility with others gradually?

➤ Do you want to completely turn over the administration of your estate to someone else, such as a trust officer of a bank, when and if you no longer have the ability to handle your assets?

➤ Do you want to create a trust for one or all of your children that will last until they are twenty-five or fifty-five?

➤ Do you want special college funds available from insurance proceeds in the event of your death?

➤ Do you want to provide a college fund for your grandchildren?

When you begin to do estate planning, you should also start making basic decisions about difficult issues, those you have probably avoided confronting because they involve a thorny situation or person in your life. One of the main reasons people postpone estate planning is that they cannot bring themselves to address these problems. For example, which child should have the family farm? To whom should I leave my diamond engagement ring? Who will most appreciate Granddad's railroad watch? What about the artwork, the antiques, and my baseball cards? Who will take good care of and cherish my grandmother's crystal? What about the family pictures, the family Bible, a few precious gems, letters from World War I?

Since answering such questions is often an emotional and exhausting exercise, we do nothing. A friend of mine was exactly like that. Because he could not decide how to divide his home between his present wife and his two children from a previous marriage, he failed to write a will. When he died unexpectedly, no will was in place to express his wishes. For that reason, his home had to be sold, in compliance with state law, to achieve an equitable cash distribution between the wife and the children. Had my friend written a will, this tragic situation could have been avoided and other ways found to permit an equitable division between all of these individuals without jeopardizing his wife's interest in the home.

If you do not have a will or you have not signed any other legal documents to handle your estate, ask yourself why you haven't. Then make a plan so that you do not leave your loved ones without any road map for their future if you cannot be around to give them directions.

Setting goals in estate planning is a process. After you think about your unique situation and begin to refine the issues you want to resolve with an estate plan, you will begin to formulate your own goals.

All of estate planning is really an evolution in which you progress from simple thinking, such as "I have a will, and it gives everything to my wife," to a more complex and comprehensive way of thinking, such as "I have a will, but I also have other even more important documents in place, so that I can divide my estate in such a

way as to benefit my wife, my kids, and my elderly mother. I can also avoid or minimize state and federal taxes, stay out of the court system, and provide for management when and if I become disabled. And I can still control and integrate all that I
own for as long as possible." Now that is a good estate plan.

Establish Your Fiscal Identity

OF EQUAL IMPORTANCE, FROM AN ESTATE planning standpoint, is how you "think"
about finances. We all have certain impressions and attitudes about financial matters that govern our economic goals and our view of life in general.

One of my own first ideas about money came from my mother. She had been
deeply impressed to learn that her mother saved her "egg money" to leave to her
daughters upon her death because "she never owned anything, and she wanted her
girls to have something of their own." From that early discovery that not one of my
grandmother's close female relatives owned anything in their own right came this
idea about elementary finances: It is important to have a "little something."

What are your ideas about finances? What do you think, for instance, about these
basic monetary questions?

➢ What are the problems you face in accumulating an estate?

➢ How can you retain what you have and add to it?

➢ How do fiscal decisions you have made affect your everyday life?

➢ What common mistakes do you make in dealing with money?

The way you think about each of these questions will be reflected in your estate
plan. Often, we don't think about these matters at all. On a day-to-day basis, we go
about the business of living without giving much thought to the financial ramifications of our lives. We try to get a good job and increase our income to meet our
short-term goals: car payments, insurance, rent or home mortgage payments. But
for the most part, most people fail to plan effectively for their financial futures. And
your financial plan is an essential ingredient of your estate plan. An estate plan without solid financial data will produce a hollow plan lacking in substance.

Therefore, you should collect critical financial information for your plan. For
example, you should begin to gather information about your bank accounts, such as
where they are located, the number of each account, and the present balances.
Similarly, you need to list your stocks, bonds, and other investments. And be precise; the name of what you own isn't sufficient. List the names of the stocks, the
number of shares, and the stock certificate numbers if you have the stock in your

own name. If you hold stock in the name of an account with a brokerage firm, you need to make notes about that account—where it is located, the name the account is in, who your representative in the firm is, the account number, and the present value of the shares. In general, you should have a clear, concise picture of your assets and liabilities, to keep for yourself and to have available for the legal and financial advisers with whom you will be working.

Talk to your professional advisers, such as attorneys, financial planners, and accountants, as well as other family members, to get a snapshot of those assets that you want to list as "yours." You can establish a good baseline for your fiscal identity by calculating your net worth.

Determine Your Net Worth

YOU MAY BE A TEACHER, FARMER, RANCHER, engineer, doctor, writer, artisan, or civil servant, but from a strictly financial point of view, you are what you own. That means you must first determine your net worth before attempting to establish an estate plan. Net worth, your true value in fiscal terms, is easy to determine. Start with the total value of your assets, such as your car, house, cash, and stock. From that total value you subtract what you owe—all of your bills, such as your mortgage, car loan, and obligations, such as the house utilities and taxes due. Here are some examples of typical assets and liabilities.

Net worth is not a difficult concept even if you are not familiar with some of the

Assets Minus Liabilities = Net Worth

ASSETS	LIABILITIES
Annuities	Bills and Debts:
Cash	Alimony
Equity in Your Business	Car Payments
Insurance	Child Support
Investments	Credit Cards
Personal Property	Student Loans
Real Estate	Charge Accounts
Retirement Funds	Insurance Premiums
Savings Accounts	Mortgages
Miscellaneous Assets	Personal Loans
	Taxes

Keep Your Goals in the Forefront

The goals of financial planning are to:
➢ obtain security;
➢ achieve maximum income;
➢ increase principal assets; and
➢ transfer assets to future generations without depletion.

The goals of estate planning are to:
➢ protect and preserve what you have achieved in your financial plan;
➢ pass on your financial achievements efficiently and cost-effectively; and
➢ make assets available for personal and medical needs during your lifetime.

basic terms used in estate planning. With good information and a thorough under-standing of your own net worth, you can make excellent estate planning decisions. To determine this number, begin listing all of your assets and all of your debts. Try to be very comprehensive in this effort. List everything you own. Attribute an esti-mated value to each asset. This includes today's cash value of your life insurance pol-icy, the value of your retirement funds (even if you cannot withdraw them), and per-sonal possessions, such as artwork or collectibles you may own.

Likewise, list your bills. Include your car, boat, and house mortgage payments and the sums you pay for all insurance premiums. Be thorough, so that you have a true picture of your debts. Do not forget anything, because it will give an incorrect picture of your net worth. It is often difficult, if not impossible, to put everything into a comprehensive package the first time, so you will find yourself going back again and again to add to or delete items. Just be patient and take a step-by-step approach to your itemization.

Why is net worth so important? Because your planning is based on whether you have a $500 net worth, a $5,000 net worth, a $50,000 net worth, a $500,000 net worth, or even more. Or if it turns out you have negative net worth—you owe more than you own—you will at least have a better understanding of how to plan so that you will achieve your financial goals in the future.

Your net worth, together with your planning goals, forms the cornerstone for your ultimate estate. Once you have estimated your net worth, you can begin planning to maximize your security and that of your loved ones.

Increase Your Estate

HOW DO YOU ACCUMULATE AN ESTATE, in the face of rising costs and the increasing needs of a growing family? How do you increase your net worth when these and other factors work against the accumulation of an estate?

After reviewing thousands of estates as a sitting judge, I have reached a few basic conclusions about how average working people accumulate an estate. I have seen in case after case that hardworking people of average means can and do accumulate estates of sizable value. A recent article, "Getting Rich $100 at a Time," in *Changing Times* magazine put it succinctly: "No hot tips. No magic formulas. No tricks. You accumulate assets by hitching to the right vehicle and sticking with it." David Speck, executive of a Washington, D.C., securities firm, states, "Real wealth comes from the orderly, regular discipline of adding something, somewhere, all the time."

In 80 percent or more of the estates that pass through our courts, the deceased made no attempt to build assets of real value. In Ohio, for instance, the average estate that goes through the probate court system has an approximate value of $50,000 to $150,000. In fact, some estates are insolvent, meaning that the person who died left more debt than assets.

By and large, however, individuals who systematically attempt to put together an estate are able to do so. Most of us think that "only people who are smarter than we are" can accumulate assets, because we say to ourselves, "It takes so much to live today. I can't save. It's impossible to put any assets aside because I need all of my earnings right now just to make ends meet." However, with a plan and a strong desire to save, we can all do better, and it doesn't have to be only the very smart or the very rich who can build an estate.

The Case of the Wealthy Miser

MATTIE WAS SEVENTY-SIX YEARS OLD when she died. For years she had lived alone in partial seclusion at the edge of a small Midwestern town, farming and taking care of her modest needs. Her few distant relatives would visit on occasion to make sure that Mattie had groceries and that she was still all right, but they were never encouraged to stay long and were not in any way emotionally close to Mattie.

At her death, she owned the small farm that her parents had left her, together with the assets she had accumulated during her lifetime. Imagine her relatives' surprise when an inventory of Mattie's estate revealed the following assets:

Mattie's Estate

ASSETS	NET WORTH
1. Real Estate	$ 173,000
2. Financial Investments	
a. Managed Retirement Fund	9,025
b. Ohio Tax-Exempt Fund	60,073
c. Bond Fund	21,427
d. High Yield Tax-Exempt Fund	91,112
e. Annuity	87,600
f. Limited Partnership Fund	24,000
g. Mutual Funds	14,337
3. Mutual Life Insurance Company	2,400
4. Bank Accounts	
a. Checking Account	6,238
b. Savings Account	50,000
5. Car (8 years old)	0

DEBT	
Debt	**0**
Total Estate	**$ 539,212**

When asked how this woman had accumulated more than half a million dollars with only modest Social Security income, her niece replied, "Her utility bills were less than $30 a month. She saved her money. She didn't spend any money on much of anything … not even food."

Actually, when Mattie inherited the farm from her parents, she had a neighbor who owned some mutual funds and encouraged Mattie to buy some, too. Since Mattie lived alone and had no interests other than planting a small vegetable garden each spring, she became interested in trying to save money and making it grow. She bought her first mutual funds when she was in her thirties, and it became a hobby for her. She watched her accounts grow by tiny increments, in much the same way that she watched her garden grow.

Also, she never spent any money, except on life's bare necessities. Although most of us would not want to live like Mattie, she does prove that if you have the desire, you can accumulate an estate.

Keys to Building an Estate

FROM THE HUNDREDS OF ESTATES I'VE seen over the years, I know there are certain keys to success.

Be serious. Think about money. Most of us live from paycheck to paycheck and use credit cards when we want to purchase something at the moment. People who accumulate money think about how serious money is; they don't buy just because they want to.

Be determined. Plan to save and have an estate. Most of us do not think like that. We think it would be nice, but we don't plan to have much, and so we don't have much. People who have money have planned to have it.

Think about how to maximize what you have. If you have money to save, make sure you're getting the best rate of return on it. People who have accumulated assets review them every month to make sure they are getting the very best return all the time on their money. That's how they accumulate more assets. They watch each and every change in interest rates, and they aggressively put their funds where they can find the best return.

Understand the importance of compound interest. Compound interest is a great estate builder. If, for instance, you leave $10,000 invested for a period of time and allow the interest to build, your money will grow dramatically. At 8 percent for ten years you will have $22,080; at 10 percent, $26,851; and at 12 percent, you will have $32,620.

A regular investment of only $100, compounded annually, at 6 percent or 8 percent interest, will rapidly increase.

The Power of Compound Interest

INVESTMENT	PERCENT INTEREST	5 YEARS	10 YEARS	15 YEARS
$100	6%	$564	$1,318	$2,328
$100	8%	$587	$1,449	$2,715

Realize that you are not going to win a lottery and get rich quickly. If you want to have financial security, then it is up to you to do something about it. Don't expect Lady Luck to show up; she seldom does. Instead of expecting her to arrive on your doorstep, reassess what you can achieve on your own without her.

Understand that the acquisition of an estate is a lifelong goal. Although you do not get rich overnight, you can get reasonably secure over time. A person can put together assets over a long period of time and make financial security an attainable, realistic goal.

Understand the power of $100. Money is like a living plant. First, you get a small plant, such as $100, and then you keep it, add to it, and watch it increase and then increase again, over and over. It's true that those who have money make money. But it is true because those who have it preserve it one dollar at a time and try to turn the meager crop of bills into larger harvests of funds throughout the years.

Understand financial basics such as amortization of loans, investment options, and certain tax rules. Amortization is a big word for a simple concept. It is the term used to calculate the payment required over a definite period of time at the charged interest rate, in order to retire the loan in full. For example, if you want to buy a $10,000 parcel of real estate and pay for it in fifteen years, what will you pay each month on the loan if the bank charges 7.5 percent on your loan? To find out, check *McGraw-Hill's Interest Amortization Tables,* by Jack C. Estes and J. Estes with Dennis R. Kelley (published by McGraw-Hill). Although other books are available on the topic, this one is the most comprehensive and the least expensive at about $10. You can usually find this book at your local bank, library, or bookstore, or at www.bn.com (the Barnes and Noble Web site). You can also find amortization tables online at www.mortgage-x.com.

To use the tables in the book, find the amount of the loan ($10,000 in this case), find the rate of interest (7.5 percent), and run your eye across the columns until you find the term of years, which is fifteen in this case. The answer? You will pay $92.70 per month for fifteen years to pay your loan of $10,000 at 7.5 percent interest. If you want to maximize your funds, you must understand interest rates and how they apply to your loans; that way you can look for the best rates available.

Know your investment options. Put your funds in the best place for you, whether that is U.S. bonds, certificates of deposit, triple tax-free bonds, stock, insurance, deferred compensation, IRAs, or annuities. Research all of these options and select—perhaps with professional help—those that are best for you from a personal, tax, and investment standpoint.

Finally, know your tax bracket and realize the consequences of it. If you are in the 28 percent bracket, 28 percent of every dollar you earn will go for taxes, and so will each dollar you receive as a dividend or in interest. Your tax bracket should influence your investment decisions. For example, consider that a bank certificate of deposit provides taxable income, and a tax-exempt fund may give you triple tax-exempt income.

Create goals and keep striving to meet them. Every expert extols the advantages of having a budget. In fact, most experts say that you should save between 10 and 15 percent of your net income. If this seems to be an unrealistic goal for you, perhaps a more realistic goal is to attempt to save $10 a week for a month. If you succeed, try to save $20 a week for the next month. Or set a goal that, in your opinion, is realistically attainable and build on your success by increasing your goal. One way to think about it is to pay yourself first each month, sending money to your savings or brokerage account just as you would any creditor, so that you set aside some funds for savings.

Be tenacious. Never give up. Keep trying to build an estate, little by little, and you will succeed. It's similar to a diet. You try to lose those extra pounds, but you really want that dessert tonight. So you try again tomorrow, and one day, you do lose weight. If you keep trying, you will eventually save some money.

Eliminate one expense each month. In the credit-card age, which makes an extra movie or dinner out painless until later, try to do without those extras, even if it is only once a month. Put aside the money you save.

Avoid instant buying. The experts say it all the time: Don't see it and buy it. Eliminate impulse buying. Think about your money. If you see the perfect suit to buy, for example, try thinking about it for three days before you make a buying commitment, and then purchase it only if you feel that you absolutely need it.

Cut back on credit card use. People who build estates usually have one or no credit cards. They are very mindful of the interest they are paying for the luxury of credit cards, and they buy on credit only sparingly so as not to pay more interest on their credit card bills than they receive on their investments. Interest on an investment may be 6 percent; interest charged on your credit card debt may be twice or even three times that much. This makes credit cards the single most expensive "convenience" in our lives.

Start small but think big. Visualize your success. If you are saving for a car or a home or a vacation, see yourself as a winner. You can save for those items if you decide to do so. But you don't have to buy the nicest car; purchase a reasonably priced car instead.

Read publications about financial matters. Open your mind to money issues.

Educate yourself about the world of finance. As with any subject, you need to learn about money. You start by reading books, magazines, and newspapers on the subject. Here is a list of reading materials to help you get started:

➤ *Barron's*
➤ *Consumer Reports*
➤ *Don't Die Broke,* by Margaret A. Malaspina (Bloomberg Press, 1999)
➤ *Fortune*
➤ *Guide to Your Investments 2000,* by Nancy Dunnan (Dun and Bradstreet, 1999)
➤ *Kiplinger's Personal Finance*
➤ *Money*
➤ *SmartMoney*
➤ *Staying Wealthy,* by Brian H. Breuel (Bloomberg Press, 1998)
➤ *USA Today* money section
➤ *The Wall Street Journal*

Don't count on anyone else. You are your best success story, so count on yourself. Like everything else that is worthwhile, it takes hard work day after day and year after year, but the end result is rewarding both to you and to future generations of your family, who will reap the rewards of your efforts and build on them to create even larger estates.

Never stop working. Industrious people work all the time. Lazy people can never accumulate assets … or anything else. The most successful people are those who are busy, busy, busy, whether they are full-time homemakers, stockbrokers, civil servants, or retirees. "Couch potatoes" cannot accumulate an estate. Busy people simply have full lives and produce the energy to save, accumulate, and concentrate on building their estates.

Make estate planning a generational goal. Although an estate may be acquired in a single generation with hard work, concentration, and planning, it certainly can be done by two or three generations of a committed, hardworking family devoted to saving, sacrifice, and careful management of assets, plus a focus on estate planning issues. Families can build an estate that will last for decades, provided each new generation pledges to be good stewards for what they receive from their elders and each succeeding generation pledges to add to what they inherit.

Building an estate is a difficult long-term project. It is beset with obstacles and conflicts every step of the way. Do you need to buy something for your kids? Do you need a pair of shoes? Should you get a gift for the friend at the office? The enticement for spending is constant. Is there a day or a week that you don't "need" some-

How to Find a Good Attorney

OFTEN, MEETING YOUR estate planning goals requires the assistance of a good attorney. If you decide you need one, you should seek out someone who can listen to your problems, who has the necessary expertise to understand the issues involved, and who can propose solutions.

If you have never sought legal representation before, don't be discouraged; many resources exist to help you make a good decision. First, identify the issue you would like the attorney to help you with. Do you need an attorney to draft a will, advise you on the different types of trusts available, or help you sort out which of your assets are probate and which are non-probate?

Next, ask friends, family, and professional colleagues for their suggestions and recommendations. If your friends are satisfied with their attorney, chances are you will be, too. The only danger with this more informal approach is that all too often friends are likely to tell you that they like the attorney's personality, which does not necessarily tell you anything about his or her expertise. Try to focus on the expertise aspect, because in the final analysis, the results you seek will depend on your attorney's skills, not on his or her personality.

thing? That you don't want to go to a movie? Rent a tape for the VCR? Buy something at Wal-Mart or K-Mart or some other "mart"?

We can't even watch television without someone trying to sell us something new —a car, a truck, or a boat, not to mention beer, lotions, vitamins, and "stay forever young" products. Even with these constant temptations, with persistence, one can still succeed in accumulating an estate. Which one of us doesn't want to buy a car or a suit, go to a game, or buy a new TV? But people who accumulate estates control their spending, and that is the bottom line.

Put It All Together

YOU NOW ARE BEGINNING TO LAY THE groundwork for estate planning by identifying certain important issues: your particular situation, concerns, goals, and net worth. These concepts form the foundation. Next you will begin to integrate these basic

You can also look in local newspapers and Yellow Pages for lawyers' advertisements. However, advertisements are just that. They don't give you any insights into the attorney's proficiency. One of the best sources of information can be found at your local library: *Martindale-Hubbell Bar Register of Preeminent Lawyers 2001.* It not only lists names and addresses of attorneys but also rates them and specifies their areas of expertise. This is a reliable, objective source of information.

Each state has referral sources, and many states now have lists of attorneys who specialize in various aspects of the law. Several state bar associations, such as those in Florida and California, have Web sites that list the names of attorneys and their specialties (www.calbar.org and www.flabar.org). The Web has many other sources for lists of attorneys, too. Search under www.dogpile.com to seek additional names of attorneys who specialize in estate planning.

But don't settle for the first attorney who will see you. Make sure you interview at least two attorneys before you select one to represent you. Keep in mind that you want an attorney whom you can talk to easily, who is knowledgeable about your problem, and who can give you solid legal guidance in all areas of estate planning.

concepts into an estate plan. You may change your plan many times over the years, but good estate planning is a lifetime project. Don't be discouraged if you can't decide everything at once. Just take one step now toward getting things organized for your planning. And remember that you aren't expected to have all of the answers today. Work on the issues until you can narrow the solutions to several choices, and then select some options to start exploring, seeking out professional advice when necessary. (See above for some tips on finding a good attorney.) Use the ideas in this chapter as a framework to get yourself started. If you stay focused and tenacious, you will create an estate and a plan that is just right for you and your family.

Chapter 3 *Three*

Classifying Your Assets

F OR THE AVERAGE ESTATE PLANNER, it is essential to have a thorough understanding of the ideas that form the foundation of your estate plan. If you understand these basics, you can move forward with effective estate planning. In fact, you may find that you have a few bits and pieces of an estate plan already in place that you didn't even know you had. And you may find that what you have put into place is not what you want or intend at all. The first step in this journey is sorting out and classifying your assets.

The Title Role

WHETHER OR NOT YOU HAVE a million-dollar account or an asset worth a hundred dollars, the value of your assets is not the key to good estate planning. What is important is how you "title" your assets, not what they are worth, which ones you think are collectibles, or what your family wants to pass on as family heirlooms. How you title what you own has far-reaching ramifications you may not even realize. This is because the legal nature of your assets determines the way that they will be handled in the event of your death or disability. It also determines whether your assets are under your sole control and whether they provide for your security or that of your family.

At your death, ownership of all your assets flows from you to others through either a probate or a non-probate process. Property does not transfer from, say, a deceased father to his children automatically. A probate asset is one that does not have a designated beneficiary on the title. (This is true even if the beneficiary is named in the will.) A classic example is a house with one owner listed on the deed. Because no beneficiary or heir is named on the deed itself, the house must be transferred to the beneficiary named in the will through a legal, or probate, proceeding.

A non-probate asset is titled in such a way that the asset passes to another person or entity automatically, without court involvement. A life insurance policy with a named beneficiary is a good example. Or suppose a husband and wife own a house and the deed is in both their names, with the language "for their joint lives with the remainder to the survivor of them." These words on the deed make their house a non-probate asset. If one of them dies, the title to the house goes to the survivor outside of any probate process. The words of the deed are controlling in determining exactly how title to this asset will pass.

In the non-probate process, property can be transferred by contract, survivorship (joint tenancy with right of survivorship), operation of law, or a funded trust. These terms are explained later in the chapter.

The probate and non-probate processes are separate procedures. Therefore, the way in which you title an asset will determine the process necessary to transfer it from you to another, or to transfer control of it from yourself to others if you become disabled. This, in turn, determines exactly which of many legal documents you need to complete your planning objectives. The case of Jim Johnson, who did not give these issues any thought at all, demonstrates that you need to know the status of your assets in order to have your wishes carried out properly.

The Case of the $10,000 Probate Asset

JIM JOHNSON OWNED a bank savings account of $10,000 when he died. The signature card at the bank where Jim established the account clearly indicated that Jim owned the account in his sole name. The card did not specify who was to receive the account at the time of Jim's death. Therefore, the account is designated as a probate asset, because it requires a legal process to transfer the asset from Jim's name to another. The probate process decided the "ownership" of the $10,000 when Jim died, because he had not elected to designate a beneficiary on his signature card.

If Jim had left a will, his account would have passed to his named beneficiary, who most likely would have been his wife. She could have used the money to pay the bills for his extended illness. Since he left no will, his state created a statutory will on his behalf. Imagine his widow's surprise when she found out that she would have to share the account with Jim's children by a previous marriage, none of whom had seen him in more than seventeen years!

Another issue was that Jim's widow wanted to have him cremated, according to his wishes. The children retained several attorneys and fought to prevent this, as well as to gain a portion of his savings account. Finally, Jim's widow told the children they could bury Jim instead, provided they prepaid the funeral. The children agreed, and the savings account was divided among the widow and the four children.

The next morning, when I arrived at my office, the attorneys were there waiting for me. The children either would not or could not pay for the funeral, so Jim's original wishes were carried out after all, and he was cremated. Unfortunately, however, the widow still had to share Jim's account with his children.

Probate Assets

AS WE HAVE DISCUSSED, SOLE OWNERSHIP of an asset automatically makes it a probate asset. An alternative is co-ownership of an asset, or, as it's more commonly known in legal jargon, "owners as co-tenants." Such assets are titled in the name of "A and B." However, without any qualifying language, such co-ownership does not change the asset's probate status, because there is no language on the deed to indicate who is to receive the property interest at the time of death. Assets owned by co-owners or co-tenants are probate assets, just as those titled in the name of a sole owner are probate assets.

This is often a difficult concept for people to comprehend. Many people make the mistake of thinking that because they include their spouse's or parent's name on the property deed, their loved one will automatically receive the property at the death of the owner. This is not always so and leads to much litigation and misunderstandings in families.

There are, however, many non-probate assets that permit the designation of named beneficiaries or permit the establishment of legal title in such a way that they avoid all probate proceedings. Although every state has slightly different laws, avoiding probate proceedings is possible in every state by using different legal options now available for this purpose.

For instance, if two sisters own a home together and the property deed reads that it is owned by "Mary and Melissa," each one of them owns an undivided one-half of the property. If Mary makes a will giving her interest to her children, then her children inherit her interest in the property. Melissa can do likewise. If the sisters wanted to be sure that the surviving sister inherited the other's share, they could change their deed so that it read that they owned the property as joint and survivorship owners. To do that, they would have to add language to their present deed. The language on the face of a deed determines whether the title to the property will transfer to others outside of the probate process as a non-probate asset or whether the property must pass through the probate system.

Non-Probate Assets

As long as a beneficiary is named, the following assets qualify as non-probate assets:

- Annuities
- Deferred compensation plans
- Insurance contracts
- IRAs
- Joint-and-survivorship assets
- Keogh plans
- Life estate deeds
- Living trusts that are funded
- Payable-on-death accounts (PODs)
- Pension plans
- Profit-sharing plans
- Transfer-on-death accounts (TODs)

Annuities

IN MANY WAYS, ANNUITIES WORK in the same way that a life insurance policy does. Annuities have become popular in the past several years as people become more and more interested in avoiding probate and postponing ordinary income recognition. An annuity contract avoids court proceedings and provides some tax advantages as well.

An annuity is a contract that an individual makes with an insurance company. Instead of paying additional monthly premium or lump-sum payments—the usual payment methods for life insurance—an individual pays a lump sum to the insurance company, designating a certain beneficiary to receive payments of a certain amount of income monthly, quarterly, or annually, usually beginning at some future date. The annuity is invested in stocks, so the returns on the funds may go up and down with the stock market. You can also purchase fixed-rate annuities, but the rate is not always guaranteed for the life of the annuity.

A good example of the use of an annuity is a situation in which a parent wants a child to receive small monthly payments over a period of time instead of a lump-sum payment, as might occur upon the death of the parent. Thus, the owner or purchaser can determine exactly how the proceeds of the annuity contract will be paid, whether in a lump sum or in periodic payments extending over a period of years.

For example, a man buying an annuity can bind the insurance company to pay any proceeds to his wife for her life, with any funds remaining after her death to be paid equally to his children. He can also require the company to pay him a certain monthly amount if he names himself as beneficiary of the annuity. Is court action required to make this transfer? No, because the contract already indicates how the company is to handle the assets. Thus, these assets are non-probate assets. Can the owner of the annuity make the assets probate assets? Yes, by inserting language into his annuity contract providing that any proceeds remaining in his annuity at his death are to be paid to his estate. In this way, he converts his annuity to an estate asset subject to the action of a probate court.

Let's say that Mr. Jones has purchased an annuity of $25,000 naming his son as beneficiary, but he has a will in which he leaves all of his property to his wife. Will the wife receive the annuity? No, because the annuity contract takes precedence over the will. Therefore, the son will receive the annuity, even if that is the husband's *only* asset.

Insurance Contracts

THE BEST EXAMPLE OF A NON-PROBATE asset is the standard life insurance policy. What occurs when Mr. Jones owns a life insurance policy on his life, with his wife designated as the beneficiary of the policy at his death? The insurance proceeds are paid directly to his widow when he dies. Is the probate court involved in any way with the distribution of the life insurance proceeds? No, because the insurance policy is a contract between the insurance company and Mr. Jones. In other words, in exchange for the premiums paid, the company insures his life so that when he dies, the company promises Mr. Jones it will pay his wife a certain sum of money. Mrs. Jones receives her money as a direct consequence of the contract of insurance, which clearly states exactly how the insurance is to be paid at the time of Mr. Jones's death. Because this asset passes from one person to another by means of a contract, the life insurance policy is clearly a non-probate asset.

In recent years, life insurance policies and their close cousins, annuities, have been joined by six other non-probate tools. Three of the most important non-probate plans Americans use today are the traditional IRA, the Roth IRA, and the Keogh plan.

Retirement Plans

THE IRA, THE ROTH IRA, AND THE KEOGH plan are usually established at a financial institution to set aside tax-advantaged funds to be withdrawn at retirement. By putting away money regularly, the individual both saves money for future needs and may also, depending on the plan, save substantial taxes in the process. Earnings accrued on the principal funds may receive either tax-free or tax-deferred treatment, a significant benefit to the beneficiary of the fund. Funds are held until the taxpayer or the taxpayer's designated beneficiary withdraws them, which may be years in the future.

Although the IRA, the Roth IRA, and the Keogh are actually savings and retirement plans aimed primarily at providing the saver with funds at retirement, they also receive non-probate classification. This is because the owner who sets up these accounts almost always designates a beneficiary (a person, trust, or institution) to ultimately receive the funds by direct transfer from the financial institution or employment plan. Therefore, as long as your IRA, Roth IRA, or Keogh plan designates a beneficiary, it is a non-probate asset.

Pension Plans

PENSION PLANS COMPRISE an enormous amount of wealth in the United States. The assets vested in pension plans in this country total billions of dollars. The same applies to profit-sharing plans. Such plans are becoming increasingly popular in the United States and are widely used by private corporations. A company establishes a profit-sharing plan to divert some of its profit for the benefit of its employees at their retirement.

The majority of pension plans, profit-sharing plans, and deferred compensation plans in the United States are non-probate plans. Pension plans established by small companies, large corporations, or governmental entities, such as the state and federal government, address the issue of beneficiaries by (1) having employees name the beneficiaries who will receive the pension funds in question or (2) designating beneficiaries automatically if the employee does not.

In the event the employee does not name a beneficiary, the employer's plan will generally state that the spouse of the employee is the primary beneficiary, the children of the employee are the secondary beneficiaries, and that the lineal descendants, other than the children, are tertiary (or third) beneficiaries. In other plans, the employee's estate may be the sole beneficiary. Each plan is different and for that reason, you should be knowledgeable about the beneficiary issues since they are very important to the welfare of your dependents.

For estate planning purposes, the question to ask is this: Are these plans considered probate or non-probate assets? In the early days of pension and profit-sharing plans, companies and governments weren't too concerned about the niceties of these issues. They were mainly concerned about establishing affordable plans for their employees that were reasonable for retirement purposes. How to pay for the plans was the central question. However, with the passage of time, larger issues came into focus, among them the question of how to distribute these vast sums of money in the most efficient manner to the employees or to the employees' beneficiaries.

These issues of distribution are complex and vary from plan to plan, state to state, and company to company. If you participate in such a plan, you should know how it works. You may learn that you can avoid the probate process in your state by simply filling out a form naming your beneficiary. Today, as noted previously, the vast majority of pension and profit-sharing plan assets are non-probate assets.

A deferred compensation plan differs from a pension plan in that the former is an employees' plan to defer earned income each month as part of a personal savings and tax-deferral plan, while the latter is a plan to which both the employee and the employer typically contribute. Thus, deferred compensation plans are also non-probate assets when they properly designate a beneficiary. No court is involved, because the contractual planning is between the employee and employer, and the distribution of funds at a future date is predetermined by contract.

One key point cannot be emphasized enough: Only if an individual designates a beneficiary for the assets in a life insurance plan, annuity plan, deferred compensation plan, IRA plan, Keogh plan, pension plan, profit-sharing plan, or Roth IRA will those assets be non-probate. Any plan lacking a named beneficiary will go through a probate process.

"Unique Language" Non-Probate Assets

SOME ASSETS REVOLVE AROUND THE test of unique language. In other words, certain accounts may become non-probate ones only if unique words are inserted into the title. If this special language is missing, then the accounts may not be treated as non-probate assets. This language "qualifies" the account, or stock, for special non-probate status. For instance, if you own a checking account in your own name, the ownership will read James Smith. That account is a probate account and will be disposed of by a probate court. The reason is that although the ownership is clear during James Smith's life, there is nothing to indicate what happens to the account after death.

On the other hand, if you own a checking account in your name and your daughter's, the ownership might read James Smith and Mary Smith, joint and survivorship. This is inherently a non-probate account, because the "survivor", either James or Mary, will inherit this account when the first person dies. Simply entering the ownership option you want on the signature card at your bank can make all the difference in the way your accounts are handled at the time of your death. You have the right to make that decision, and you can elect to make every account you own a non-probate account.

You may be able to modify your stock, certificates of deposit, bonds, treasury notes, and other similar financial holdings in this way to make them non-probate. To find out if this is possible, write to the company that sold you the asset and ask for information about the options available to you to convert your asset into non-probate property.

There are three non-probate forms of assets that may be established *only* by specifying certain language on your bank account card, your stock certificate, or other assets:

1 Joint-and-survivorship assets
2 Payable-on-death accounts, better known as POD assets
3 Transfer-on-death accounts, better known as TOD assets

Each account you establish may be titled in your name alone or with the name of another person, and you may select a variety of ways in which to title the account. You may ask the bank officers in charge of accounts exactly what your options are. For instance, you may be informed that you have the right to own your account in your individual name or in your name with another person as a co-owner. You may also be able to establish the account in your name with another person as a joint and survivorship co-owner. One other option is to set up an account in your name alone, but with a payable on death option, which means that at your death the account would pass to someone you have designated. Check with your individual bank to see what options it offers; not all banks operate in the same way, and not all states permit the same options.

For instance, when a husband and wife set up a joint-and-survivorship account for a certificate of deposit (CD) at a bank, the signature card will commonly read "A and B, or survivor." The nature of the ownership is clear, and the distribution of the account is certain. The addition of the words "or survivor" or "joint and survivorship" indicates that the particular account in question contains the directions for disposing of the assets in the event of the death of one of the parties. If A dies, then it is clear that B, as the survivor, will receive all of the funds in the joint-and-survivorship account.

Suppose Mary provides in her will that "All certificates that I own at the ABC Bank I give to my daughter Alice." Will Alice receive the account that is titled "John and Mary, joint and survivorship"? The answer is no, because the title of the CD takes precedence over the will. Therefore, this particular certificate will transfer to John at Mary's death.

Throughout the United States, the joint-and-survivorship account is quite common, although different states may have different rules for interpreting these accounts, as well as specific taxation rules that apply to them. However, if you open such an account, using language established by state law, this option often allows you to avoid the probate process by designating the survivor on the account as the beneficiary, as provided by the law of the state where the account is established.

Note that there is a significant difference between co-ownership and joint and survivorship ownership. You may have another person's name on the deed of a house: "Jane and John." This is a form of co-ownership, but is not a survivorship ownership, as it does not say so on the deed. It only says "Jane and John." If Jane dies, her half interest goes to her estate. But if the deed reads "Jane and John, for their joint lives with the remainder to the survivor of them," this is clearly a joint and survivorship deed. In other words, if Jane dies, her half interest passes to John. This same concept is true of stocks and other financial instruments. You must specify on the paperwork that documents your ownership of the instrument exactly how your ownership interest is to read.

One note: although there can be more than two joint-and-survivorship owners on a deed, adding more names creates complications. For instance, suppose there are five people on the deed. Throughout the years, each person may marry. If the property were to be sold, all five spouses might have to sign, in addition to the five people originally named on the deed. In the event of divorce or remarriage, things can get extremely complicated. Each time a name is added to the deed, it creates more and more complexities regarding the sale, ownership, and control of the property. Therefore, most attorneys advise clients to have only two names on a co-ownership deed.

The other type of bank account that is becoming more common in the United States is the so-called payable-on-death account, or the POD. It differs from the joint-and-survivorship account in that one person owns it during his or her lifetime, but the proceeds are payable at the owner's death to another person. The original title owner and the POD beneficiary cannot own the account at the same time.

The joint-and-survivorship account permits all persons named on the account to own and to control the account during their lifetimes, regardless of who contributed the funds to the account. In a POD account, ownership and control of the account stays with the owner; title goes to the beneficiary only at the death of the POD account owner.

Therefore, the POD account is useful when a person wants to leave an account to another individual at the time of death but does not want that other person to have any control over the assets during the owner's lifetime. A grandmother, for instance, could open an account in her name alone so that she has sole control of the account during her lifetime, but when she dies, the grandchild will receive title to the account.

Often grandparents use POD accounts to make sure that each grandchild receives something from them as an inheritance. One grandfather, who had eleven grandchildren, established eleven $1,000 accounts with his name on each POD to each grandchild. At his death, each of the grandchildren automatically received the $1,000 gift.

However, a POD account with a minor child does have a drawback because children under eighteen with such an account must, in some states, have a legal guardian until they reach age eighteen. This involves court proceedings, court costs, and often legal fees. The guardian may be required to file annual accounts with the court and keep in contact with the court each year during the child's minority. These laws are in effect for a good reason: adults have used the assets of children for their own purposes, and when the child reached age eighteen, no funds were left.

If you want to leave funds to a minor through a POD account, you as the depositor should add this language to the account: "This POD to this minor child is made 'subject to the Uniform Transfers to Minors Act (UGMA).'" The depositor names a "custodian," usually himself, for the minor to conduct all of the business for the trust. The custodian is under legal obligation to supervise and invest funds properly; otherwise sanctions are imposed against him or her. These may include simply telling the custodian to do a better job, terminating the custodian from the job, or taking legal action to force the custodian to return or replace funds. If there has been fraud, legal proceedings against the custodian may be filed of either a misdemeanor or felony nature. The job of a custodian for a minor's assets is a serious one, and the law imposes a duty upon that person to act in the minor's best interest or to be held strictly accountable for not doing so.

In some states, such as California, the POD account is referred to as the "ITF account," meaning "in trust for." Almost all states have some form of the POD

How to Transfer Your Property

NO MATTER WHERE you live, your assets, regardless of their value, can be transferred from you to others in only five ways:

1 By contract

2 By your will

3 By survivorship accounts and deeds

4 By operation of state law

5 By a funded trust

account, although it may be called a different name and be handled by the financial institutions and courts in different ways.

Similarly, many states now provide for a TOD account. This is a transfer-on-death designation available for use with various stock and bond accounts. Each state determines whether, by legislative provision, to make the TOD available there. Check with a local stockbroker, who should know what your state law permits. The TOD "title" works in the same way that the POD account does. For example, John Jones has a $10,000 interest in a certain stock. He lives in a state that permits the transfer of the stock through the TOD designation. John is able to title his stock to his son so that the ownership will transfer to him upon John's death.

As the owner of your assets, you may select a variety of options available in your state. You may decide to leave everything you own in your name alone, or you may have joint-and-survivorship accounts for some assets and TOD or POD accounts for others. You may have all of your assets titled to go to your spouse, your children, your parents, or a favorite charity at the time of your death. Often you may determine the manner and time of the distribution of your assets, depending on the legal option you exercise. The choice is yours. If you make no decisions, then most, if not all, of your assets may become probate assets, and your heirs may be burdened with the accompanying time and expense that are necessary in that venue.

Trusts

THE OTHER NON-PROBATE ASSETS ARE those that are controlled by certain types of trusts. There are many varieties of trusts and many ways to use them. Suffice it to say that a trust may be drafted with the purpose of circumventing probate. A properly drafted trust may also save a significant amount in taxes, and also control the time and manner of future distributions of assets. Chapter 9 will discuss trusts in more depth.

How Title Affects Your Estate Plan

YOU SHOULD APPLY TWO BASIC THRESHOLD tests to each of your assets before you begin to create your estate plan:

1   What is the legal nature of each of your assets?
2   How does the title of each affect your estate plan?

How you title each of your assets determines whether it is probate or non-probate. You yourself determine how your assets are titled when you first acquire them and designate the title to each item. An asset cannot be both probate and non-probate. Ask yourself:

➢ How is my car titled?
➢ Who owns the title to my house?
➢ What is the nature of the titles for all of my other assets, such as boats, campers, expensive artwork, and so on?
➢ If I don't know or am not sure, how do I find out the nature of these titles?

Start by looking at the title to see if anyone else's name is on the face of it, or if there is any other language that tells you to whom the asset will belong after your death. If it is in your sole name, it will have to be administered by a probate process or special statutory procedure.

This is important, because legal principles have little significance unless you can understand and use them to meet your needs and goals. Therefore, first you need to determine whether your assets are probate or non-probate. Then you need to ask yourself: How does this affect my long-range estate plan? Consider that you must integrate your house, your retirement plan, your living will, your power of attorney, and your trust, together with your insurance plans, to develop the best possible strategy for your entire family and for yourself during your lifetime. After all, the real essence of an estate plan is to mesh all of your assets and real-life concerns into a comprehensive scheme to meet your objectives.

The following real-life cases give an indication of how assets may, and sometimes may not, meet people's planning goals.

The Case of the Outraged Daughter

JULIE JACKSON'S MOTHER, HELEN, died early in 1994, leaving a will in which she gave all of her property to her only daughter, Julie. Helen had a lifelong friend, Alice, and through the years she and Alice had become co-owners of several pieces of property.

Julie anticipated that all of the assets in her mother's name would come to her under the will. However, when her attorney examined the deed to the house, it read as follows: "This property is owned by Helen and Alice, for their joint lives with the remainder to the survivor of them." This joint-and-survivorship language means that after the first co-owner dies, the survivor inherits the entire interest in the property. This probate-avoidance language completely bypasses the probate process.

Does the will prevail, or does the deed? The deed does. The survivorship language makes the house a non-probate asset—one that is not subject to court jurisdiction. The house goes to Alice, in accordance with the language on the deed. The will cannot give away what Helen does not own. When Helen died, the real estate title passed immediately by operation of law to Alice.

To make matters worse for Julie, she discovered that all of her mother's bank accounts were titled as joint and survivorship with Alice, so Julie had no right to these assets, either. The only assets Julie inherited under her mother's will were her household goods and jewelry. These were owned solely by her mother, and they are therefore probate assets and subject to the probate court where the will was admitted.

Julie's outrage is understandable. She has in hand her mother's will, giving her all of her property. Yet she finds that her mother's interest in the house, which Julie believes she should inherit, is totally inaccessible to her.

It is very common for people to name different beneficiaries on their accounts, in their wills, and on their IRAs. Many times this is intentional; other times it is not. Often people make decisions about, say, a life insurance policy without realizing the consequences that may have on their wills, trusts, POD, TOD, or joint-and-survivorship accounts.

People often act randomly over a period of time in aligning their assets, and they seldom have every asset titled the way they want. Even with the best plans, an asset will be forgotten, or the way in which it is titled is not current with the individual's circumstances. That is why it is important to stay organized and to review your estate plan at least every other year.

The Case of the Surprised Surviving Spouse

JOE WROTE A WILL IN WHICH he left his second wife all of his estate, valued at $200,000. He then deposited his $200,000, essentially all of his assets, in an account with his stockbroker. Joe instructed the broker to title the account in his name and the name of his daughter by a previous marriage as a joint-and-survivorship account. He and his daughter signed the account registration card, and they both began to actively use the account.

At Joe's death, his daughter claimed all of the assets of the $200,000 account. Can the husband disinherit his surviving spouse in such a way? In most states, yes. The assets flow to the surviving owner of the account if the co-owners actively use the account. The assets are not deemed "probate assets," so Joe's will does not apply to the $200,000 stock account. In this particular case, Joe and his daughter knew exactly what they were doing when they began using the account. They were well aware that this would invalidate his wife's claim to the account.

Needless to say, there is much litigation and pending legislation on this issue. Every state differs; however, in most states, the survivorship account still determines ownership of the assets. A will controls only probate assets. If assets are established as non-probate before death, the title set up during the person's lifetime controls those assets.

The Case of the Cabin in the Woods

JOHN AND SAMMY WERE high school friends who often went hunting together. After high school, they went their separate ways but met in Michigan to go hunting together whenever they could get away. On one trip, they saw an old cabin for sale, and on a whim, they stopped, talked to the owner, and bought the cabin.

The deed to the property read "John and Sammy." There was no other so-called "qualifying language" or unique language on their deed, so there were no other words to establish any condition of ownership other than the names of the two men.

Over the years, John and Sammy fixed up the cabin, added plumbing, electricity, a porch, and some comfortable furniture. Their families met there over the years and enjoyed the cabin, which by then was really a nice, comfortable home.

When John died, the question came up immediately: "What about the cabin?" Under John's will, all of his property went to his wife. But would the cabin in Michigan go to Sammy, under the deed to the property?

The attorney for John's estate immediately looked at the deed to the cabin, since the title to an asset determines the way its ownership will be established. When he saw that the deed was titled to "John and Sammy," he immediately saw that John's half-interest in the cabin would pass to his wife.

Had the title to the property been joint-and-survivorship—that is, if it had read "John and Sammy, for their joint lives with the remainder to the survivor of them"—then the title to the property would have passed to the survivor, Sammy.

Fortunately, the men, early in their ownership of the cabin, decided that they would make sure their families inherited the interest each had in the property, instead of the survivor inheriting the other's share. By making good decisions from the outset, they assured a smooth and equitable transfer of the property at John's death. This enabled John's wife and their family to continue enjoying the cabin and to retain it in the family, while Sammy still had the same undivided half-interest as before John's death.

The Case of the Lifetime Savings Account

JIM AND SALLY, BROTHER AND SISTER, have owned a savings account together since they were children. Although Sally's husband died some years ago and she has children, Sally and Jim have agreed that any funds in the account are to be used for their funeral expenses when they die. Such oral agreements about personal property are often enforceable if they constitute value of less than $5,000 to $10,000, depending on state law. (Note, however, that oral agreements about real estate usually aren't enforceable.)

At the time of Sally's death, the account had $10,000 in it, of which one-half, or $5,000, belonged to Sally. Does her interest in the account go to Jim, so that he can pay for her funeral, or does it pass to her children? Sally's will left all of her property to her children.

To decide how this account will be transferred, the signature card at the bank must be inspected, since it establishes ownership. The title card indicates that Sally and Jim owned the account. It does not specify that the account was joint and survivorship, nor was the transfer-on-death or payable-on-death option selected, so the account cannot pass to Jim directly.

Sally's ownership interest in the account is one-half of its value as of the date of her death. The account is a probate asset, which means it must be distributed to Sally's children in accordance with her will.

Sally's children received their funds—the $5,000 that was her half of the account—and they refused to pay the funeral bill, since Jim had chosen the funeral home and made arrangements to pay that bill. The children felt that they should have been the ones entitled to make the final burial arrangements for their mother. Jim filed suit against the children but lost his case. He paid the funeral bill, although it took him several years. It was a sad ending for this family.

The Case of the Power of Attorney

U NCLE CLEM GAVE HIS NEPHEW James his power of attorney for financial matters, so that if he became sick or died, James could take care of his bank accounts, bills, and household accounts. He also told James to distribute his estate after death to four of his seven family members. James agreed to do this for his uncle and immediately began paying all of his bills and depositing his social security and pension checks, and James managed his investments for more than six years.

After Uncle Clem died, James discovered that the laws in every state provide that a power of attorney is good only during the lifetime of the person granting the power. In other words, once Uncle Clem died, the POA ended, and James had no authority to make any distribution of his uncle's estate. He wondered what to do with the assets he had been using to pay the bills.

James went to his attorney and explained the dilemma. The attorney asked if his uncle had left a will. James replied that he had not. Uncle Clem mistakenly thought that giving James his POA and telling him what he wanted done meant that he didn't need a will.

The attorney explained that the power of attorney is a special document created only to convey to another person certain authority under specific, defined circumstances during life. James, therefore, did not have the authority to distribute Uncle Clem's assets as he had wished. He couldn't even write checks or pay bills, as he had been doing, and he certainly could not distribute any of his uncle's assets to anyone else.

The court opened the estate and appointed James administrator. Since there was no will, Uncle Clem's assets were distributed according to the laws of descent and distribution, meaning that his property went to all of his relatives in equal shares under state law. So the four relatives to whom he wanted to leave his estate each received a one-seventh portion, instead of the one-fourth he had intended. Had he left a will, his favorite four would certainly have received the gifts he intended. That the one relative whom Uncle Clem didn't like received a one-seventh portion was just poor planning on his part.

The Case of the Property from the Second Marriage

ANNE AND HERB EACH HAD children from their previous marriages and one child together. Anne owned her home when they married. They decided that Anne's house should be put in both of their names so that if she predeceased Herb, he could live in her house for his lifetime, and at his death the house would go to her children. Anne had a deed executed, which she signed, putting the title to the house in the name of "Anne and Herb." She felt that Herb should have the right to live in the house for his lifetime and that her children would have the ultimate benefit of the ownership of the house after he died.

Very shortly after Anne signed her deed, she died unexpectedly, having been married to Herb for only two years. Immediately her children wanted to know if they owned their mother's household goods or if Herb did, and if, in fact, he owned the house.

Since title determines ownership, it is immediately clear that under the deed, Herb owns outright a one-half interest in the house. But what about Anne's portion? Does he have a right to live in the house for his lifetime, or does Anne's half interest go to her children?

Herb and the children decided to go to the same attorney to hear the legal issues from the same source. The attorney informed all of them that Herb did not own a life estate in Anne's portion of the house, since there is no language in the deed to state that intention. Anne had made a will that gave "all of my property to my children." Thus, the children had a right to receive their mother's half of her home.

However, in all states, a surviving spouse has the right to elect to "take against the will" of the deceased spouse. Under the statutes of their state, he could take up to a one-third interest in the estate, plus he had the right to purchase the home from her estate, which he did. He received a one-third interest in her one-half interest in the house, and then he paid into her estate the amount needed to purchase the other two-thirds interest so that he would own the home outright. The children inherited the funds paid into her estate.

Herb also had the right to the household goods, but in an amicable settlement, he gave all of Anne's furniture, family photographs, and heir-looms to Anne's children. When the dust settled, Herb owned the home, and the children had the cash and all of the household possessions that had belonged to their mother.

What about Anne and Herb's child? Herb continued to raise the child, who received a portion of his mother's estate equal to what the other children received. In addition, Herb reached an agreement with Anne's children that a portion of the household goods would be held for the child until he came of age. All cash assets owned by the child were held in a custodian account in the child's name, with Herb as the custodian until their son came of age.

Was everyone satisfied by this outcome? No, not everyone. But it solved some problems and allowed the children to receive what they cherished the most: their mother's things. And it allowed Herb to purchase the house so that he could continue to make a home for their son. Everyone wanted to keep the peace so that all of the children could see each other and participate in the life of the youngest child. It was a reasonable settlement, if not the one Anne initially intended.

The Case of the U.S. Bonds

JANICE HAS CO-OWNED U.S. BONDS in her name with her son, Bill, for many years. They were purchased for her and Bill by her first husband. After her first husband's death, she remarried. In her will, executed after her second marriage, she willed all of her property to her second husband, Ralph. They had agreed to combine property so that they could purchase a small home together.

Janice died after an extended illness, leaving Ralph with many medical bills. He needs money and believes that under Janice's will, he is entitled to receive all of her property, which he thinks should include the U.S. bonds.

Bill and Ralph agreed that they would have their attorneys bring the matter before the court for a decision and that both of them would abide by that decision. Ralph's attorney filed an action known as a declaratory judgment action, in which the parties set out the facts, and asked the court to determine the legal rights of the two parties.

The courts ruled that the title to the bonds indicates that each of the co-owners owns one-half of the bonds. At the death of one of the owners, in the absence of any other language to the contrary, one-half of the legal interest in the bonds would go into Janice's estate, and then under her will, they would transfer to the surviving spouse, Ralph. At the same time, the court ruled that Bill owned a one-half interest in the bonds, so he is entitled to claim half of them as his property.

Chapter Four

How State Laws Affect Estate Planning

YOU SIMPLY CANNOT DO GOOD, effective estate planning without realizing the impact of state laws—not only in the state where you live now, but in those states where you acquired or plan to acquire property. The underlying rules that govern all of your actions are made by state legislative action, and they have a direct impact on your estate plan.

Most people don't realize that their estates may be directly affected by these far-reaching state laws and that these laws have a wide, and often unexpected, impact on their families. Many think that the most significant concerns revolve around probate and taxes—how to avoid probate and how to minimize the impact of state and local taxes. But just as important, if not more, are the state laws that govern such wide-ranging issues as inheritance by intestacy, spousal rights of election at the time of death of a spouse, and process and procedure. In addition, the transfer of assets between spouses, or the prevention of that transfer, is of great importance.

Estates are actually governed by one of three rules of law, and often a combination of all three may have a direct influence on your estate. And, just as frequently, the results are unforeseen and radically different from what the decedent intended.

First and foremost is the traditional body of probate law, which is in effect in the majority of U.S. states and is used exclusively as a basis to establish all process and procedure in the decedent's estate proceeding. Nine states, known as community property states, follow an entirely different process for property owned by spouses. This process takes precedence over all matters that affect spousal rights at the time of death. Finally, sixteen states apply the Uniform Probate Code to probate estates.

Because the laws in effect in the state where you live have a direct impact on your estate planning, it is important that you understand some of their basic provisions and how they may influence your estate planning goals, your assets, and your intentions about those assets. Make no mistake about it: regardless of your goals and legal instruments (or lack of them), if your state laws mandate that your estate must be handled in a certain way, they will take precedence over your own desires.

Do You Live in a Community Property State?

IF YOU ARE MARRIED AND YOU NOW LIVE, or once lived, in a community property state, your estate will be settled under specific statutory provisions. In some states, community property must go through a probate process, and in other states, it doesn't. But even more important than the probate consequences is the nature of the ownership of property.

The nine community property states are:

➢ Arizona
➢ California
➢ Idaho

➢ Louisiana
➢ Nevada
➢ New Mexico

➢ Texas
➢ Washington
➢ Wisconsin

In addition, the state of Alaska allows spouses to sign a community property agreement electing that system of law to govern their property rights instead of the traditional law that currently applies to estates in that state.

Community Property Defined

COMMUNITY PROPERTY IS PROPERTY THAT you or your spouse acquire during marriage. If you live in a state that applies community property laws to determine spousal property rights, then any property you or your spouse acquire during your marriage in that state, and any and all property you or your spouse acquired in the past while living in another community property state, is deemed community property. This means the property is owned one-half by each spouse. Also, all of the earnings of the spouses during marriage, if they live in community property states, are community property, as are all of the assets purchased with those earnings.

This system of law changes the entire nature of the ownership of all assets acquired by spouses. In traditional states, if a husband acquires property, he owns it. Often, if the property is personal property, such as stocks, cash, bonds, collectibles, or antiques, he can transfer those assets to others without the consent or signature of the spouse, who has no legal interest in the property.

In community property states, however, the wife would have an interest—perhaps up to 50 percent of the value—in all property the husband acquired during marriage. In fact, community property states treat spousal property as if it were property of a business partnership, in which each spouse owns a 50 percent interest in all of the assets designated as community property. This becomes very important in divorce cases, but it is just as critical, if not more so, in probate matters at the death of the first spouse, particularly if that individual wanted to give property to individuals other than the surviving spouse.

Does a spouse have the right to own property as an individual? Yes. Property held in the name of a sole spouse is known as "separate property." This means that property a spouse acquired before marriage by inheritance or gift and property owned before the marriage is, and can remain, separate property of a spouse, with this provision: separate property must be kept separate and must not be commingled with community property during the marriage or it will become community property.

What is commingling? This means mixing separate property with community property until it can no longer be identified as separate property. For instance, suppose you have an account in your name with $1,000 in it, and you add $500 of that money to a community property account titled in your name and that of your spouse. Not only have you transferred $500, but you have altered the separate property owned solely by you to a community property asset owned by you and your spouse by commingling your assets with his.

Because the designation of spousal assets is very important, it is essential that spouses keep accurate records when they acquire property in community property states: when the acquisition was made, how title was applied to the asset, and the source of the funds used for the purchase. Each of these factors may become critical, especially when the first spouse dies.

You may be wondering whether this means that spouses can't own their homes as joint tenants with the right of survivorship (so that the surviving spouse will automatically own the home when the first spouse dies). In Arizona, Nevada, Texas, and Wisconsin, spouses can use joint tenancy for their real estate; in California and New Mexico, there is a simplified process for transferring community property to the surviving spouse. In all of the rest of the community property states, community property must go through probate, just like other kinds of property.

Community property may also have a major impact on estate tax issues. When the first spouse dies in a community property state, the tax, or cost, basis for the entire spousal community property is established. In traditional probate states, only the portion of property owned by the decedent spouse is appraised and a tax, or cost, basis established.

The cost basis of an asset determines what tax may be due when an asset is later sold or transferred to others. If community property spouses are unaware of these facts, they may not understand the full significance of the appraisal of the spousal property or its potential future effects—that is, when capital gains taxes may be due upon the later sale of the community property.

It is therefore important to plan to minimize taxes and simultaneously make sure the surviving spouse is protected after the death of the first. Further planning is also necessary to ensure that the title to community property will smoothly pass to beneficiaries of the couple at the time of the survivor's death, or to beneficiaries of both spouses, if that is an important goal for the couple. Below is a typical example of a community property estate.

The Case of the Community Property Estate

SAM AND JANET LIVED in California, a community property state, and paid $100,000 for all of their property, which they accumulated there during their marriage. The $100,000 represents their cost basis (or simply "basis"), with a basis to Sam of $50,000 and a basis to Janet of $50,000. When Sam died, the property was appraised at $180,000.

Janet wants to sell the property but fears she will have to pay a lot of capital gains tax on the increase in the value of the property. If she has to pay a lot of taxes, then she can't afford to sell the property. At the same time, she can't keep up the property and pay the real estate taxes on it that they could afford when there were two of them working and paying all the expenses of home ownership. She is so upset, and the bills are beginning to mount to the point that she has to do something. What can she do?

When Janet went to see her attorney and explained her problem, he told her that although she and Sam each had a basis of $50,000 when they bought the property, Sam's death gave her an automatic increase in basis equal to the amount the property was worth at the time of his death. Since the property was appraised at $180,000 at that time, Janet can sell the property for that amount without any tax consequences. In non-community states, Sam's one-half interest in the property might have received a step up in basis, and her basis might have remained at $50,000. The moral of this story is that the couple owned property that they could not afford in the event of one of their deaths. A sale had to take place.

The tax consequences of such a sale can be devastating. Fortunately, the way both federal and state laws handle the assets of the first spouse to die is usually to give the surviving spouse a break. The law gives a step up in basis to the assets of the first spouse to die, and this gives a significant break to the surviving spouse. In this case, Janet was able to sell the house, make a profit, avoid a capital gains tax that might have ruined her financially, and walk away from a house she could no longer afford. Janet was lucky; in another state, she might not have been able to escape heavy tax consequences as readily. The moral of this story is to be knowledgeable about capital gains taxes and how they affect property values at the time of death.

Clearly it is important to understand the effects of ownership of community property, not only upon the title to the property but also on your personal tax situation. Note that the Taxpayer Relief Act of 1997 lowered capital gains as follows:

➤ 20 percent for property held for twelve months or more before sale;

➤ 28 percent for collectibles; and

➤ 25 percent for depreciation recapture on real estate.

For assets purchased after 2000 and held for more than five years, the capital gains rate is 18 percent for individuals, trusts, and estates, if complex requirements are met.

Is It Joint Property or Community?

IT IS ALSO IMPORTANT to understand that how the assets of the husband and wife are titled on a deed, account, or stock may not determine asset ownership in community property states. If the property is titled in the name of the wife but assets for the acquisition came from community property of both spouses, it will probably be designated as a community property asset.

Community property law is often very confusing to those who are not accustomed to dealing with it. However, the concept is very simple: Marriage is a partnership, so that the parties in this partnership own all property acquired during the marriage in equal shares, just as in a business partnership where all assets and all debts are treated as belonging equally to each partner. Much litigation surrounds the issue of whether or not a particular asset is community or separate property if it was acquired during marriage or while domiciled in a certain state. When there is conflict at the time of divorce or death, many issues can arise about how the property of the marriage was acquired in the first place and how it should be divided when death, dissolution, or divorce ends the marriage contract.

Generally speaking, a spouse who resides in any one of the nine community property states must initiate the estate planning process by determining the exact legal status of each asset acquired while residing there. An inventory should be made of all assets, including real and personal property, such as cars, boats, pension plans, insurance policies, second homes, stock, bonds, and bank accounts, to determine which assets, if any, are separate property and which are community property assets. Such an itemized list should include each asset owned and its legal status, as well as its current market value.

When you are married and you either move into or live in a community property state, your status (and your spouse's) as the owner of your property is governed by that state's law, which allocates and imposes ownership shares between the spouses in portions deemed "fair." The following community property checklist indicates the many possibilities for ownership in a community property state. Property may be owned as community property, as separate property of one of the spouses, as quasi-community property (property acquired in another state that could have been community property if that state were a community property state), or as a combination of all of these.

You should use this checklist to help categorize each of your assets. After you decide which of them are community property, separate property, or quasi-community property, it may then be necessary to determine, by examining the title to each asset, which may be probate and which may be non-probate assets.

For estate planning purposes, the title to your assets must be clear and readily identifiable. You must know what you own that's solely yours (separate property) and what you own as community property with your spouse. But if you have income flowing into and out of an account, for example, how do you know what is what? And how do you determine ownership of the house? The car? Investments?

One of the most important aspects of community property is seen when couples in community property states own property as co-owners or as joint and survivorship owners. In traditional states, co-ownership or survivorship ownership is simple; if the

Community Property Estate Planning Checklist

IN A COMMUNITY PROPERTY state, your assets can fall into several categories:

➢ Community property
➢ Wife's separate property
➢ Husband's separate property
➢ Property owned by husband and wife as tenants in common (could be separate or community property)
➢ Property owned by husband and wife as joint owners with the right of survivorship (could be separate or community property)
➢ Quasi-community property of the wife and husband, which is basically defined as property acquired in another state that could have been community property if that state were a community property state

couple co-owns property, then each spouse owns a one-half interest in the property; if they own property as survivorship co-owners, at the death of the first spouse, the surviving spouse receives the property pursuant to the language of the legal instrument creating the ownership interest. This may be language contained on a deed, account, stock, or fund.

However, in community property states, if spouses have either of these ownership rights, they may own them as their own "separate property" or as "community property", depending on how they acquired the property and the source of the funds used to acquire the property. Whether or not the property is separate or community determines how the property will be distributed to others at the time of the death of the spouses. For this reason, clarification of assets held in community property states is very important.

The only sure way to know is to enter into a written contract with your spouse and make a list of those items that are his separate property, her separate property, and the community property they both acknowledge as belonging to them together. In most community property states (unlike in other states) spouses can contract with each other. Therefore, by entering into a written contract with each other regarding these issues, at least there is a list of assets and an understanding about the owner-ship rights for each of them. The assets may change, be sold, or disappear, but at least you have a written instrument in hand that safeguards both parties from future disputes over the ownership of the property.

The Case of the Confused Spouses

ALICE AND JOHN WERE MARRIED in Ohio in 1970. At that time Alice owned two parcels of real estate and a painting valued at $5,000. John owned no property. In 1985, Alice and John moved to California, a community property state. Over time, they accumulated a house, savings accounts, stock, and pension funds. Some of the assets they titled jointly and some separately. When John and Alice began to make plans about their property, they found they were very confused. Should the property that they purchased in California with proceeds from the sale of their real estate in Ohio be counted as community property? Are their pensions, which are titled separately, community property? What about stocks, savings accounts, and other investments—some titled separately, some jointly, and some with their children's names? What about Alice's painting, which is now worth a great deal more than $5,000? Is that her separate property or community property?

Finally, in frustration and confusion, they went to see an estate plan-ner. The attorney had them list all of their assets. He told them to include where they purchased their property, when they sold it, and how they used the assets from the sale. In other words, Alice and John had to con-struct a picture of their complete marital assets and trace the assets from any sales of property to decide whether they had used separate or com-munity assets to purchase their home.

Then they had to list the assets they owned in their separate names. They also noted whether those assets were purchased from community assets or from the separate assets they had in their own names.

What about the painting? It belonged to Alice and still does. It is her separate property. As such she can give it away, keep it, or will it to any-one she chooses.

The marital home they own? Since it was purchased by assets belonging to both spouses, it is community property. Each spouse owns a one-half interest in it. Their pensions may stand in their separate names and belong to each individual as separate property.

These issues can be ironed out between amicable spouses, who usually need to clarify all of these matters in the process of doing their estate planning. The big problem comes when there is discord, divorce, and dissolution of the marriage. Then, every asset belonging to either or both spouses comes into conflict, and it may take months and much litigation to determine the exact nature of a couple's assets.

This story demonstrates that it is important to know how the title to all of your assets is held. Also, when you move into or out of a community property state, be aware that there are far-reaching financial consequences.

There are a few exceptions to the rule that spousal community property gives each spouse a one-half interest in those assets. For instance, suppose a husband takes funds from the community property assets and purchases a life insurance policy, in which he makes his daughter from a previous marriage the beneficiary. Many community property states allow the daughter to receive these funds on the basis that insurance law takes precedence over community property laws. Such inconsistencies make it essential for those with complex estate plans to consult with tax and legal experts in community property states, as only those well versed in the intricacies of and exceptions to community property laws can give good advice about important issues to spouses who want to achieve particular estate planning goals.

The Bottom Line in Community Property States

THE ACTUAL DETERMINATION of what is or what is not community property is made by statute, by a court of law, or by agreement of the parties in community property states. Regardless of how the determination is made, in these states all spousal assets, excluding separate property, are deemed to be owned one-half by each spouse. No effective estate planning can take place in a community property state until the exact legal status of the property involved is determined.

Needless to say, if you are married and live in a community property state, a list that designates each spouse's community property treatment with regard to each asset, as well as its probate and non-probate status, is the cornerstone for your ultimate estate plan. Although these determinations appear to be complex, they become very clear as you begin to work through your assets and decide which of them are "his, hers, or ours." Then, from that fundamental understanding, you need to work forward to decide how you want your assets handled at the time of disability or death. Actually, many people believe that the treatment of spousal assets is more equitable in community property states than in the traditional or Uniform Probate Code states, as both spouses are fifty-fifty owners of all marital assets. This is not so in other states.

If You Live in a Uniform Probate Code State

OUTSIDE OF THE NINE community property states, eighteen states have adopted the Uniform Probate Code (UPC) to govern all matters pertaining to a decedent's estate. Unlike community property states, which dictate how spousal property is owned and treated by spouses, the Uniform Probate states do not alter property ownership rights between spouses except when a spouse dies intestate (without a will). The UPC states concentrate on trying to make probate of a decedent's estate an efficient administrative process. Thus, the approach taken by the UPC states is essentially procedural, and this process has a direct impact on estate planning issues. It also details how property is distributed if a spouse dies intestate.

The Uniform Probate Code reflects what is generally considered to be the most efficient and progressive thinking on how probate matters should be handled throughout the United States. Approved in 1969 and amended several times, this code was approved and recommended by the American Bar Association and the Commissioners on Uniform State Laws, who seek to unify all of the probate laws throughout the country. Such unification would make one law in fifty states for the convenience of all of the people in the country.

States can adopt part of the code, all of it, or none of it. Although to date only sixteen states have accepted the Uniform Probate Code almost in its entirety, many other states have significantly modified their antiquated procedures as a result of the code. Thus, many states have been and will continue to be strongly influenced by the Uniform Probate Code. In fact, all fifty states, including community property states, have updated their procedures in some ways due to its recommendations. It has been a powerful influence for legal reform in almost all traditional probate states and has made probate a much more efficient process in the majority of states.

States that have adopted the Uniform Probate Code, with some modifications, are:

- ➢ Alaska
- ➢ Arizona
- ➢ Colorado
- ➢ Florida
- ➢ Hawaii
- ➢ Idaho

- ➢ Maine
- ➢ Michigan
- ➢ Minnesota
- ➢ Montana
- ➢ Nebraska
- ➢ New Mexico

- ➢ North Dakota
- ➢ South Carolina
- ➢ South Dakota
- ➢ Utah

If you live in a Uniform Probate Code state, will your property rights be affected as they are in community property states? Not at all. As noted previously, the Uniform Probate Code does not change property rights. Rather, it attempts in a broad and sweeping manner to update all of the procedures usually in place in traditional probate court processes.

For instance, in traditional probate states, historically there was no short-form or abbreviated probate process for modest estates. All estates, no matter how small, were required to go through the same formal step-by-step process in probate. This, of course, has been a real hardship to those involved in small estates, as it is not unusual for the funds the decedent has left to be entirely consumed by fees and court costs in the administration procedure (this often requires notices to be filed in newspapers, certified mail to be sent to heirs and beneficiaries, and additional due process legal actions that are often time-consuming and costly).

The Uniform Probate Code was the first attempt to address this problem and recommend short procedures for handling small estates. Since 1969, more and more updating has followed, until the code today represents the best probate thinking of those who advocate both uniformity and efficient administration in all probate proceedings.

If this code is so efficient and modern, why don't all probate courts follow it? There is a large body of law that has been developed over the years that has as its basis the cautious, conservative handling of property. The theory is that when a person dies, probate courts have the duty to make sure that due process is followed, all assets are carefully handled, rights of creditors are protected, hearings are established to ascertain control of the estate, and firm accounting is undertaken to ensure the proper and correct distribution of assets. In many traditional probate states, these goals take precedence over expediting probate, because of concerns that speed could lead to errors, problems, and more complications for the beneficiaries and heirs of the estate.

The Case of the Widow in a Uniform Probate Code State

JIM DIED IN SOUTH DAKOTA without leaving a will. His wife, Amy, had no assets in her own name. She and Jim had married very young, and he took care of all of the checkbooks, financial matters, and household bills. She didn't have title to any of his assets: the farm, cars, cattle, or crops. Several months have passed since Jim died, and now the bills are piling up on the kitchen table. Amy doesn't know what to do. After many a sleepless night, she gets the name of a local attorney from a good neighbor.

The attorney explains to Amy that South Dakota is one of the sixteen states that has adopted the Uniform Probate Code in its entirety, and since Jim didn't leave a will, his estate will be distributed strictly in accordance with the code. Although not all Uniform Probate Code states are alike, in South Dakota, the legislature mandates that Jim's widow will inherit his entire estate if no heir survived him. Amy explains that Jim has a grown child somewhere, but she doesn't know where he is located.

The attorney files an estate proceeding, and he tries and fails to find Jim's son, although he hires a search firm to look for him. The firm advertised in newspapers where the boy and his mother were supposed to have lived, but no trace of him could be found.

The Uniform Code mandates that if the descendants of the deceased are not descendants of the surviving spouse, the survivor receives the first $100,000 of the estate, plus one-half of any balance of the intestate estate. In this case, the son's half of the estate is said to have "escheated to the state," meaning that it goes to the state, to be held until such time as the son should appear and claim it. There are literally millions of dollars in state treasuries around the country waiting for people to return and claim their inheritances, and most never come. States usually have laws that allow their general funds to use these monies eventually.

Amy was able to use her inheritance wisely and has financial help, too, although she writes her own checks and pays her own bills. The son has never been found—but maybe one day he will hear of the newspaper ad and come forward to claim his inheritance.

Most of the Uniform Probate Code states distribute a decedent spouse's estate in the manner outlined in this case. States that have not adopted the UPC make other provisions for surviving spouses when there is intestacy, but each state sets various portions aside for the surviving spouse, although the treatment varies by state.

These are only a few examples of how your current or past state residency influences: (1) the procedure that determines probate administration, (2) the rules and regulations that will govern it, and (3) the substantive ownership rights of spousal property that will take precedence over your will and other legal documents, if you live where state law dictates spousal property issues.

Therefore, it is important to understand what the laws are in your state of residence before you begin to do your estate planning. As you proceed into more and more complex legal planning, you may find that you benefit more from being a resident of one state than another.

State laws are far more complex than most people realize, because they mandate legal ownership concepts between spouses, establish set procedures for handling a decedent's estate, and establish rights of inheritance in the event of intestacy. It is impossible to overemphasize just how pervasive these laws are and how directly they may affect you and your family. For this reason, Chapter 5 discusses the workings of the traditional probate process used in most states, so you will have a fundamental grasp of how your estate may be handled at your disability or death.

Chapter 5 *Five*

The Probate Process

MANY PEOPLE TALK ABOUT THE probate process in our courts, but few really understand the function or purpose of probate, and, more important for estate planning purposes, few comprehend the important *limitations* of probate courts. Just as there are fifty states, so are there fifty different methods of explaining the so-called probate process. Each respective state legislature has created its own form of probate law to govern the residents of its state. No matter where these courts are located, however, one statement can be made about all of them: Probate courts are more involved with the property and families of people who have died than any other court. No courts have a wider impact for estate planning purposes than the probate courts of this country.

Most people are vaguely aware that our laws have evolved from the British common law and have been "Americanized" to suit the needs of today's growing and complex society. However, keep in mind that as the law has evolved and changed through the years, the probate process, which was formalized into law in the nineteenth century, is one area of the law that has maintained a rigid, precise administrative structure, much like that created in past centuries.

However, unlike other courts that may handle a variety of problems, the probate court of today is designed only to administer estates (those of people who have died, and also those of minors and incompetent adults). In this specialized court, strict rules must be meticulously followed; failure to follow all of the steps and procedures of the system often causes complicated, expensive, and time-consuming problems.

Through an intricate process, the court deals on a step-by-step basis with taking an inventory and ultimately selling or transferring all of the assets of the deceased, from the family pet to the furniture, stamp collections, real estate, boats, boat motors, lawn chairs, cash, bonds, glassware, antiques, and any other assets that the deceased owned. Due to the importance of property and ownership in our country, the probate process was developed to assure guidance and equity for the transfer of property from a decedent to others.

Some critics of the system, however, refer to the probate process as a "quagmire" because of its rigidity, rules, and multiple hearings. Although the process is indeed laborious, it is in place in every state in the United States, and almost every family is at some time involved, either directly or indirectly, with this court and its rulings. Therefore, a basic understanding of its purpose and process is helpful for the estate planner, because this knowledge can help you decide whether the probate court is the best venue for transferring assets or whether it is a process best avoided.

If you want to know the specifics of the probate process in your state, be forewarned that they are not always easy to find. You can call your local probate court to inquire whether they have any brochures available. State bar associations often have brochures on wills, but seldom do they publish anything on the process itself.

The best possible source of information is the actual law, which may be found in the statutory laws at your local bar association law library. This is cumbersome and often confusing, but it does give you an idea of what is involved in the process.

The Reasons for Probate

THE PURPOSE OF PROBATE IS FOURFOLD:
1 to clear title to property passing from the decedent to beneficiaries;
2 to protect the decedent's estate and beneficiaries from claims of creditors;
3 to protect creditors of the decedent by providing a format within which they may pursue their claims; and
4 to distribute the decedent's property in a proper and orderly manner.

Source: *Estate Planning Simplified,* by Doug Morey, Professional Education System, Inc. (1990)

Although the probate process may differ from state to state, almost all states have a general probate process that usually consists of common legal steps to collect or marshal assets, settle the decedent's final debts, and transfer legal title to property. The statutory language sets forth the entire process the court must use to handle an estate. Notices are given to interested parties for hearings, and dates for the completion of certain steps are established so that issues can be resolved and the entire process can be completed in a timely manner.

As you might guess, any time you have rules and hearings and notices and reams of paper, you also have impatience, expense, and time-consuming hours. This is why the probate process is often best avoided if possible and why in recent years state legislatures have expended considerable time and effort to streamline these procedures to make probate courts more efficient.

In the case of a small estate where state law permits abbreviated proceedings, it may even be possible to swiftly advance through the probate process by what is known as "short-form probate procedure." Nearly every state has such a procedure for administering small estates. These are relatively brief procedures with modest court costs of less than $50. Some states permit this for estates under $15,000, some for those under $5,000 and some for estates of less than $25,000. To find out if your state offers a short form of probate, call your local court, bar association, or attorney for more information.

Also note that more probate-avoidance options have become available in recent years. Once you understand the probate process, you can decide whether you want to use it in your estate plan.

How Does Probate Work?

AS NOTED AT THE BEGINNING OF THIS chapter, the process of probate administration works in fifty different ways, depending on the state. In most states, a complete statutory process begins automatically when a person dies and leaves behind probate assets. Because the court has no jurisdiction over non-probate assets, only those assets that are probate in nature can be administered by a probate process. This process decides exactly how the decedent's property will be legally transferred to others. Here is a detailed description of the entire probate process.

Step 1: The Will ... or Lack of It

THE WILL IS THE CORNERSTONE OF THE entire probate process and is the central document the court uses to determine all matters that may come before it. It is a basic frame of reference if there are disputes, claims, or a need for clarification regarding the property or the intentions of the decedent.

First, the will is filed in the probate court, a procedure called "admitting the will to probate," wherein the will becomes a matter of public record. Its genuineness may be tested at this point. If found to have been revoked by a later will, it is not admitted; if found to be the authentic testament of the decedent, it is admitted to probate, and its terms are followed throughout the administrative process, unless later they are set aside in a will-contest proceeding.

If there is no will, the court makes the determination that the decedent died without leaving a will and that the estate will be processed as intestate. Intestacy means that the court must process the estate in accordance with state laws. Final distribution is made according to "intestate succession," as defined by the decedent's state of residence. "Intestate succession" is a term used to indicate that the property of the deceased will descend to his lineal descendants, those to whom the decedent is related by blood, or those whom the decedent has legally adopted.

When disputes arise between a spouse and blood relatives of a decedent, the courts must do a balancing act. More often than not, such disputes arise when one spouse dies and leaves behind a spouse and children from a previous marriage. If there is also a will in which the decedent specifies how his or her property is to be distributed, courts will enforce that will. However, if a spouse dies without leaving a will, the courts look to succession laws that specifically designate how the property of the decedent is to be allocated between the surviving spouse and the decedent's children. Each state has different proportions it gives to the spouse and the heirs, but in all cases, the spousal rights take precedence for a certain percentage of the estate, with the balance of the estate going to the children.

What happens to the property of all of those individuals who die without having a will? The legislative statutes of the deceased's resident state include a provision called "The Law of Descent and Distribution." This is the law of intestate succession, essentially the state's estate plan for the deceased. In other words, if you don't write a will, the state writes it for you, and that is the law that applies to your assets at the time of your death. Although this may seem unfair (because the state does not know your wishes), at least it does serve the public interest to make sure that your property is disposed of in an orderly manner.

Once the court determines that the will is the valid declaration of the decedent, it begins the process of appointing the fiduciary. This person is also called the executor or executrix (female), conservator, or administrator, depending on the state involved.

Step 2: Put Someone in Charge of the Estate

AFTER A WILL IS ADMITTED TO THE probate process, the first job of the judge is to appoint a fiduciary: someone to be in charge of the estate proceedings. If there is a will, the judge appoints the executor named in the will; if not, then the judge will appoint an administrator specified by statute to serve in that capacity. Each state has different rules about who is entitled to serve as fiduciary, but usually statutes provide that the surviving spouse, children, and grandchildren, in that order of priority, have the right to serve as administrator. A person appointed under the authority of a will is known as the executor, or, if a woman, as the executrix. One named to administer the estate of a decedent who died intestate is known as the administrator or administratrix, as the case may be.

The fiduciary's duties are determined by state law. Each fiduciary must carefully perform those statutory duties. If the fiduciary fails to fulfill any duty, the court may remove that fiduciary, who may also have liability to others if statutory duties are not performed.

The fiduciary basically is in charge of the estate: usually the fiduciary retains an attorney to assist in the administration of the estate and to give advice on how to complete the process. Because the process often appears rigid and complicated to a layperson, an attorney may be able to provide advice to expedite the process.

The fiduciary has several duties to perform. First, he must collect, inventory, appraise, and preserve all assets during the estate process, and then he must permit all creditors to file claims for payment of debts due them from the decedent. Next, he or she pays taxes and debts that are due. Finally, he formally transfers, by deed or other legal document, all of the estate assets to the decedent's beneficiaries under the will, or, if the decedent left no will, to the lineal heirs, in accordance with the laws of intestate succession for the decedent's resident state.

The fiduciary sends a notice of death to beneficiaries named in the will, to heirs at law, and, in many states, to creditors of the decedent. State law may require that this notice be published in a newspaper in general circulation in the county of the decedent's residence or that notices be sent by certified mail or by ordinary mail. This notice is a due process requirement, and each state handles this issue differently, depending on the legislative intent of the state involved. In some states a legal notice of someone's death must be published in a newspaper once a week for six weeks; in other states, the notice must appear in the paper for three full, consecutive weeks. Some states do not require a newspaper notice at all. Expenses of this nature are generally paid from the decedent's estate, as are court costs and the costs of appraisals and attorney and fiduciary fees.

It is then the duty of the fiduciary to inventory the assets of the decedent, to have them appraised and insured if necessary, and generally to preserve and protect them until transfer to the proper parties. This aspect is crucial, because the value of the estate will affect other aspects of the estate proceedings, such as the estate taxes to be paid to the state and federal taxing authorities and the fees to be paid to the fiduciary and the fiduciary's attorney.

Debts due from the estate (such as utilities, personal loans and other debts) must usually be approved for payment by the probate court. Taxes due on the estate (for estate and income tax purposes) are determined by state and federal regulation. Finally, fees for fiduciaries and attorneys are usually set by court rules and allowed by the court. In essence, the fiduciary collects assets and income due or owned by the decedent (all of which are assets of the estate), holds all of the assets temporarily so he can pay fees, expenses and taxes, and then ultimately makes distribution of the balance of the assets to the beneficiaries of the estate, according to the law of the state where the person lived at the time of death.

In the meantime, the court determines the names of the beneficiaries in the will and each one's share. If there is no will, the court will hold hearings to determine the heirs who will inherit the estate and the portion each will receive under state law. Unknown heirs, children born out of wedlock, and others who believe they should inherit have a right to file their claims and receive a hearing. The court then determines the individual(s) who will inherit and the portion each is entitled to receive by law.

The fiduciary completes pending lawsuits and defends any will contests, prepares and pays all local, state, and federal taxes, pays creditors, transfers property to the proper parties, and finally files an accounting of proceedings with the court to complete the estate administration. The fiduciary has the responsibility to handle the decedent's estate in an efficient, cost-effective manner, which is often time-consuming and difficult. Fortunately, fiduciaries are paid a reasonable fee, usually based upon a percentage of assets handled, when the estate is closed. (See Appendix A for a more comprehensive discussion of their fee arrangements.) Also, the fiduciary can obtain the services of an attorney to assist with all aspects of the estate proceedings; an accountant for help with tax matters and income tax returns; and appraisers to evaluate the decedent's assets. These professionals are paid from the assets of the decedent's estate.

Finally, the fiduciary is required to file with the court a final accounting, which is a full and complete financial snapshot of all of the assets of the decedent, all of the debts, the disbursements made in the course of the estate proceedings, and finally, the record of all beneficiary distributions the fiduciary has made. Often this filing must be accompanied by the canceled checks, so the court has actual evidence that there has been correct financial management of the estate during its administration. The financial management of the fiduciary is open to the scrutiny of the heirs and beneficiaries and also of the court. Objections can be filed at any time during the proceedings about the way the fiduciary has handled the finances of the estate. Also, the fiduciary is personally responsible for using good investment judgment, or face the consequences: removal as the fiduciary, fines, or penalties. In some cases, if there is fraud, the fiduciary may be prosecuted on the basis of a misdemeanor or felony—very serious offenses.

Throughout the probate process, the fiduciary has wide latitude for handling the decedent's estate probate assets. However, that doesn't mean that the fiduciary can exercise independent judgment in all matters. The fiduciary must consider the intentions of the decedent, understand the attitudes of the beneficiaries, and use the legal duty of care statutorily required of all fiduciaries: to apply the "reasonableness of a prudent person."

This is especially important if the fiduciary is required by circumstances to manage an ongoing business or to make investments during the course of administration. Risks are ever present for loss or waste of assets. The fiduciary may be held liable for these losses if the "prudent person" rule has not been followed.

Another area of conflict may arise when the fiduciary wants to distribute assets to beneficiaries and heirs. How this is accomplished, either in cash or in kind, is often a matter for litigation and dispute. Make no mistake: the job of a fiduciary is not an easy one. And it is often made more difficult by family members who tell the fiduciary that "Mom wanted me to have Dad's watch before she died." The fiduciary must either resolve the difficult and diverse problems during administration or bring them to the attention of the judge for hearing and resolution.

Also, throughout the estate administration, claimants, creditors, heirs, and beneficiaries can file objections to the fiduciary's handling of the estate, and they often file objections to the final account of the fiduciary. In many cases, court hearings are necessary to determine how best to divide assets, how to make distribution equitably, and how to make sure the fiduciary is not personally liable for his actions in making distributions from the estate.

This is probably one of the strengths of the probate process: it can bring finality to an array of issues that may plague the family and the administration of an estate. Of course, it is also expensive, because each motion and hearing leads to legal fees, additional fiduciary fees, and court costs. Even so, the systematic resolution of complex issues may be best accomplished in a legal setting. Others may argue that a good trustee or family counselor may solve these matters outside of the probate setting and do so much more economically. Although that may be true in some instances, it's probably still true that a court of law can impose order and decisiveness in a complex setting more efficiently than another venue.

Step 3: Take an Inventory of the Probate Estate

PERHAPS THE MOST CRUCIAL AND MOST OFTEN misunderstood part of an estate proceeding is the inventory filing. In each probate process, the fiduciary must file with the court an inventory of the probate assets of the decedent. Inventory is important because it plays a significant role to:

➢ establish values that determine inheritance taxes due, and that may affect income taxes to be paid by the estate;

➢ determine the tax basis for assets that will have a major impact upon tax issues many years in the future;

➢ set values on certain property that the surviving spouse may, by state law, have an option to purchase; and

➢ determine legal fees and fiduciary fees.

Often the fiduciary has problems including all of the decedent's assets in an inventory. Family members and others may claim that the decedent didn't in fact own a certain item in dispute, or that the item belonged to another, or that the decedent gifted the item just before death. The surviving spouse may also take the position that all of the household property is hers, for example, or that all of the assets belong to her, since it was her employment that paid for certain valuable items, particularly if there are valuable household items or collectibles.

In case of disagreement concerning what should or should not be included in an inventory or the value of any item of probate property listed in the inventory, the fiduciary has a legal duty to file a motion with the court for a hearing on all matters in dispute. Typically, relatives of the decedent and those individuals or entities named in the decedent's will receive written notice of the hearing and will have the opportunity to obtain legal counsel before the court hears all of the evidence and makes a ruling on each issue. After the court rules, the parties can appeal the decision. If they do not, the estate proceedings move forward. Many problems can be avoided prior to death by discussions within families; however, these conversations seem never to take place. Failure to solve issues of this nature within a family before death makes it almost certain that these problems will become magnified after death. Family members will be burdened with them, and costly litigation may be required to finally solve a long-standing problem.

How thorough does an inventory have to be? The detail required depends largely on the value of the tangibles, household items, and collectibles involved; tax issues that may be present; and the final distribution of the decedent's assets. If a controversy between a second spouse and the children of a first marriage is likely, if the value of the assets is substantial, and if the ultimate distribution of the estate is not clear, a very detailed accounting may be necessary. This may include itemization, photography, and evaluation of each and every item the decedent left, including personal clothing, items owned as a hobby, even towels, washcloths, and shoes, in the extreme case.

The courts and tax authorities usually do not require this level of detail; however, the situation may be such that the fiduciary wants all of the parties involved to be satisfied that an accurate record has been made and that the items listed are correct. If any of the inventory items are not correct, then interested parties can bring this to the attention of the court for hearing, and the inventory may ultimately be amended.

Often, if the surviving spouse is the only beneficiary, the fiduciary may feel quite comfortable in attributing a value to the decedent's inventory that is reasonably accurate without compiling a list of assets and appraising all of them. However, a fiduciary must be very careful in exactly how the inventory in every estate is completed, as this basic duty is critical to the process and has so many ramifications for future legal and tax issues.

Step 4: Calculate and Pay the Decedent's Debts

ONE IMPORTANT REASON FOR THE probate process in its present form is making sure that the decedent's debts are paid. In short, we have probate because of the rights of creditors. The probate proceeding is not only the collection of assets and their distribution to beneficiaries and heirs but also ensuring that the creditors are paid in full before property is passed to others. Thus, probate is a major cog in the wheel of the economic life of the nation, because it mandates payment of bills.

In recent years, this mandate has been diluted as state legislative bodies give way to the pressure to expedite probate proceedings. Therefore, in many states today the rights of creditors to payment of debts are secondary to the rights of beneficiaries and heirs to complete probate as rapidly as possible. In these states, there is no settlement of debts in the estate administration, because creditors are no longer entitled to notice at the death of the decedent. This often means that creditors are not required to file their claims directly against the estate but may elect to take legal action against the beneficiaries and heirs who inherit the decedent's assets.

Some fiduciaries, in order to protect the beneficiaries, heirs, creditors, and themselves, insist that all claims be brought within the probate process in order to seek finality on debt issues during the administration process. This seems to be a more businesslike approach; however, those who want their money as soon as possible from the process may not be very sympathetic to the probate delay necessary to hear from creditors.

A related issue in the forefront of probate controversy today is that of probate avoidance versus debt. Because probate courts have jurisdiction only over probate assets, it is not unusual for the fiduciary to be appointed by the court only to find that all of the decedent's assets are non-probate, such as life insurance policies and real estate held by joint tenancy. The fiduciary may find that the decedent left behind thousands of dollars of debt due to various creditors but that there are no probate assets to pay these debts, as illustrated in the case presented below.

The Case of the Disappointed Creditor

JOHN AND MONA WERE MARRIED for ten years and had three children. When John was sixty-seven, he died quite suddenly. He left a home titled to himself and Mona as joint tenants with the right of survivorship. In addition, he and Mona had several certificates of deposit and bank accounts totaling around $23,400, also held as joint tenants with right of survivorship.

Although John left a will with all of his property going to Mona, he left no probate estate to be administered by that will. All of their property was held in joint-and-survivorship titles, so that upon his death, all of the assets—the house, bank accounts, and certificates of deposit—went automatically to Mona.

Now Mona has received a letter from a credit card company demanding that she pay John's credit card balance of $30,000. Does she have to pay this bill, which she did not know about?

State laws vary on this question. Some state laws take the position that all assets go to the surviving widow under joint-and-survivorship ownership and that she has no legal duty to pay a spouse's bills if she did not cosign on the loans. Other states mandate that if the surviving spouse received assets, she should pay the bills to the extent of her benefit.

In Mona's case, she and the credit card company agreed that she would pay one-third of the claim and the credit card company would discharge the rest of the claim. Mona gave more than she wanted to, and the credit card company got far less than it wanted to accept. But this compromise worked, and the problem was resolved.

Step 5: Find Out How Much Tax Is Due

WHOEVER SAID THAT THE ONLY SURE THINGS in life are death and taxes was surely correct. The tax collector has an interest in estate proceedings in the majority of states, both for state and for federal tax purposes. California, Florida, and a few other states have no death tax as such but do have what is known as a "pickup tax," a minimum tax based on the federal estate tax return credit. However, it is safe to say that for the thousands of estates that pass through the probate process throughout the United States, tax issues are of paramount importance.

If you think about it, you will realize why taxing estates for "death taxes" is so attractive to the tax collector: the decedent, who is no longer with us, cannot complain. And not surprisingly, local, state, and federal governments usually obtain some tax benefit from an estate, either through an income tax or an inheritance or estate tax.

Usually tax matters are of paramount importance at the time of death, either to determine the amount due for payment of inheritance taxes, or to determine some federal tax ramifications for the future of the surviving spouse, or to fix a basis in real estate, or to determine tax issues that may affect a business interest. It is usually necessary to file a state and/or federal estate tax return at someone's death, even if there is no tax due to be paid.

Taxes, or the amount to be paid or to be avoided, remain one of the most important aspects of estate planning today, primarily because you have so many excellent opportunities to save money by good advance planning. This aspect alone leads people to seek guidance from professional estate planners, since the savings can amount to hundreds of thousands of dollars.

Often people become so involved with saving tax dollars that they want all of their assets to be classified as non-probate assets in the belief that non-probate assets automatically avoid tax. This is a misguided and erroneous assumption. Taxes may be due on a non-probate asset as they are on probate assets. Whether an estate is probate or non-probate has nothing to do with whether taxes are due or the amount. Taxes are derived from the value of the assets owned, so the amount of estate tax due at death is not significantly related to the assets' probate or non-probate status.

States vary in how life insurance, for instance, is treated for tax purposes. In some states, if the decedent owned life insurance, the state law may provide that no tax is due if the surviving spouse is the beneficiary. If another person is the beneficiary, then the funds paid out in accordance with the terms of the insurance policy may be added to the estate taxes due from the decedent's estate.

No inheritance, whether the result of a distribution under an insurance policy or a gift from the decedent under the will, is taxed as income to a named beneficiary unless it is distributable income held by the estate during estate administration. If another person is the beneficiary, then the policy may be taxed as an asset of the decedent's estate under inheritance tax law.

One of the basic reasons for estate planning is to give you, the planner, an opportunity to determine your net worth, collect your assets and debts, and then go to a qualified tax planner to determine what taxes may be due from your estate or your survivors at the time of death. If you complete this planning in advance, you have many legal options that may be a real benefit in the future, as will be further explained in Chapter 6.

Step 6: Distribute the Decedent's Estate

ONCE THE ASSETS OF THE DECEDENT have been collected and appraised, debts have been paid to the satisfaction of all of the creditors, taxes have been settled, and claims and other matters in contention have been resolved, the fiduciary is now ready to make distribution of the decedent's estate.

If the decedent left a will, the fiduciary will make the distribution to the beneficiaries named in the will. However, if there is a surviving spouse, that spouse has the right in many states to "take against the will." This means that the surviving spouse may elect to take his or her statutory share, as specified by the law of the state where the decedent resided.

The Case of the Surviving Spouse

JIM AND JAN MARRIED LATE in life and wanted to make sure that their children by previous marriages were protected. They made wills providing that they would both own their home, which they had bought jointly, during their lifetime. At the death of the first spouse, the surviving spouse would have a life estate in the home, meaning that the surviving spouse would actually own the right to live in the house for his or her lifetime. At the death of the surviving spouse, the home was to be sold and the proceeds of sale were to be divided equally among their children.

However, when Jan died, Jim found he was unhappy with the terms of her will, under which he would have only a life estate in the home. And as a result of longstanding laws in effect in many states, known as the "spousal laws of election," Jim had the option either to accept the terms of Jan's will or to accept a statutory share from her estate, an amount designated by state law that is a percentage of the total value of her estate. Only spouses have this right of election, which permits them to receive property under the will of the deceased spouse or under the election laws of their state.

Jim decided to accept a statutory share and not that portion due him under her will. Therefore, when Jim decided to elect the statutory share of Jan's estate, he received one-third of the estate, and he also had the right to purchase the marital home at a fair market value as determined by appraisal. In addition, state law gave him the right to take by purchase, or as part of his statutory share, all of the household goods.

Imagine, if you will, the anger Jan's children felt when they learned that their mom's home was going to become Jim's and that he also was going to have all of her keepsakes, furniture, and other sentimental articles in the home. This scenario is very common, especially when second marriages are involved. After Jim exercised his right to elect to take against the will, he received a one-third credit for his share of the value of Jan's estate and deposited the balance of the funds due to become the owner of the marital home. He also "elected" against the estate to take, by purchase or statute, all of the household goods.

The upset children went to the attorney who drafted the wills. His records and correspondence indicated that he had advised Jim and Jan in writing of the possibility of the election provision available to the surviving spouse. In a handwritten note, the couple indicated they knew of the right of election and wanted to sign their wills anyway.

Spouses do have, in almost all states, certain statutory rights that they can claim against the estate of the decedent spouse. They have not only the right to elect to take against the will but also the right to purchase the marital home, the right to a year or more widow's allowance from the decedent's estate, and other significant rights. Those rights continue to exist even if both spouses sign wills and other documents. At the death of the first spouse, these statutory rights are not extinguished; they continue to be rights of the surviving spouse.

For that reason, when a fiduciary is dealing with spousal estates, one of his or her most important duties is to obtain from the surviving spouse a document, in writing, in which that spouse either accepts the will's provision or elects to assert his or her claims against the estate. If the surviving spouse accepts the provisions of the will, the fiduciary is free to make distributions to the people designated in the will.

If there is no will, the fiduciary will make distributions to those individuals designated by the law of the decedent's resident state. In Ohio, for example, if the decedent died without leaving a will, the surviving spouse receives a statutory sum of money and a fractional percentage of the estate, depending on whether or not there are children. The balance of the estate is divided first among any minor children, and then to the other children. It is possible, and not unusual, that between the distribution for the surviving spouse and the distribution for the minor child or children, there may be no estate assets remaining for the adult children.

Trying to make distributions of an estate for which no will exists is very difficult in most instances, as the family expectations are seldom met by the statutory provisions, which often seem unfair and inequitable to those involved. That is why it is good planning to make a will so that you can be sure that you, and not the statutory provisions of your state, determine the distribution of your assets.

Step 7: Finalize the Estate Process

ONCE ALL OF THIS HAS BEEN RESOLVED, the fiduciary must file the final account. This is a financial statement, often with canceled checks attached, showing each and every transaction in the estate. This is the last official document the fiduciary is required to file, and it contains a concise financial account: what assets were collected, what bills were paid, and what distributions were made. The balance of assets remaining in the hands of the fiduciary must be zero. Some state laws require copies to be attached of all checks written, all bills paid, and all receipts from recipients of distributions. Current law is moving away from this comprehensive accounting due to the cost of filing it and the time involved in preparing such a lengthy document.

In any case, after the court reviews this process and finds it satisfactory, the fiduciary is released, and the case is closed, unless some unhappy heir or beneficiary is dissatisfied with the accounting. At this point objections may be filed to fees, transactions, distributions, and any and all other matters relating to the financial management of the estate. Hearings may be required, and motions and affidavits may be filed with the court. It is here that the final complaints can be heard. After all of these matters are resolved one way or the other, the court will finally accept the account with whatever modifications were required, and the estate is finally at an end. The fiduciary is released from the legal duties imposed, and all matters in the probate process are brought to a conclusion.

Planning for Probate

IT IS NO WONDER, GIVEN WHAT MANY people perceive as the red tape involved in probate proceedings, that there is a general trend away from using the probate process. Today individuals not only are trying to formulate estate plans to avoid probate but also are attempting to combine their financial plans with their estate plans so that they can manage the entire complexity of their finances and life decisions under one comprehensive plan. This means that many estates may eventually be composed of non-probate assets—none of which will be involved in the probate process. Because you are the person who decides how your assets are titled, you have an excellent opportunity for good estate planning if you concentrate your efforts to maximize your estate and minimize misunderstandings and costs. How you title your assets and how you plan now for the future are decisions that have far-reaching consequences.

As you begin the estate planning process, keep the following in mind:

➤ You are the person who decides how your assets are titled and how those assets will flow at the time of your death.

➤ The title of an asset determines whether it is a probate or non-probate asset.

➤ If an asset is a probate asset, it will pass through a probate process, which is determined by the state of your residence at the time of your death. If you leave a will, it takes precedence; if you don't have a will, your state of residence has one for you. Even if you have a will, there may be other circumstances that permit a different final distribution from what you intended.

One of the most important things individuals should do when embarking on estate planning is to find out about a few basic laws in the state in which they live. Consider, in particular, the following:

➤ Do you live in a community property state?

➤ Do you live in a state that has adopted the Uniform Probate Code?

➤ What happens to your property if you die without leaving a will?

➤ What kind of a probate process do you have in your state?

➤ What are the rights of your surviving spouse to elect to take against your will?

The probate process has expedited procedures for the small estate, usually estimated at under $25,000, which may require the filing of only a single document. However, for larger estates, clearly there is a defined, at times protracted, process to handle the estate in a step-by-step manner aimed at helping to resolve potentially difficult issues. On the whole, however, the following are often true:

➤ The probate process is time-consuming.

➤ The probate process is costly in both financial and emotional terms.

➤ You have little control over the probate process, because it is statutory—that is, prescribed by law.

➤ The chances are that you and your family will be involved in some form of probate process unless you take specific steps to avoid it.

Your actions can determine exactly how your property will be handled at the time of your disability or death. You have full authority to direct the manner in which your assets will be controlled at all times. However, if you do not put your wishes in writing, via specific legal documents, then the probate process will intervene and make those decisions necessary to control your estate, both during your lifetime (if you become disabled) and at the time of your death.

As probate still remains a little-understood, mysterious, and intimidating process, most people may be wise to avoid it. A good estate plan can include a comprehensive method to avoid probate by combining certain financial and legal tools to control and direct your estate along other more efficient, cost-effective pathways better suited for you and your family. Part Two discusses these tools in depth.

Part Two

Estate Planning Tools

C h a p t e r **6** *S i x*

Financial Tools:
The Building Blocks of
Estate Planning

JUST AS IT TAKES MANY DIFFERENT tools to build a house, fix a car, or repair a sidewalk, it takes a variety of tools to create an estate plan. Although the tools available to the estate planner are many, each one is designed to suit only one particular need at a time. In theory, the more needs you have, the more tools you may need to employ; the more sophisticated your goals, the more sophisticated the selection and design of each tool will be.

Therefore, appreciating the uses of each planning tool is important. For instance, you should understand exactly what a will can do for you and, just as important, what it cannot. It is not relevant in the least that one will is two pages and another twenty-two pages. The key issues are whether it addresses your planning needs and whether it reflects your wishes about the distribution of your assets.

As you begin to think about the various options available, you will begin to realize that some are just right for you and that you will have little, if any, interest in others. This evaluation process will help your plan take shape and emerge.

Your friends may mention various legal documents, such as their wills or trust instruments. They may tell you about the plans they have made with their children concerning the use of power-of-attorney instruments, or how they have set up their bank accounts and stock investments. Although it is often interesting to compare notes with friends, it is not always a good idea to plan your estate according to information you receive from them. You should make all of your decisions based on your own unique estate planning needs. Each legal tool has specific functions, each accomplishes a specific purpose for the planner, and each is a single piece of the total estate plan puzzle.

If you are like most Americans, you have certain estate goals you want to achieve. You may be a single person who wants to ensure that if you become ill for a period of time, someone else, such as a family member or good friend, will have the medical and legal authority to make decisions for you during your period of disability. You may be a married person concerned about your spouse's needs in the event of your death or about your children's security if you are not here to assist them.

In any set of circumstances, each goal may require a separate financial or legal instrument or a combination of them. Below is a list of the most common and useful estate and financial planning tools, followed by a brief discussion and explanation of each one. To help you work through the options and decide on the best combination for your needs, you may want to seek the advice of an estate planning or financial planning expert. But read through the list first to get some ideas.

Your Estate Planning Tool Kit

➤ **Annuities**
  Fixed
  Variable
➤ **Business plan options**
➤ **Charitable gifting**
➤ **Deferred income plans**
  401(k)   *Keogh*
  IRA   *SEP*
➤ **Descent and distribution**
  (state intestacy laws)
➤ **Disclaimer**
➤ **Financial investments**
➤ **Gifts**
➤ **Incorporation proceedings**
➤ **Insurance**
  Liability insurance
  Life insurance
  Medical insurance
➤ **Life estate transfers**
➤ **Marital deduction planning**

  Annuities
  Generational trusts
  Gifting
  Trusts
➤ **Partnership planning**
➤ **Pension plans**
➤ **Powers of attorney for**
  financial matters
➤ **Powers of attorney for**
  health-care matters
➤ **Profit-sharing plans**
➤ **Property ownership types**
  Co-ownership
  Joint and survivorship
  Payable-on-death accounts
  Sole ownership
  Tenants in common
  Transfer-on-death accounts
➤ **Rental plans**
➤ **Retirement plans**

IRA
Keogh
Roth IRA
Work-related plans
➤ **Trusts**
Charitable trusts
Irrevocable trusts

Living trusts
Medicaid trusts
Revocable trusts
Testamentary trusts
➤ **Wills**
Living will
Will

These options are like "Fortune's Toolbox," because you can keep—or lose—a fortune, depending on which tool you use and exactly how well you use it.

A brief explanation follows about each of the financial tools available for your use, because the more you know about the many options open to you, the better your decisions will be about which tools will best fit into your overall estate plan. No effort is made here to discuss these options from a scholarly point of view, because this is not a dissertation on the technical aspects. Rather, this is a brief overview to give you an idea of what is out there for your use so that you can begin to understand the options available for good, solid estate planning.

Annuities

AN ANNUITY IS A SPECIAL TYPE OF investment plan. Although traditional insurance plans were designed to protect against the loss of a home or life, today's annuities protect against loss of income. For instance, you can buy an annuity that will preserve your investment or collect tax-deferred income. The annuity will then pay you back in the future, either by lump-sum payment or monthly payments, depending on the plan you select.

Annuities offer two estate planning advantages. First and foremost is the opportunity to invest in a tax-deferred plan that will grow over time. Second is the opportunity to use the annuity as a non-probate asset, which can avoid the probate process by naming a beneficiary who is to inherit the annuity in the event of the death of its owner.

Annuities earn interest on the principal sums invested; then the interest earns interest. The income you accumulate is tax-deferred—that is, the taxes you would ordinarily pay are deferred, so you actually earn interest on the sums you might have had to pay for taxes. Taxes will ultimately have to be paid, but often they can be deferred over a very long period of time, and the beneficiary who receives the proceeds of the annuity will pay the tax after inheritance.

Not everyone is a good match for an annuity. But say, for example, a grandfather wishes to invest some money for his newly born grandchild, this is an excellent way to provide the child with tax-deferred funds in the future. The grandfather has the opportunity to invest for his grandchild without paying taxes on the accumulating assets, and at the same time, he can designate his grandson as the beneficiary on the annuity, thus completely bypassing the probate process. This makes the annuity an excellent estate planning device.

There are two kinds of annuities: fixed and variable. Simply stated, the fixed annuity guarantees a certain fixed rate of interest that will accrue to the funds initially invested. The variable annuity plan applies a variable rate of interest to the invested funds. Often that rate is at "market" or "established" rates, depending upon the interest rate that the company calculates as being applicable to your portion of its overall investment portfolio. Annuities have become popular in the past several years, basically because of the tax-deferred aspect of these funds, which operate in many ways like an IRA (without the $2,000 annual limit that applies to IRAs).

In addition, annuities permit the purchaser to name himself as the beneficiary or to name another person, such as a spouse or child, for a return of income over a future period of time. This may be particularly helpful if the annuity holder wants to provide for periodic monthly payments in the future to a member of his family who, he feels, may not be able to handle a large lump-sum payment.

Tax deferment, however, is still the main attraction of annuities. This means that if you invest $10,000 in a fixed annuity to mature at the end of ten years, all interest is tax-deferred during those ten years.

There are disadvantages to the annuity. Some experts believe that the annuity is not as flexible as a trust, and that annuities tie up your money too long for too much risk, because they may not be insured. Others feel that purchasing tax-free municipal bonds or other tax-exempt investments are much better financial decisions.

The biggest disadvantage to an annuity as an investment may be that if you must cash in your annuity for some reason, you could pay up to 10 percent to the IRS as a tax penalty and up to 6 percent to the insurance company. These are all factors to consider before you invest in any annuity. For some, annuities may be excellent estate planning tools; for others, it may simply be the least desirable of many other options that would better serve them.

Before you make a commitment to purchase an annuity, you should be convinced that it is the best possible investment for the funds involved. Make sure that you can comply with the terms of the annuity, which include leaving the funds in the annuity account for a certain period of time, and that you are accomplishing some special purpose with an annuity that you could not do any other way.

Charitable Donations

CHARITABLE GIVING IS AN IMPORTANT tool for estate planners to consider. The simple act of giving weekly to your church or making an annual donation to the United Way or to the college or charity of your choice can help satisfy sophisticated gift and tax goals. In fact, Americans who give to charity today receive even greater benefits during their lifetimes than they did in the past.

For those who intend to contribute to charities, the possibilities for tax savings and estate planning are many. Charitable giving has always played a large role in the United States, and most Americans continue to make charitable giving a periodic event. Because many people gift to their religious institutions, their favorite charity, or to a special educational institution, it's important to understand the tax advantages. To encourage gifting to charities, the IRS permits an itemized deduction with limitations for the fair market value of the gift. This means that if you give your house of worship $300 a year, you may claim an itemized deduction on your tax return for the year in which you made the gift.

Smart planners are now encouraged to donate "appreciated property" to charities. For instance, if you purchased stock in 1991 that cost you $1,000 and that stock is now worth $10,000, you may donate the stock to the charity at the appreciated value and receive an itemized deduction for the full value of the stock—a nice gift for the church and a nice deduction for the taxpayer. This is particularly attractive to those who would otherwise pay significant capital gains taxes on the sale of the stock. Many IRS rules govern gifting that involves transfers of assets to avoid taxes, but charitable gifting offers the estate planner a better way to give during one's lifetime instead of through a will because of the many benefits to the donor as well as to the recipient.

You may want to create a charitable trust, whereby you transfer assets into a trust and receive the income during your lifetime; at your death, the trust transfers the assets directly to the charity outside of any court or other legal procedure. Many variations are available on this theme, enabling you to plan your gifting to charities to avoid probate and save taxes. If you regularly gift to charities and own appreciated property, this estate planning tool may be an excellent choice, allowing you to transfer the property to a trust, which then sells the property. At the time of the sale by this special charitable trust, no tax is due on the sale, even if appreciated property is involved. The charity that received the property then pays you an annuity over your lifetime (or over the lives of those you select). This increases your cash flow, avoids estate taxes at your death, and avoids what could have been large capital gains. The assets remaining in the trust are then paid at your death to the charity or charities you have chosen. In addition, you are allowed to use, at the time of the gift, a discounted value of that remainder interest as a charitable contribution on your federal income tax return, thus saving you income-tax dollars.

In his article, "Do Your Heirs a Favor: Plan Your Estate for Taxes," written for the Web site www.moneycentral.msn.com, Jeff Schnepper explains, "In the classical example, these tax savings are used to buy estate tax-exempt life insurance to replace the wealth going to charity rather than to your family. The net result is no capital gains on the sale, more cash in your pocket, the same wealth transfer to your family, and big dollars to the charity. Everybody wins except the IRS."

Gifts

CLOSELY RELATED TO CHARITABLE gifting is the concept of gifting to family members. As you begin to plan your estate to minimize court and tax involvement, you may be tempted at one time or another to say, "The heck with this. I'm just going to give it away, and then I won't have to worry about it, and I know all of my assets will go right to my kids without any fuss or muss."

Alas, even if you were tempted to give away all of your assets, you would not be wise to do so. You could create even bigger tax and estate problems for your children. Likewise, if you intend to make gifts to your religious institution, favorite charity, college, hospital, or other charity, you should talk to your accountant about which of the several gifting options would be in your best interest from a tax point of view.

Most important, do not make gifts unless you can get along without the assets you want to gift. Realize that once a gift is made, even if you later need the asset returned, it will not come back to you. Things happen that are unexpected: the child you made the gift to may become too ill to return it, or become embroiled in a divorce. Any number of circumstances can arise to make the return of the gift to you impossible. If you make a gift, you should consider it permanent. And never make a gift unless your attorney or accountant has explained the tax ramifications of doing so.

Another situation in which well-meaning people, especially grandparents, may cause more problems than they solve arises when they make gifts to minors. Throughout the United States, any significant gift made to a minor (someone under eighteen years of age) may require the appointment of a guardian by a court so that the guardian will be responsible for the funds of the minor. To avoid having to appoint a guardian, it may be possible to make a gift to a minor by depositing the gift in a bank in the name of the donor, some other adult, or even the bank, with trust powers specifying that the gift is to be held by the adult "as custodian for the minor under the Uniform Transfers to Minors Act."

This transfer is permitted in the majority of states, although you should check with banking authorities in your state before attempting this form of gift. This particular procedure allows the gift to flow to the minor in a special account without the appointment of a guardian. If permitted in your state, the Uniform Transfers to Minors Act is an excellent tool for gifting to children, as that statute has provisions that safeguard the funds, the investment of the funds, and, further, makes provision for continuity of the custodial aspect of the account in the event of the death of the initial custodian.

The same provision can be made with assets other than money. For example, stock, mutual funds, life insurance, and annuities may also be handled in this way. Note also that income received from assets held in custodial form may be taxed at the top marginal rate of the child's parents.

It is often very important, however, to make gifts, because there are so many advantages to the estate planner. Why? Because your estate taxes, for both federal and state estate purposes, will be reduced as a result of the gift. Since you have an annual gift exclusion of $10,000 per person for gifts made to anyone, this means you can give away that amount each year to your family members or others, on a per-person basis, thereby reducing the value of your estate and diminishing your estate taxes. In addition, you can do so without paying any taxes on the gift yourself.

For a married couple, the annual exclusion allows each of them to gift up to $10,000 annually to each of their children or grandchildren without any tax impact. It also allows heirs to receive gifts that they may need now, while they are raising families. Correspondingly, their parents' estates are reduced, thus reducing future estate taxes for the parents. In addition, grandparents also can make gifts in any amount and pay no gift taxes as long as such gifts go for tuition and are paid directly to the college. And, further, a grandparent can give an additional $10,000 free of gift tax, to pay for room and board, directly to the college or university.

In addition, the Hope scholarship tax credit may be applicable if a child (or you) is in school. This tax credit reimburses parents up to $1,500 a year for tuition aid during the first two years in college. There is also the Lifetime Learning credit, which applies after the first two years of college. This credit has been increased to $2,500 for 2001 from $1,000.

All of these gift and tax benefits are examples of excellent estate planning, in which one generation uses its assets to obtain current tax relief while helping its children or grandchildren obtain an education. In addition, the Education IRA is an excellent planning tool to help children get an education.

Insurance

Life Insurance

INSURANCE PLANS ARE PROBABLY THE most widely known estate planning tool. "Whole life insurance" is an insurance plan you purchase by paying either monthly or annual premiums based on your age for a designated amount of insurance. Because you are purchasing the plan, it has cash value, against which you may borrow during the life of the policy.

For example, a husband buys a $20,000 policy and names his wife as the beneficiary. The face value, which will be paid directly to the wife if the husband dies, is $20,000, but the husband can cash in his policy or borrow its cash value (which is a fluctuating figure that depends upon the age of the policy, the amount of premiums paid, and other related variables). The easiest way to determine the cash value of any whole life policy is to ask your insurance company for a letter informing you of this value.

Unlike a whole life policy, which has continuing value for the policy owner, term life insurance requires a single premium for a single year. For instance, a husband pays one premium for a $20,000 policy. If he dies during that year, his wife will receive the $20,000; however, if he doesn't die, he has expended his premium for one year of insurance coverage.

When universal life insurance emerged a number of years ago, financial planners claimed it was the best type of insurance the industry had ever created. It may be, in fact, a much more flexible type of coverage, but it is still a form of whole life insurance. Its main feature is that the purchaser of the policy can designate what percentage of his premiums should go to cover insurance on his life and what remaining percentage can go into a "savings plan" invested with the insurance company.

Variable life insurance is a variation on universal life that offers many of the same features but offers the purchaser a much wider array of investments, from stocks to mutual funds. Both financial and estate planners debate whether life insurance offers a good investment opportunity for your assets. Putting that issue aside, the real question for estate planning is: Do I really need to buy life insurance?

The fact of the matter is that every proper estate plan considers insurance, if for no other reason than for the payment of bills and taxes at death. Most people need to purchase whole life when they are young and have dependents that must be provided for if they die. But most people can't afford whole life at this stage of their lives and must fall back on term, which does not provide any cash value. When they can finally afford whole life, perhaps in their forties or fifties, they no longer need it as much, because their children are grown.

Nevertheless, as much as none of us wants to spend hard-earned funds on insurance premiums, we must at least consider the feasibility of having some insurance in our overall plan, for our own protection and that of our families. Statistics indicate that most people probably need insurance of some kind in their planning. Just which kind you want and can afford are the essential questions.

Health Insurance

EVERYONE TODAY NEEDS HEALTH INSURANCE. In the event of illness, no one can be without medical care. If you are a stay-at-home mother whose husband's job provides your life insurance, no question is as pertinent as whether you will have health insurance if your spouse becomes disabled or dies. Although many people receive health insurance coverage at their place of employment, part-time workers, employees at small companies, and self-employed people must buy their own coverage.

Health care coverage is today, and will continue to be, one of the most difficult issues to resolve in the United States. More people today are not covered by any type of health insurance than at any time in our history, and this has become a national dilemma: how to give prescription drugs and health care to all citizens affordably without raising taxes precipitously or taking vital money from other important government programs.

In all fifty states, Medicaid covers those who are not covered by private insurance. But to qualify for Medicaid, a person must meet certain eligibility standards that vary from state to state, are encumbered by red tape, and are weighed down by budgetary restrictions. Even Medicare cannot always bear the weight of those who are in need.

There is, for those who can afford it, private Medigap insurance, which is designed to fill the growing gap between medical bills and what Medicare covers. It doesn't, however, fill those gaps entirely.

Long-term-care insurance is available to cover the costs of nursing home care. This is a relatively new field, so buyer beware. If you are interested in this type of coverage, explore several programs offered by reputable companies. Outstanding programs are available, but there are many more that are completely worthless.

All health insurance is expensive, regardless of who is paying for it. Even so, no estate plan can be complete without a serious review of your health needs and the health insurance you may need.

Just as important as life insurance is disability insurance, which pays you a monthly benefit if you become disabled. As an essential estate planning goal is to protect and preserve the family and assets during your lifetime, it is a very prudent idea to anticipate that at some time during your working life, there will be a period when you are not able to work. Disability insurance helps cover the lost income during such times of disability.

Disability insurance may actually be more important than life insurance, since it protects one of your most important assets: the ability to work and earn income. You can select from a variety of plans the premium you wish to pay and the length of time you would like to be covered if you are disabled. All of these factors affect the cost of the insurance, but regardless of the policy, it won't cover all of the loss of your paycheck. Most policies cover between 60 percent and 70 percent of your salary. Nor does this insurance cover every kind of disability; each policy specifically defines the kind of disability it covers, the circumstances that trigger payment, the length of time benefits will continue, and how payments are terminated.

Although one can easily imagine that the head of a family would want to retain disability insurance to cover loss of income while he is disabled, one might ask: should a single person have disability insurance? Actually, it is arguably more important for a single person to obtain this insurance, as this individual would have no financial support system in the event of disability. Check to see if your employer offers this option, or, see if your union or credit union offers it. If not, most large insurance companies offer a variety of disability plans. Stick with those rated A-plus by A. M. Best, a prominent insurance rating firm. A. M. Best publishes its ratings annually; you can usually find this book in the business or reference section of your local library. The book *Staying Wealthy: Strategies for Protecting Your Assets,* by Brian H. Breuel (Bloomberg Press, 1998), offers a good discussion on the importance of including disability insurance in your overall estate plan.

Retirement Plans

HEALTH NEEDS AND RETIREMENT planning often become twin issues when long-term planning is involved. This is because health and retirement issues require estate planning that will offer the planner a secure foundation for future years, when there may be serious health problems to face without a paycheck to count on. This is why retirement plans are so very important: they help provide the finances needed to meet daily bills and expenses, and, further, to pay medical bills when they arise.

Today, the most popular retirement plans are individual retirement accounts (IRAs), Keogh plans, employer pension plans, life annuities, and deferred compensation plans. All of these retirement plans do three important things: (1) they defer the payment of current taxes, (2) they provide for future income, and (3) they serve as non-probate assets for estate planning. These excellent benefits are good reasons for people to do retirement planning early in life, when the potential future benefits can be maximized.

IRAs

PROBABLY NO SAVINGS PLAN IS AS POPULAR in the United States today as the individual retirement account, or IRA. Although some of its tax appeal has been limited in recent years, it still offers planners some major benefits. The newly created Roth IRA is the newest IRA to join the list of very popular investment plans that return significant tax savings to investors.

IRAs, both the traditional and the Roth, encourage saving $2,000 per year per person. The former allows an annual tax deduction for the $2,000; the Roth allows no deduction, but the interest that accrues on this savings accumulates tax free over the years. For some, the way in which the $2,000 is taxed as income without a deduction, as with the Roth IRA, may limit its appeal; for others, this is another way to save and accumulate income without paying income taxes on the appreciation.

IRA rules are strict, but the benefits are great. For that reason, you should consider IRAs for your estate plan, so be sure to check on current laws regarding your contributions to an IRA to determine whether investing in such a plan is advisable.

Remember, even if you do not qualify for the annual tax deduction, you may still wish to contribute to your IRA to:

➤ create a "forced savings" plan;
➤ take advantage of the tax deferrals; and
➤ make more money on your investment than you would with other forms of investment.

This has great appeal to many investors and is a way to defer taxes on interest earned, keep a savings plan intact, and still control the manner in which the funds are invested.

The diversity that IRAs offer investors is one of their most attractive features. There are, in fact, all kinds of IRAs:

➤ The **Individual Retirement Account (IRA)** is an account set up with a bank, broker, or mutual fund. Many kinds of stocks, bonds, or mutual funds may be invested in this IRA.

➤ The **Individual Retirement Annuity** may be purchased from an insurance company through its annuity plan.
➤ The so-called **SEP-IRA**, known as the Simplified Employee Pension, is established by employers for their employees.
➤ A **Spousal IRA** is set up by a married income earner for the non-income-earning spouse.
➤ A **Rollover IRA** is set up to receive funds from a qualified retirement plan.
➤ An **Inherited IRA** is inherited by a non-spouse.
➤ An **Educational IRA**, established after January 1, 1998, can provide funds for a beneficiary to obtain a higher education.
➤ A **Stretch IRA** is simply an IRA designed to stretch the IRA benefits across generational barriers to maximize the tax benefits to future beneficiaries.
➤ A **Roth IRA**, established in January 1998, has become very popular with many people, particularly young adults in search of a tax-saving vehicle.

By far the most popular investments today are the traditional IRA and the Roth IRA, but all IRAs in general are popular because they allow the taxpayer to reap super benefits in the long term that may not be available in any other investment format. Today, it is not simply a matter of earning a good income, it is how to keep the tax on that income as minimal as possible so that your funds will not be diluted in the process. This means that the smart investor is always seeking options that allow for maximum tax-saving opportunities, and IRAs provide just that option.

What are the tax consequences of the IRA? The traditional IRA allows for a $2,000 tax deduction for each year you contribute. However, and this is important, all of the future distributions from the IRA, including interest, dividends, and capital gains accrued through the years, are taxable at ordinary income rates when you start withdrawing funds from the account.

The Roth IRA works in the reverse, and for those who are fortunate enough to qualify, the tax benefits are dramatically increased over the traditional IRA. Your annual contribution to the Roth is not deductible in the year it is made. And although you pay taxes now on those contributions, the funds that you will later withdraw from the Roth are not taxable, provided you hold your Roth for no less than five years and reach the age of fifty-nine and one-half. Imagine having an account in which you can invest and have all of the income, dividends, interest, and gains accrue over the years until that day when you want to start withdrawing—and then not having to pay any taxes on the benefits that have accrued. That is why so many taxpayers are investing in IRAs and will continue to do so over the years.

Since the Roth IRA was created primarily to help low and middle income individuals save for retirement, the law doesn't allow upper income taxpayers to open one. However, a maximum of $2,000 a year can be contributed to a Roth IRA plan by single taxpayers with adjusted gross income of $95,000 or less. Between $95,000 and $110,000, a partial contribution is allowed. No contribution is permitted above $110,000.

For joint filers who have an adjusted gross income of $150,000 or less, a $2,000 contribution from each taxpayer is permitted. Between $150,000 and $160,000 a partial contribution is permitted; over $160,000 no contribution is allowed.

Finally, note that another often overlooked aspect of the Roth IRA is that there is no age limit. This means if a senior citizen meets the adjusted gross income requirements, then he or she can open a Roth IRA.

There are many rules applicable to IRAs, and they are often made cumbersome by special terms: adjusted gross income (AGI), conversion, rollovers, transfers, qualified plans, qualified compensation, earned income, phaseout range, stretch IRA, qualified distribution. These are just a few of the terms in common IRA usage. The IRS rules are also complex. Seek an expert in this field to see how an IRA investment might benefit not only you but also your children or parents.

IRAs are a good way to invest in stocks, bonds, and other investments and keep them in one neat, easily managed account. Some investments, however, are excluded by law from IRAs: leveraged investments (which are those made with borrowed money); collectible items, such as stamps, artwork, and antiques; and mortgaged real estate.

The IRA is primarily a financial planning tool aimed at providing funds when the investor who does not have some other qualified pension plan retires. When the IRA is established, the investor must designate for the account both a beneficiary, who is the primary person who will receive the account if the investor dies, and a contingent beneficiary, the person who would receive the assets if the primary beneficiary died before the investor did.

When the owner names a spouse or children as the beneficiaries, the funds go directly to those beneficiaries, completely bypassing probate. IRAs have generational benefits: the owner/investor of the IRA can defer income on the funds and can pass these assets on to a spouse or children probate-free. Also, the next generation will be able to enjoy the benefit of these funds.

There are, however, tax ramifications involved. If children receive the IRA funds as beneficiaries, they will be taxed to the extent of the gain incurred in the IRA. This means they must report the IRA as ordinary income and pay income tax on the gains. To prevent this, some professional estate planners recommend passing along the account, rather than the funds from the account. The children can then withdraw funds and pay taxes according to the IRS life expectancy charts. This is called a "stretch-out" IRA. If the beneficiary is a spouse, she can take all of the IRA funds and pay all taxes at that time or place the IRA proceeds into a rollover account to continue deferring distribution and taxes, at least until the age of seventy-and-one-half.

Most planners believe that everyone should have some form of IRA. However, you may want to consider a wide array of investment tools that may provide similar or even better planning options than IRAs to meet your goals.

Keogh Plans

A KEOGH PLAN IS SOLELY FOR self-employed individuals. If you are self-employed, this is *the* plan to understand. Essentially, the Keogh works very much like an IRA, except for two crucial differences. First, a self-employed individual may invest up to a certain sum each year. Second, if you, as an employer, elect to participate in a Keogh plan, you must cover your employees under the plan. This means that if you elect to invest 8 percent of your earned income in the plan for your own retirement benefit, you must invest 8 percent for each of your employees.

Thus, a Keogh plan may prove to be too expensive for a small company. On the other hand, if you are a small-business owner, can you afford to be without a plan to supplement your modest monthly Social Security benefits at the time of retirement? Advantages of the Keogh plan are similar to those of the IRA: forced savings and deferred taxes on all accumulating funds.

There are two types of Keogh plans: (1) defined contribution plans and (2) defined benefit plans. Under the first plan, you decide how much to put into the plan annually; at retirement, you will receive a set sum based on how well the plan has performed over time. The exact amount is unknown until the investor decides to begin withdrawing money from the plan. The defined benefit plan is similar to the plans corporations establish for their employees. Each month or year, the employer contributes a set amount of money to the plan; the sum to be received upon retirement is predictable.

If you are a self-employed person operating a sole proprietorship or a small company, the Keogh plan is well worth considering. Again, it is aimed primarily for use as a retirement plan, and because the planner names the primary and contingent beneficiaries, it is a non-probate vehicle that avoids the probate process.

Simplified Employee Pension Plans (SEPs)

ANOTHER INDIVIDUAL RETIREMENT PLAN is the simplified employee pension or SEP plan, often referred to as a SEP-IRA. This is quite popular with sole proprietors and owners of small businesses. Sponsored by an employer for the benefit of employees, SEPs work much like traditional IRAs. You can contribute up to 15 percent of your salary annually to a SEP. The money will grow tax free, and you may name a beneficiary for the plan, so that it becomes a non-probate asset at the time of your death. For more tax information, see the SEP section of *IRS Publication 590*, free upon request from the IRS, or download it from www.irs.gov.

What is the benefit of such a plan? The funds invested in the SEP are not included on the employee's W-2 for the year of investment. This not only saves income taxes but may put the taxpayer into a lower tax bracket, so that the end result will be less taxes due. SEP funds also defer taxes on interest earned.

The SEP has two unique aspects. The employer/owner who sponsors the SEP for the company SEP plan can contribute up to 15 percent of his or her salary, for a maximum annual contribution of $22,500, as long as a contribution of an equal percentage is made to the company employees. Also, unlike other types of retirement programs, all of the money once contributed becomes the property of the employee, without any vesting time. This means that the employee doesn't have to work for the company for, say, five years before he or she receives an ownership interest in those SEP funds. In this way, both the employee and the employer receive a great estate planning benefit. Assets are invested now to grow tax free through the years. Plus, there are a variety of investment options available, and all of the assets accumulate and pass to the beneficiary directly without any probate process whatsoever.

401(k) Plans

THE 401(K) IS NAMED AFTER THE provision in the IRS Code that created it. Basically, the 401(k) allows companies to establish a qualified plan (meaning it meets IRS standards) into which the employee can contribute up to a certain sum annually that is not treated as income. The effect is tax-deferred treatment of all accumulating income. These plans offer a wide variety of investment options, from mutual funds with fixed rates to a portfolio composed of an array of stocks.

Companies want their employees to save in 401(k) plans for reasons that are beneficial to them, and therefore some companies will even make contributions for their employees into such plans. In many cases, employers will partially match employees' contributions into the plan to encourage them to use it. Investment options in 401(k) plans are varied and permit a wide assortment of choices.

A 401(k) has the estate planning benefit of most other retirement plans: it defers the payment of current taxes, provides for future income, and will pass from the owner of the plan to named beneficiaries as non-probate assets.

In addition, a 401(k) has several important and usually overlooked benefits. First, balances you have in your 401(k) are excluded from most college aid calculations, which is of great assistance when seeking financial aid for college, and loans from your 401(k) are permitted under certain specific circumstances for your child's education. These are nice estate planning examples of one generation helping the next, and both generations benefit.

Businesses as Retirement Plans

ALTHOUGH MOST PEOPLE DON'T CONSIDER the estate planning benefits of business entities, it is one area that offers some nice opportunities for excellent planning. There are four major business entities in general use in the United States today:

1 Sole proprietorships
2 Corporations
3 Partnerships: limited and general
4 Limited liability companies

The sole proprietorship is an informal business entity that requires very little except a listing in the Yellow Pages; the other entities are creatures of statute and require a formal application to state or federal agencies, supervision, inspection, and annual registration.

One special benefit of formal entities is that there is little if any personal liability. The sole proprietor has personal liability, so that his or her personal assets may be tapped by creditors of the business—and financial ruin is the risk.

Of estate planning interest are the formal entities that limit personal liability and have other important benefits:

➤ Ownership interests can be divided among multiple owners. This makes it possible for a parent, for instance, to gift stock or other benefits to children as part of a business strategy, reducing the parent's estate and passing along to children assets, which in turn reduces taxes at the time of the parent's death.

➤ Centralized management can be provided even when there are multiple owners. This benefit allows for control of a business to be fragmented among many owners but at the same time provides for one manager to "run the business," thus preserving it when various owners have diverse financial interests in it.

➤ Individuals can take advantage of certain business tax breaks that may be allowed only to legal entities, including various fringe benefits such as health insurance, pension plans, and profit distributions, which may not be subject to self-employment taxes.

If you run your own business, the best thing you can do for yourself is to seek advice from your tax specialist to make sure that you are receiving all of the advantages possible and that you are using the business entity for proper estate planning purposes. This is one of the most overlooked areas of estate planning. Few business people seem to realize that they can use their businesses to maximize gifting, to receive tax, health, and pension plan benefits, and at the same time, to distribute business assets to the next generation for efficient estate planning.

For more information on this issue, see www.nolo.com and www.netplanning .com, the Web site of the National Network of Estate Planning Attorneys. Deloitte and Touche, the international accounting firm, also has an excellent site, www.dton line.com.

Social Security

NO DISCUSSION ABOUT RETIREMENT PLANS is complete without some mention of the biggest retirement system in the world: our Social Security system. Most Americans know that at some point in their sixties they can retire, and if they have contributed to the Social Security system during their working years and for the required period of time (forty quarters), they will qualify for monthly Social Security payments for the rest of their lives.

Most people don't know, however, the exact amount of money that they will be able to count on from Social Security at the time of retirement. Just as you should know about how much it will cost you to live at retirement, you should know the approximate amount of income you may receive from Social Security when you retire.

Fortunately, the Social Security Administration has a form, Form SSA-7004, which, if filled out and mailed in, will tell you the approximate monthly amount you will receive from the Social Security system upon retirement. This is an excellent way to communicate with the Social Security Administration as an introduction to that system. You may obtain this form at any Social Security office.

If you need any information about Social Security, just drop in at your local Social Security office. Each office has brochures on a variety of topics. Social Security is one of the most accommodating departments in the federal system. (Also see www.ssa.gov, the official Web site of the Social Security Administration, where you can now sign up for Social Security online.)

Stocks, Bonds, and Mutual Funds

EQUITY INVESTMENTS ARE OFFERED FOR sale to the public every day. And because these investments are now, or most likely will be, part of your estate, you should understand how they fit into an overall plan.

First, I will share with you a lesson I gradually learned: don't be intimidated. For years, I thought that all of these investments were only for the wealthy. I couldn't have been more wrong. Everyone today is participating in these investments by necessity. As interest rates in bank savings accounts have fallen to 3 percent and below, people have shifted their assets by the billions to better-interest-bearing investments, such as stocks, bonds, and mutual funds. There are as many reasons to invest in these various instruments as there are people. Most people, however, invest in order to increase the value of their assets and to increase their income.

Ask yourself three important things before you make any investment: Are you investing for security? For income or for growth? What is your tax bracket? Define your investment purposes before making each investment. Your investment goals are central to your investment decisions, and your tax bracket may have a direct impact upon what you can expect your returns to be from your investments.

Whether you invest for security, for income, or for growth reasons, or in order to attain maximum benefit for each and every investment, you must understand the tax implications so you will receive the best yield on your money. Basic to your investment goals is understanding how much yield you'll actually realize from your investment.

Yield is the amount of money you make on the principal invested. It is actually the income earned by an investment divided by its price. But note that this is an oversimplification of yield, because you should not think about the percentage of yield without considering your tax bracket, which has a direct impact on yield. So, to determine whether you are making the correct investment decisions for your assets, first determine your tax bracket by checking last year's tax return. (Of course, it may be different this year if your income stream is considerably higher.)

If you are paying too much tax on the return on your investment, maybe you should consider investing in tax-free issues. If you are in the 31 percent tax bracket or higher, you may be a candidate for tax-free investments. Investments that yield income and interest that are not tax free—such as interest on a certificate of deposit or dividends on stock—may increase your taxable income and therefore cost you more to own than tax-free investments.

When in doubt, talk to your financial adviser or accountant. Once you understand your yield, your tax bracket, your stage in life, and your goals, you are ready to put together a portfolio that will become your estate to build on for the future.

Investments play a major part in everyone's estate today. They cut deeply across every estate planning aspect:

➤ Estate tax computations: How will your investments be evaluated at the time of your death?

➤ Marital deduction planning: How should you balance your estate plan between your investments and your real estate?

➤ If you think your investments will be substantial at your death, will you need to buy life insurance to pay estate taxes to preserve your assets?

➤ How will your pension, profit-sharing, or stock plans at work affect your personally held investments?

➤ How should your investments be titled for probate avoidance?

➤ Should you use your investments for gifting?

➤ How do you want to title your investments, especially if you live in a community property state?

➤ What is the best way for your investments to be transferred to beneficiaries, avoid probate, diminish taxes? Should you use a will or a trust?

➤ If you become disabled, whom do you trust to give power of attorney for finances to manage your investments during your disability?

These are some of the many issues you need to think about regarding your investments. That is why investing is a dual issue: on the one hand, you want to invest to build an estate; and on the other hand, you want to preserve and transfer your investments.

All of the financial tools mentioned in this chapter have one goal in common: the accumulation and preservation of wealth. However, just as important is the goal of planning for the control and transfer of that wealth to others in such a way that the wealth is not diminished by taxes, probate proceedings, family dissension, or other issues detrimental to you or your family.

The goal of a good estate plan is to bind together all of these aspects of wealth, preservation, accumulation, and transfer so tightly that the assets and the plan become one unified entity that is cost effective, meets your individual needs, and will stand the test of adversity, lending strength and stability to your everyday life.

Remember, the more you know about your financial options, the more likely you are to be able to maximize your assets, the basic goal of financial planning. If you are having difficulty sorting out your investment and financial options, seek out a qualified professional financial planner to help you establish a plan. Once you maximize your financial planning, you can integrate your investments into your estate plan to achieve an outstanding plan for life and death.

Wills

IN ADDITION TO THE FINANCIAL vehicles described in Chapter 6, into which we pour a large part of our wealth, a variety of traditional, basic legal instruments form the very bedrock of estate planning across the United States. Although from time to time one may become more popular than others, several legal instruments are usually necessary to achieve an effective, solid, and well-balanced plan.

In some ways, integrating the legal vehicles in your estate plan is easiest to understand if you visualize it as a large pyramid composed of blocks of fundamental tools. Each person must determine which step of the pyramid is most important to him or her as an individual. Your final estate plan will consist of carefully placed blocks of legal tools, held firmly in place by sound fiscal management. Such a plan is the ideal creation.

Legal instruments should be selected with care and integrated into your personal and financial life. As you begin to think about what you want to accomplish in your estate plan, you will choose the tools that fit you and your goals. You'll begin to decide which ones are essential today and which ones you will need in the future.

Each legal tool has a specific purpose. One of the most common legal tools in use in the United States today is the last will and testament. Read on to find out what this tool is, what it can do for you, and what its limitations are.

The Last Will and Testament

NO LEGAL TOOL IS MORE DISCUSSED and less understood by the general public than the ordinary last will and testament, more commonly known simply as the "will." Generally, few people really understand this document and what it does and, more important, what it does not do.

Most people believe that a will "takes care of things when I die." Well, maybe it does, and maybe it doesn't. Simply put, a will is a document that meets state requirements for being a "will." In most states, it must fulfill three basic requirements.

1 **A will must be in writing.** A will cannot be oral, with a few rare exceptions, nor can it be an oral promise to make a will. Your neighbor may tell you he'll remember you in his will for all the times you have cut his grass, but in most states, this oral promise isn't enforceable. Thus, if you want to make sure that someone receives a gift from you, you'd better put it in writing.

2 **A will must be signed and witnessed.** Some states require two witnesses; other states require three. Many states, in addition, require a notary to acknowledge the signature of the signer of the will.

3 **A will must make a disposition of property.** Once a will is written, signed, witnessed, and notarized as required by the state of your residence, it has to dispose of your property. A will can't be a general statement of your philosophy of life and still qualify as a will. The will generally provides for the payment of all bills, gives funeral instructions, appoints a fiduciary (executor) to be in charge of your estate, and provides for how your property will divided after death.

A will is the vehicle that determines how and to whom a person's probate assets will flow after death. (An example of a typical will appears on the following page.) The advantages of having a will are these:

➤ If you own probate assets, a will distributes those assets in accordance with your wishes after your death.

➤ You can put a person in charge of your probate matters.

➤ You can appoint a guardian for your children in a will.

➤ Your will is a public, historical record for future generations of your family.

A will has limitations, however. The main one is that a will does not distribute non-probate assets, such as your pension funds, IRAs, joint-and-survivorship property, life estate interests, TOD and POD accounts, and real estate holdings. In other words, most of your assets are not influenced at all by a will.

Sample Last Will and Testament

I, (Name), of the City of Anytown, State, make and publish this, my Last Will and Testament.

I.   I revoke all previous wills made by me.

II.   I direct that all of my just debts and funeral bills be paid.

III. I give to my wife my entire estate. In the event she should predecease me, then I give my estate to my children A and B, share and share alike.

IV.   I appoint my wife as my Executrix to serve without bond. In the event my wife predeceases me, then I appoint my children A and B, or the survivor of them, as fiduciaries of my estate to serve without bond.

IN WITNESS WHEREOF I sign this, my LAST WILL AND TESTAMENT, at Anytown, U.S.A., this 3rd day of June, 2001.

(Signature, Witnesses, and Notarization per applicable state law.)

Wills and all documents filed in a probate process relating to them are matters of public record. Your will and all filings in the probate process, including the inventory of your probate assets, are an open book to anyone. In the event you disinherit a family member, make unequal distributions to children, or make any other disposition in your will that is likely to be unpopular, these facts will be open to all to inspect. Many family members of celebrities have discovered to their dismay how public a will is after death.

There are so many things a will is not empowered to do. You cannot, for instance, use your will to control payment of income over a period of years to your parents. Nor can you control any of your non-probate assets, which usually comprise the bulk of your estate. You cannot delay any distribution of assets, and you cannot reduce your tax bill.

But there is one important thing that a will can do, and that is to put someone in charge of your assets after your death. This person whom you appoint in your will is the fiduciary, also known as the executor, and he or she will handle your financial affairs after your death. This is an important and potentially very complex job, as the executor's duties are many and varied. These duties include the following:

➤ Collect all of the decedent's assets and debts.

➤ Retain an attorney and accountant if legal procedures or tax returns are necessary.

➤ Obtain appraisals on all assets if their value is unclear.

➤ Initiate the probate process if necessary and file all necessary legal documents in that proceeding in a timely manner, after giving proper notice to heirs, beneficiaries, and creditors.

➤ Decide, perhaps with the assistance of an attorney, who will inherit the property of a decedent. If there is a will, it will indicate who inherits what property and in what proportion; if there is no will, then the assets will be distributed by state laws, known as the laws of intestate succession.

➤ Determine whether the property of the decedent can be used by others during the pendency of the proceedings; decide whether property must be sold and if so, sell the property.

➤ Find out whether assets can be at least partially distributed to the proper parties during administration proceedings, or whether all distribution must be held up until all the probate steps are completed.

➤ Take care of the mail; pay all bills, including hospital bills and utilities; notify Social Security, pension funds, brokers, creditors, landlords, and others of the death.

➤ Create an estate account so that all business can be conducted through this account; keep careful records and keep copies of everything.

➤ Litigate issues that are necessary, such as actions to settle title on real estate and controversies between heirs or beneficiaries; determine who are the legal heirs of the decedent; implement tax appeals.

➤ Handle all property located out of state.

➤ Finally, distribute all of the assets of the decedent to the proper parties.

With all of these duties to handle, it is easy to see why you want to appoint an executor in your will who has outstanding abilities and who is:

➤ honest, trustworthy, and diligent;

➤ reasonable, organized, and impartial;

➤ businesslike;

➤ knowledgeable about your business matters if possible;

➤ imbued with good common sense; and

➤ willing to do the job.

Most people make a will in order to provide for a distribution of their property after they die. They think they should not leave any loose ends, and generally, they're right. What a great many people fail to realize is that a will does not cover all of the assets they own. It covers only probate assets, which are only a small percentage of your total assets. This is why the will is really a "10 percent document." It may take care of a small percentage of your assets and business affairs at the time of your death, but it does not affect big-ticket items like your retirement benefits, IRAs, joint bank accounts, and other significant accounts.

So why have a will if it doesn't even cover some of your most significant assets? Because a will indicates who is in charge of your *probate* assets and how they are to be distributed at the time of your death. It takes care of those loose ends that we all leave even with the most careful planning, and it can help avoid sad situations like the one described below.

The Case of the Superstitious Procrastinator

WHEN I WAS PRACTICING LAW, I met a woman in the hospital where we were both patients. After we were discharged from the hospital, she came to my office and asked me to draft her will.

There was nothing unusual about the provisions she made in the will, because she left all of her estate to her husband of many years. But she felt that when and if she signed a will, she would die.

Although she knew this was irrational and superstitious, she put off making her will just because she felt that signing it would be signing her death warrant. After preparing the will, I telephoned her to come in. Month after month went by, and she did not come in to execute her will. When she died of a heart attack several years later, her will was still in my files … unsigned. As a result, her property was divided among her spouse and her minor children, a distribution of assets she would never have wanted.

This division of property had an important long-term consequence. Since the widower did not actually have the full legal title to the home, he was unable to refinance his mortgage and get a new longer-term loan, one that would have permitted him to keep the home for himself and his minor children. As a result, the house had to be sold. The children's portion of the sale was put into separate accounts for each of them; their father used his share to buy a smaller home with a more modest mortgage payment. It was a sad day when the family had to pack up and move out of "their" home.

There is one more vitally important aspect of having a will that applies to parents with young children. You can appoint guardians for your children in your will so that if you should unexpectedly die during their minority (before they reach eighteen years of age), someone will be legally appointed to take care of them.

But whom do you trust enough to appoint as your children's guardian? This is a very difficult decision for parents to make. Often grandparents are too old to serve; other relatives may live too far away. Best friends may already have children of their own. How do you decide whom to appoint? Consider these ideas:

➤ Has the guardian been well known to you and the children over a period of years?

➤ Do you and your spouse share common ideas with the guardian about life, family values, religious ideas, and important life goals for children?

➤ Do you have confidence in this person? Will the children's best interests always come first? Are there other children in the home? Will this be good for your children?

➤ Can you provide enough financial support for your children to assist the guardian in raising them?

➤ Does the guardian have the interest, the time, and the love to take care of another person's children?

➤ Would the children have to move to where the guardian lives? How would this affect their schooling and future educational prospects?

One fact often overlooked by young parents who are so busy with their everyday lives is that if they don't name a guardian for their children, a court of law will name one for them, and often the person selected would not have been the parents' first choice. Often, too, family dissension and lawsuits stem from disagreements over who is best suited to take care of the children. If the parents have not named a guardian, this typically comes up only after the parents' death, at a time when the children are still grieving their loss. By naming the guardians in a will, the parents make the decision. The courts almost always enforce the written wishes of the parents, and the children's futures are secure.

Most guardianships of children involve a single guardian to take care of both the children and their assets. However, most states allow you to name one guardian to take care of the children's upbringing and a different guardian to manage the estate of the minor children. In many cases, giving the financial responsibility to a different person, so that he or she can focus on handling bills and finances and investing the assets left for the children's care, may work out better for all concerned.

What about leaving your minor children your property in your will? Laws in all of the states require that an adult manage the assets of a minor until the child reaches eighteen, the age of majority. If you leave assets to a minor child, courts must appoint a guardian to look after the assets, which means that the guardian must file annual or biannual reports with the court, attend hearings, and usually obtain the services of an attorney. If you want to leave property to your minor children, there are simply better ways of doing it than using a will, unless you leave the gift to your child under the Uniform Transfers to Minors Act (UTMA), which has been enacted in almost all states.

The UTMA provides the framework for you to name a guardian who acts as custodian for the minor's funds. It is less formal than setting up a trust for a grandchild, for example, but it does have statutory safeguards for the handling of the funds, and it ends when the child reaches the age of twenty-one, or in a few states, twenty-five. If you use this provision in your will, it simply reads: "I leave all of the assets in my accounts at ABC Bank to my sister, Ann Powers, as custodian for my daughter Mary under the Ohio Uniform Transfers to Minors Act." This language is sufficient to create the custodianship, if and when it is ever needed.

Are there better ways to protect your minor child's assets? Yes. You could set up a simple trust for each child, or you could set up a pot trust, which means you set up a blanket trust to cover all of them. Also, you can name a guardian of the estate of your children to handle your children's upbringing and finances, with court supervision. And you can use a life insurance trust to provide for asset management and distribution, based on your children's needs when they are minors. Life insurance trusts can also provide for educational needs when children graduate from high school.

One other thing that a will may be used for is to disinherit family members. This is more commonly done than the general public realizes. As families become separated, children increasingly live far from parents and sometimes drift away from them, while the parents age and perhaps experience poor health. Some parents are coming to the conclusion that only the child or children who look after them should have the benefit of their assets.

Sometimes there is such strife between parents and a child that the parents want to legally disinherit that child. Then, too, there are situations in which one spouse would like to disinherit the other spouse. Although state laws are uniform in permitting disinheritance of children if they are older than eighteen, the laws on allowing one spouse to completely disinherit the other vary.

One purpose a will should not be used for today is to make a donation of organs or of your body to a medical hospital for study or transplant purposes. Today, the proper way to make this gift is to sign a donor card with the hospital or foundation involved. This card identifies you as a donor, and at your death, the donation will take place, provided your family does not object and the facility is informed in time and has the ability to accept the gift. Almost all state departments of motor vehicles have donor cards, and many states are now printing information on your driver's license to indicate whether you are a donor. Be aware, too, that if your family objects to this donation and refuses to sign consents, your wish may be defeated. However, if you want to make this gift, get your donor card signed, discuss this with your family, and chances are the gift will benefit someone, someplace and sometime. For more information about donations, call the National Anatomical Service at 800-727-0700.

Once you decide you need a will and have executed one, is it set in stone for the rest of your life? Not at all. A will can be changed, modified, or destroyed at any time. Here's an example of the kind of flexibility you have with wills, although it is a bit overdone.

The Case of the Perpetual Planner

ELDERLY SARAH CAME TO SEE me every year when I was practicing law. She was a warm, wonderful person whose main concern in her advancing age was that she treat her five children equally so that none would feel slighted at the time of her death.

Every year Sarah drew up a new will, and each year, pursuant to her instructions, I drafted her new will to redistribute her few possessions among her children. Instead of Joe receiving the TV, she thought maybe Annie should get it. Then Joe would get the picture of his father, which had been previously willed to Alice, and so it went. For five years, on an annual basis, until the time of her death, I rewrote Sarah's will to redistribute the same five possessions to her five children in different ways.

The point here is that establishing an estate plan doesn't mean you lack the flexibility to change your mind in the future if you're so inclined or if your circumstances change. However, assuming you have a will that meets your needs at the present time, how often should you review it? The American Bar Association recommends a review at least every two years, and more often if there is a major change of circumstances. Such changes might be any one or more of the following:

➤ If a new beneficiary is born or dies.
➤ If you change your mind about whom you want to leave your property to.
➤ If there is a change in your marital status: if you get married, divorced, or acquire a life mate.
➤ If anyone named in your will (the executor or beneficiaries) dies, becomes disabled, or becomes unable to serve.
➤ If the descriptions of the assets in your will do not readily identify them. If, for instance, you give Jane your "antique table and chairs" and you acquire another antique set, you will want to make clear which items you are gifting.

How do you change your will? Some legal professionals believe that once the new will is drawn up, the old will should be destroyed. However, today most attorneys simply add a codicil, which is an amendment to your will, to add or delete simple portions of the will.

If you are going to substantially change your will, you should think about executing an entirely new one and include in it the proviso that you are revoking all previous wills.

Again, wills address only your probate assets. You may be able to achieve all of your estate planning outside of a court; if so, all well and good. But in many cases, court involvement can be beneficial. The court offers one more estate planning option that you should consider carefully. You should keep the option open whether or not you want the court involved for some particular reason. It may serve a useful purpose, and occasionally it can bring order out of chaos.

Most of us will leave some probate assets, the proverbial "loose ends," and we feel better knowing that a person of our choice will be in charge of our probate "estate" when we pass away, if for no other reason than to make funeral arrangements. Incidentally, those plans should be made well in advance and should not really be included in our wills. This is because the will may not even be read until well after the person's death. Also, it might not be seen by the estate representative before the funeral, so any instructions included in a will may not be followed.

The Living Will

ANOTHER TYPE OF WILL IS THE SO-CALLED LIVING WILL, which has nothing whatsoever to do with property. It is a document that deals exclusively with health care issues. More precisely, it addresses the issue of what kind of health care you want—or don't want—when you are in a vegetative, brain-dead, or permanently unconscious condition (as defined by attending physicians) and death is imminent. Do you want your health care providers to continue to use every medical process available, including ventilators, to keep you alive? Or do you want them to stop treatment and allow you to die? These are the issues covered by the living will and another document, the durable power of attorney for health care.

The forms for these documents are different in each state. Some states require the living will and the durable power of attorney for health care to be written as separate distinct legal forms; other states combine them into a single document. Language and options are different as well. You can usually get a copy of both from your state attorney general's office, your local hospital, or the department of aging office in your state. Also, your family attorney will have these documents or can draft them for you.

These documents, often called "advance directives," serve as your written instructions on your health care wishes, to take effect when you are not able to make these wishes known to health care providers. The durable power of attorney for health care is covered in Chapter 10, "Legal Tools for Disability Planning."

The living will is discussed here due to the general public's confusion about the difference between a last will and testament and a living will.

The purpose of a living will is to increase your control over medical treatment decisions at a time when you may not be able to make decisions yourself or verbalize your wishes. For instance, if you have a stroke or a heart attack, or you are in a serious automobile accident and are unable to make clear what you want in a critical care situation, a living will allows a person you have appointed to act for you. Even more important, it states the kind of health care you want—and don't want.

There are two kinds of living wills in use in the United States: the informal living will and the formal statutory living will. The informal living will was in common use before the more formal document, and many are still in use today. (See an example of an informal living will, at right.)

Informal Living Wills

THESE PRIVATE LIVING WILLS are not legally binding documents, because they don't meet the formal statutory requirements of state laws, but they serve as one's

Informal Living Will

To my Family, Physician, Attorney, and Medical Facility:

I, (Name), being of sound mind, voluntarily make known my desires concerning medical treatment when I am dying.

I believe that death is a natural part of life. Dying should not be unnecessarily prolonged. I have a right to make my own decisions concerning treatment that might unduly prolong the dying process. I request that I be fully informed as my death approaches. If possible, I want to participate in decisions regarding my medical treatment and the procedures that may be used to prolong my life.

If I should become unable to make those decisions and have an injury, disease, or illness considered incurable and terminal by my physicians, I direct my physician and all medical personnel to withhold or withdraw all life-sustaining procedures that would serve only to artificially prolong the dying process. I do, however, ask that treatment be administered that will provide me with maximum comfort and freedom from pain.

This statement is made after careful consideration and reflection. It is my intention that these directions be honored by my family and physicians(s) as a final expression of my legal right to refuse medical treatment, and I accept the consequences of this refusal.

Signed (Name)

instructions to family, friends, and physicians that no heroic medical measures should be taken to keep the patient alive if and when death is inevitable.

In the early 1980s, the problems with these documents were many. First, they were not legally binding on either the medical community or on the courts. Second, they did not become "effective" until the death of the person, at which time, of course, the decision whether or not to prolong life was moot. Finally, there were those who thought (and many people still do) that the idea of ending life by the removal of the patient from a life-preserving machine is morally wrong and is in fact euthanasia, "mercy killing," or a murder of another human being.

From the 1980s until the early 1990s these informal living wills floated in a sea of uncertainty, yet they were the only documents in existence that addressed this particular issue. More and more clients were going to attorneys' offices to see what legal remedies they could use so they would not be kept alive and in nursing homes over a long period of time. However, there were no legal remedies available for this problem. It was impossible to halt medical treatment. Physicians felt they could not stop treatment of a terminally ill patient even if the patient was brain-dead. At one time, more than 10,000 patients in a vegetative, brain-dead condition were sustained on medical equipment in hospitals and similar facilities across the country.

Then came a tragic case of a young woman that altered the way these cases were handled and, in the process, permanently changed the course of laws and medical treatment in the United States. Nancy Cruzan was her name, and that name will be immortalized in the annals of the U.S. Supreme Court. Nancy was a young adult in her twenties who had been in a vegetative state for eight years as the result of an automobile accident. She had resided in a variety of facilities in this condition, the last a state hospital. Her life was maintained by several pieces of life-sustaining equipment.

In an effort to release their daughter from this tragic condition, the Cruzan family requested the courts to allow them to instruct Nancy's attending physicians to remove their daughter from this life-sustaining equipment. This case took the issue of removing life-sustaining equipment from a brain-dead person all the way from a small Missouri courtroom to the United States Supreme Court.

The legal issue was: What would Nancy have wanted? Was there any evidence of her thoughts about such a situation? The wishes of Nancy's parents alone proved insufficient to determine what Nancy would have wanted. Nancy had no living will. She had not expressed to her parents that she would have wanted to be released from life-sustaining equipment. Years of waiting, followed by appeal after appeal in the courts, yielded no relief to the parents—or to Nancy. The case was finally resolved years after the first documents were filed in the Missouri courts, due to the evidence of a long-lost friend of Nancy's. The friend had not known of Nancy's condition, but after she learned of the situation, she came forward. She was able to recall and later testify that she had had a conversation with Nancy in which Nancy said she would not want to be kept alive artificially. The machinery was removed, and Nancy was allowed to die in peace.

Had Nancy had a living will, the courts, as well as the physicians, would have known exactly what medical treatment she would have wanted in this extreme situation. This is an excellent, though sad, example of why it is so important that we ourselves make our wishes known, preferably in writing, about what medical treatment, if any, we want if we are in a permanently unconscious or vegetative and terminal condition. The more formal statutory living will that has been developed in recent years offers a better chance of accomplishing that end.

Formal Statutory Living Wills

LIVING WILLS TYPICALLY ALLOW YOU TO SPECIFY which life-prolonging measures to use and which ones to withhold, as well as what "comfort care" may be used, such as hydration and pain medication. Some living wills are general in their scope, while others allow you to checkmark specific options you want and don't want. In other words, you can put a check mark beside "no ventilator" and also check off "yes, surgery even if I am in a terminal condition." As an example, see the excerpt from New York state's detailed living will on the following page.

Most people who have living wills have strong convictions that they don't want extraordinary lifesaving techniques applied if they become terminal, unconscious, and vegetative. However, few stop to realize that living wills have many restrictive features as well.

➤ They are extremely narrow documents, because they cover only a tiny window of time: when death is imminent and one is in a permanently unconscious state. The reality is that the majority of health care decisions that need to be made are the day-to-day health care decisions—the nursing home placements and treatment options for patients lacking the mental capacity to act—and not the dramatic end-of-life scenario called to mind by the living will.

➤ Even if one has a living will, it always needs clarification and interpretation by health care providers. If there is a dispute within a family, then even if there is a living will, health care providers are reluctant to comply with it.

➤ And what if you have a living will from Iowa and you move to Florida? Will your living will be accepted in your new state of residence? States are mixed in how they handle that issue. Some state laws are silent on this problem; some accept the living wills of other states. Most states now use the wording of the Uniform Rights of the Terminally Ill Act, which states: "A declaration executed in another state in compliance with the law of this State is validly executed for purposes of this Act."

➤ What if you change your mind about your living will while you are critically ill? What if you tell the doctor to disregard your living will and then you become permanently unconscious? Remember that as long as you are conscious and competent, you still control all of your health care decisions, even if they are

New York State's Living Will

I direct that NO treatment be given just to keep me alive when I have:

➤ a condition or conditions that will cause me to die soon, or

➤ a condition or conditions so bad (including substantial brain damage or brain disease) that there is little reasonable hope that I will regain a quality of life acceptable to me.

When I have one of these conditions, the treatments I DO NOT want include the following items that I have circled and placed my initials at the end of the line:

➤ surgery

➤ doing things to start my heart or breathing (CPR)

➤ medicine to treat infections (antibiotics)

➤ artificial kidney machine (dialysis)

➤ breathing machine (respirator, ventilator)

➤ food or water given through a tube in the vein, nose, or stomach (tube feedings)

➤ chemotherapy (cancer treatment)

➤ blood transfusions

completely different from what you have stated in your living will.

➤ What if the person who is to act for you under the living will dies? What if that person cannot be located when a decision is needed? An emergency process must be initiated in a court of law, which would appoint a guardian to make these decisions.

These questions merely emphasize that if you have a living will, you have done your best to make sure that if you are ever one of those very few people in a permanently unconscious state, your health care will be in accordance with your wishes. However, facts and circumstances surrounding the living will may be subject to change, and absolute certainty about results cannot be guaranteed. Perhaps the most important thing to tell your family is that you want excellent pain control, comfort care, and dignity in death. These, after all, are the reflected intentions in the living will.

Few legal instruments are as widely discussed as the last will and testament and the living will. Just remember, however, that both of these wills are very narrow legal instruments that apply in only limited situations. The last will and testament, although the most well known legal tool, is applicable only to probate assets; it has no impact on many of the diverse assets most people own today, such as retirement funds, investments, annuities, IRAs, and insurance policies. The living will, though well known to the public, is likewise a legal instrument applicable only to a certain window in time and circumstance, in the event death is imminent and one is in a permanent unconscious or vegetative state.

With such limitations, you might ask, "Are these legal options the only ones open to me? Since I've heard so much about them, aren't they the most important legal instruments I should consider?"

The answer is that wills are one option available to you. However, many of the other legal instruments you may use, or a combination of them, may serve your purposes far better than a last will and testament and/or a living will can to manage the wide range of health care, personal, and financial management issues that may confront you today and in the future. Estate planning is all about trying to put together the best combination of legal instruments possible and then combining them with your life goals and financial plans. In understanding what a will does and what a living will does—and what they don't do—you are one step closer to understanding that one legal tool is not a solution to all your problems.

Chapter Eight

Property Deeds

MARIANNE MOORE, ONE OF AMERICA'S MOST RENOWNED POETS, wrote, "If you tell me why the fence appears impassable, I then will tell you why I think that I can get across it if I try." The "fence" in estate planning consists of the court system, the taxing authorities, and the whole bundle of red tape and expensive fees inherent in it all. For years, estate planners have been trying diligently to figure out a sure way to "beat the system" so that their families will not have to deal with the courts, the tax system, or all of the costly related tax, legal, and financial advisers.

Avoid Probate by Changing Your Deeds

PUTTING ASIDE THE TAX CONSIDERATIONS for now, the question is, "Is there some way around the court system?" The answer is yes, if you want to make that a priority in your planning. You may title your property in such a way that it will never pass through any court system in this country. Why would you want to change the title to your assets? Because a court system does not have jurisdiction over distribution of non-probate assets.

Does it sound simple? Yes. Is it easy to accomplish? Yes. Is there more than one way to change title? Yes, there are several ways. However, as these options are discussed, try to remember that for every advantage gained in converting probate assets to non-probate assets, there may be some serious disadvantages to doing so. Like a captain navigating his boat between reefs, you must decide exactly which position is right for you. You can change the nature of your assets at any time. If you discuss this with your friends, they no doubt will advise you to do so to "avoid probate." But remember that friends, however well intentioned, aren't experts in estate planning, so if you are serious about putting a tax-efficient estate plan in place, go to experts who know the rules and can give you knowledgeable advice.

Although it is true that you may "avoid probate" in many states by putting some or all of your assets into non-probate titles, there are some disadvantages to avoiding probate and the orderly process it involves. Sidestepping this process has larger ramifications, as you will see later in the chapter. It may mean that the individuals who receive your non-probate assets have no obligation to pay any debts you leave behind, including a funeral bill. It may mean that you create huge tax problems for your beneficiaries. So use care when you decide to title your assets as non-probate ones; it is far more complex that simply signing your name to a new deed. Get advice about any tax or estate planning ramifications before you sign a single thing.

For example, suppose you want to co-own property with your only son. What could be wrong with that? Especially if you are eighty years old and want to make sure that he has some legal rights in your property if you get sick or die?

The problem with sharing ownership of your property with anyone is that we don't have a crystal ball to gaze into and read the future. If you convey all of your property, or even a part of it, to your child, you cannot predict what may happen.

Let's say you decide to put your son's name on your deed as a joint-and-survivorship owner with you. What happens if he has financial difficulties? What if your son is forced to file for bankruptcy, or becomes involved in a divorce action? Can the courts or creditors force a sale of the property to pay his financial obligations?

The answer is yes. Why? Because when you make a child (or anyone) a co-owner of your property, that child owns an interest in the property. Therefore, any future events that may occur are likely to have a direct impact on that property interest. Can you ask your son to deed the property back to you if problems crop up? Perhaps, but it is much more likely that such a conveyance would be seen as collusive, and the transfer would be set aside so that your son's interest would still be used to pay creditors or spousal obligations.

In addition, there sometimes is dissension in families that cannot be easily resolved without a court-appointed fiduciary, so you may *want* a court of law to take charge of your estate and decide issues for the family. If, however, you still want to avoid the probate process as much as possible, you certainly can do so by using a variety of non-probate legal tools.

By far the most popular device used today to sidestep probate when real estate is involved is a co-ownership legal tool, the "non-probate" deed. These unique deeds contain precise language that makes possible several different legal avenues to probate avoidance.

Non-Probate Real Estate Deeds

THERE ARE ACTUALLY FIVE TYPES of real estate co-ownership options that you may use as probate avoidance techniques:

1 Joint tenancy with the right of survivorship deeds (JTWROS)
2 Tenancy by the entirety deeds (these may be available only to married couples in some states but operate legally in the same way as JTWROS)
3 Life estate ownership of property deeds
4 Transfer-on-death ownership deeds (TODs)
5 Community property ownership (if you live in a community property state)

What does it mean to say these particular legal options can avoid probate? Suppose James J. Jones owns his house in his name only. His deed states that he alone is the owner of the property. If he dies, one of the first legal issues that will arise is how this house passes from him to his named heirs or beneficiaries. What is the most significant fact to look at in this situation? It is the face of the deed and the title language contained there. A deed thus represents more than a mere ownership concept; it also acts as a device to determine the probate or non-probate nature of the property involved.

Since the deed has *only* the name of James J. Jones on it, the property is subject to the jurisdiction of the probate process (see "The Case of the Greedy Heir"). If there is a will, the title to the home will transfer to the named beneficiaries; if there is no will, it will transfer to the heirs at law. In either case, a probate process will take jurisdiction of the title after Jones's death and will process it so that it passes to the proper heirs or beneficiaries. This will take some months and may be costly in both time and money.

The Case of the Greedy Heir

SAM AND SHIRLEY CASE WORKED at Ford Motor Company on the assembly line for many years. They raised three children, educated two of them, and then retired. Early in their thirty-six-year marriage, they had purchased a small house on thirty acres of land. When they bought the property, the only way they could own and title the property was in their names as co-tenants—that is, as co-owners. The title to their property read: "Sam Case and Shirley Case." This meant that each of them owned a one-half interest in the property, but it also meant that if one of them died, the surviving spouse did *not* automatically inherit the property. Instead, the one-half ownership interest of the first spouse was a probate asset. That one-half interest would, by state law, pass into the estate of the deceased spouse and then would be transferred either by will or by the laws of the state if there were no will.

Sam died in his mid-sixties, leaving behind his wife, his two adult children, and one minor child, who was sixteen years old. He left no will; he believed that his wife would inherit all of his property since everything they owned they had worked for and accumulated together.

Sam's one-half interest passed by law into his estate. Since he left no will leaving his property to his spouse, the law of the state required distribution as follows:

➤ first, the first $60,000 interest in the property to the surviving spouse;

➤ second, a one-third interest in the balance of the property to the surviving spouse; and

➤ third, a two-thirds interest in the balance of the property to the children in equal shares.

Some state laws require that the minor child's interest take precedence over the rights of other siblings and that the balance of the property be held and used for the care and support of the minor.

The result in this case? Shirley owned her half of the property, plus an interest to the extent of $60,000, together with a one-third interest in the balance of Sam's one-half interest. The children owned the balance, or two-thirds interest in the balance of Sam's one-half interest.

Although this sounds complicated, it isn't. The property was appraised at a value of $460,000. Shirley owned one-half, or $230,000, since her name was on the deed as a co-owner.

She was then granted by law $60,000, plus one-third of the balance of Sam's one half interest, or, stated another way, one-third of $170,000, which equals $56,667. So, Shirley owned her $230,000, plus $60,000, plus $56,667, for a total ownership interest in the $460,000 property of $346,667. The children divided the balance of $113,333 equally so that each child owned a $37,778 share. (Each state handles these percentages differently, so it is a good idea to find out how your state mandates property distribution if there is no will.)

If the children had been content to have their mother manage and control all of the property, all would have gone on smoothly. However, one of the sons had a spouse who wanted their share of the property so they could build a house themselves. This led to a partition of the property and a sale of a large part of the acreage. This caused a great deal of misunderstanding, anger, and hurt feelings, and as a result, the family became very divided and is no longer united as a family.

This is not by any means an isolated case. People buy property and put their names on their deeds, and years go by without the owners' devoting a single thought to *how* this asset will be handled at the time of death. Often, surviving spouses do not receive the assets they have been expecting. This means that dissension sets in after death because something doesn't work the way everyone assumed it would.

By sharp contrast, in co-ownership deeds, the language on the face of the deed itself allows the property to transfer entirely *outside* of any probate process and directly to the person named as the survivor on the deed. Why? Because the language on the face of the deed creates a non-probate asset by which title passes in accordance with its specific language.

It is important to understand that the language of each deed is unique. The language of the James J. Jones deed is that of a sole owner. Co-ownership language is very precise and must comply with state law. On the other hand, this means that non-probate deeds not only avoid probate, they also create extremely fast transfers of property. They also diminish, and in most cases completely eliminate, legal costs involved in the transfer of co-ownership property.

Joint-and-Survivorship Deeds and Tenancy by the Entirety Deeds

JOINT-AND-SURVIVORSHIP CONVEYANCES are the most common probate-avoidance method in common use today and are recognized in most states. However, these conveyances are not automatic. To create this particular form of co-ownership, specific language must be included within the conveying deed, stating, "From the owner of the property to A and B, as joint tenants with right of survivorship." If that language is in A and B's deed, then they have created a joint-and-survivorship deed. If A dies, B becomes the owner of the entire interest.

The survivorship feature of joint tenancy means that the last joint tenant to die owns the entire asset. Ownership of the asset passes to the surviving joint tenant by operation of law. The most obvious advantage of a joint-and-survivorship form of co-ownership is that co-ownership property passes immediately upon death from the decedent to the surviving owner. The transfer is cost efficient since no court costs or legal fees are involved, and there is no frustration or delay in transferring the title to the property.

Originally, only married couples could elect co-ownership of property and were allowed to own it as tenants by entirety. Today, thirty states recognize this concept, which is very similar to the joint-and-survivorship concept of ownership. As a result, we will treat these concepts as if they are the same for purposes of discussion.

If you are interested in having a deed drafted for a co-ownership interest in property, make sure that you see an attorney who is knowledgeable about real estate law, as each state requires different language to create this type of ownership. Ohio may use different wording from Tennessee, and that state may differ from Maine.

Disadvantages of Joint-and-Survivorship Property

ALTHOUGH JOINT-AND-SURVIVORSHIP and tenancy by the entirety have a number of pluses, this type of ownership also has its disadvantages:

➤ Probate is not totally eliminated if the decedent owned other probate property at the time of death. In such cases, a probate procedure will still be required.

➤ When the survivor of jointly owned property dies, his or her assets will be subject to probate. In other words, joint-and-survivorship deeds, while avoiding probate for the first spouse to die, do not avoid probate for the last to die.

➤ The last-to-die spouse may end up owning all of the joint-and-survivorship property, which may be substantial. As a result, estate taxes may be greatly increased. If your assets are more than $600,000, many financial planners say you are not a good candidate for joint-and-survivorship planning, since you will be far better served by creating a trust instead—a vehicle that may greatly reduce taxes. (See Chapter 9 for more information on trusts.) Too much property held as joint-and-survivorship can be very detrimental if not done properly and with an eye on the tax consequences.

➤ Including only one child (from among several) with a parent on a deed as joint-and-survivorship co-owners (an increasingly popular probate-avoidance practice in the United States) may cause family dissension. It may also serve to disinherit all of the other children.

For example, a widow with three children may think it prudent to place one of her children on her deed as a co-owner. For instance, the deed to her home may read, "This house is owned by myself and my daughter Jan." In the event the mother dies, Jan will inherit the house as the survivor. She has no obligation to share this ownership with her siblings. In fact, from the time her name is placed on the deed, she has an undivided one-half ownership in the house in most states. This means that if the mother wants to sell her house, she must have her daughter's signature and consent to the sale.

➤ After the first spouse's death, there may be some gift-tax problems if the surviving spouse adds one or all of the children to the deed as joint-and-survivor co-owners to avoid probate. The surviving spouse's assets would be exposed to claims of the children's creditors. Also, the surviving spouse could lose control over the property, and this situation could create unnecessary income- and gift-tax problems for the children after the death of the surviving spouse.

➤ In the event that any joint tenant becomes mentally incapacitated, the jointly held house could become involved in a probate guardianship proceeding, in which case no sale of the home would be allowed until the probate court permitted it. This situation also might have an impact on the Medicaid treatment of the spousal assets. The joint-and-survivorship ownership of the house would have to be explored with Medicaid issues in mind, a complicated and muddy area of the law in each of the states.

➤ Some estate planning advisers say that jointly owned assets "create taxes without the benefit of ownership." For example, if sisters Janice and Joan own a house together as joint tenants with right of survivorship, and Joan dies, title to the house will pass to Janice without going through probate. However, even though Joan's family will receive no benefit from the house, one-half of its value must be included in Joan's estate for federal estate tax purposes.

One last but very important warning: Creating joint-and-survivorship property should never substitute for a will or trust. If the joint owners die simultaneously, as a result of a car accident or other disaster, all of the property would become subject to probate and would be transferred to the lineal descendants, which the owners might not have wanted.

Joint Ownership in Community Property States

COMMUNITY PROPERTY, A STATUTORY FORM of spousal co-ownership, exists in all community property states in one form or another. (See Chapter 4 for a list of those states.) Although the statutory language varies in community property states, they all have in common this basic concept: all property accumulated by a married couple living in a community property state is owned in accordance with state law as community property; that is, each spouse owns one-half of the property.

The property belongs to the spouses as marriage partners, in the same way that property is owned by a business that is a partnership. This means that the property is owned share and share alike, with each spouse owning one-half of the whole.

Spouses not only share the property itself but also share equally in income derived from the property; they share equally in each other's salaries, wages, and all other compensation. In addition, each spouse in community property states, as the owner of one-half of the property, can give his or her share to someone other than the spouse by transfer, gift, will, or trust.

Can spouses change the community property aspect of their real estate? Yes. As they do with any other aspect of real property, individuals have the right at any time to alter their deeds. In community property states, however, it is important to make a formal record of all substantial changes from the community property status to another form of ownership. As with any legal documents that deal with real estate or personal property of substantial value (in excess of $10,000), this record must be in writing, witnessed and notarized in accordance with the laws of the state where a person resides.

Therefore, if a couple wants to convert their community property to joint-and-survivorship property, they do so by changing their property deed to include the operative words: "joint and survivorship."

The important thing to remember in a community property state is that one can change the ownership of the spousal property, but it should be done in a clear, formal manner to avoid any confusion later for the spouses or the heirs and beneficiaries.

Life Estate Deeds for Probate Avoidance

JUST AS YOU CAN CHANGE YOUR DEED from owning property as a sole owner to owning it with another person as a joint and survivorship owner, you may also change your ownership interest in your property to convey the property to others and still retain a life estate interest in it. Deeds may be in many forms, depending on state requirements, but almost all states recognize life estate deeds that both avoid probate and allow you to convey to your children or others an immediate interest in your property, while allowing you to live in and control your property for the rest of your life. The conveyance form used to accomplish this is referred to in some states as a life estate deed and in other states as a life-right deed.

If you, as the sole owner of your home, want to put your daughter Anne's name on your deed in such a way that you will have the right to live in your home the rest of your life, and at the same time you want to provide that the title of your home will pass directly to your daughter outside of any probate process, you can sign a life estate deed. Typically, this would read: "From Jane Doe *to Jane Doe for her lifetime, with the remainder interest to my daughter, Anne.*"

This deed allows you to live in your home during your lifetime, pay all of the bills and taxes on the property, maintain it for as long as you live, and enjoy all of the rights of ownership. What happens when you die? The property, pursuant to your life estate deed, transfers the "remainder" (or the property interest remaining after your death) directly to your child.

Suppose you want your house to go to your daughter and then to your grand-child, without letting your son-in-law acquire any interest in your property. You can create a life estate deed that contains life estates for various individuals, with the remainder interest vesting in future years to your grandson. You execute a deed that reads like this: "From Jane Doe *to Jane Doe for her life, at her death to Anne for her lifetime, with the remainder interest to John, my grandson.*" You have thus created a life estate for yourself and a consecutive life estate for your daughter, free of any legal claim your son-in-law might put forth. You also have stipulated that your grandchild will ultimately inherit your property—and you have avoided probate in the process!

But note that estate planning attorneys are not comfortable with recommending to clients the management of real estate transfers over several generations through a life estate deed. I can well remember my surprise the first time I saw a life estate deed that had the mother retaining a life estate in her modest home, giving all of her eleven children a consecutive life estate in the property, and making a provision that the last of her children living was to receive the remainder interest. In this case, the property was involved in one bankruptcy proceeding, several divorce proceedings, and numerous disputes over who should pay for the upkeep of the property when some of the children lived in the house and some did not. Still, the use of a life estate deed on a more sensible basis is an excellent device to provide for generational transfer of property outside of probate.

If and when you are thinking of sharing property ownership with your children, here are some guidelines to follow:
> Make sure you know what you are doing, and be certain that sharing the owner-ship of your assets is to your advantage, regardless of the benefit to others.

➤ The old adage that "you should make no gifts or loans to others unless you can absolutely afford to" is excellent advice in this situation. When you make transfers or gifts to others, don't do so with the idea that if you need the funds or property back, it will be given back to you. If you do have that idea, this is an indication that you should not be making the gift in the first place.

➤ Instead of sharing ownership with someone else, consider placing the property in a simple trust instead. This is the best idea of all. It will protect you—regardless of future financial problems.

➤ Once you sign a deed, it is considered a permanent transfer. Don't do this unless you are prepared for a permanent, irrevocable consequence.

Some attorneys also recommend what is known as a "joint-and-concurrent life estate." This refers to the language used in a life estate deed stipulating that each co-owner, i.e., each of the spouses, will have a life estate in the property, and they can then name their respective children as the remainder beneficiaries.

In some states, there is now also the so-called Lady Bird Life Estate Deed, so named because Lady Bird and Lyndon Johnson supposedly created this ownership concept, also called an "enhanced life estate deed." It was developed to give the benefits of life ownership and at the same time avoid many of its difficulties. Under this form of ownership, the owner retains a life estate and grants a remainder, but by law can mortgage or sell the property during his or her lifetime, regardless of the remainder person's interest. The traditional life estate deed splits the ownership of the property in such a way that both the life owner *and* the remainder owner are required to agree and sign a deed of sale. Thus, if the remainder person, who might be the daughter, refused to sign a deed of sale when her mother, who is the life tenant, wanted to sell, no sale could take place.

In this enhanced life estate deed, which is not available in every state, the mother could keep all rights of ownership, including the right to sell her property if she desires. The remainder person does not have to agree to sign anything, and owning the property does not disqualify the mother for Medicaid in most states. The grantee receives the property at the time of the mother's death without any probate process and also gets the step-up in basis that is so very important for tax reasons.

The step-up issue highlights some important tax advantages that come into play when you transfer real estate to your children. For example, suppose you buy property for $50,000 and add $5,000 of improvements to it. Therefore, the basis of the property for tax purposes is $55,000. If, at the time you sell the property, it is sold for $75,000, you have enjoyed a gain of $20,000, on which you must pay a capital gains tax.

Let's say you still own the property at your death; it is appraised and valued at $75,000. The tax code permits what is called a step-up in basis to $75,000. This new basis is very advantageous to heirs and beneficiaries. If they sell the property for $75,000, they do not have to pay capital gains tax on it.

In addition to the tax consequences, you also need to be aware that Medicaid will scrutinize any and all transfers from an elderly person to others. The manner in which a home, farm, or other asset is disposed of by an elderly person who requests Medicaid and Medicare coverage of all nursing home and medical expenses is an area fraught with problems. Can a person transfer a $75,000 asset to her children, seek admittance to a nursing home, and expect to have all of her care paid for by public funds? No!

Therefore, if you are thinking about transferring property and you think you may have to go into a nursing home for care, be sure to thoroughly investigate your state's laws about this entire area. Otherwise, you may very well find that the transfer you wish to make will actually disqualify you from receiving any assistance for nursing home or medical needs.

One last life estate concept should be mentioned, although it should be used with care: the "quit-claim deed with remainder interest and retained power to modify remainderman by will," or CRID. A quit-claim deed with proper CRID language permits property to bypass probate because it contains the life estate and remainder language. However, the owner of the property reserves the right to change the remainderman under his or her last will and testament. That may sound appealing to some, but in some states, it has the potential to create a defective title. This makes a probate process essential to clear up title issues, and it might make litigation more probable between remainder persons named in the deed versus those named in the will. That said, in states that permit the use of the CRID deed, the transfer goes through without any problems more often than not. Used with care, it can be a good way to transfer property outside the probate process.

Transfer-on-Death Deeds
ONE OTHER NEW CO-OWNERSHIP DEED now available in Kansas, Ohio, and a few other states is called the transfer-on-death deed, or TOD deed. This deed is similar to a payable-on-death (POD) bank account and transfer-on-death (TOD) stock designation, both of which have been standard options in commercial areas for a long time.

Transfer- or payable-on-death language allows the owner of an asset to designate the name of the beneficiary whom the owner wants to inherit the property at the time of the owner's death. At death, the property is automatically transferred to the beneficiary, thus avoiding probate. In many ways, this is similar to the owner of a life insurance policy designating the beneficiary of the proceeds of the policy at the time of death. The transfer of the assets takes place outside of any probate administration and in accordance with the language of the insurance contract. POD accounts and TOD stock accounts work the same way; transfer is made pursuant to the beneficiary named on the documents involved.

The advantages to such deeds are:

➤ Property is transferred to a beneficiary quickly and at less cost than would be the case if court costs and attorney fees were involved.

➤ Privacy between the parties is preserved, since the assets are not subject to probate and do not have to be entered into the inventory records of the court, to which the public has access.

➤ Similarly, the owner of the property can have more flexibility, since what the owner does with this asset is not under the scrutiny of unhappy relatives.

➤ The named TOD beneficiary has no right of ownership or interference until the death of the owner, which gives the owner total control of the property during his or her lifetime. You can change the TOD owner during your lifetime.

What is the operating language that must be included in a deed of this nature? The deed, like all other deeds, must include a proper description of the real estate to be transferred and the signatures of all the property owners. Signatures of the beneficiaries are not necessary, although the beneficiary's name must appear on the deed. This must be filed in the local office for recording of deeds, often known as the recorder's or registrar of deeds' office, prior to the death of the owner. After the owner's death, the beneficiary must file a certified copy of the owner's death certificate. See the following page for a typical TOD deed.

Note that if you want to ensure that each of your beneficiaries receives a specific amount of money or portion of an asset, you should specify each beneficiary on the deed. Otherwise, if you entrust one beneficiary to distribute your assets to the others, there may be some very unhappy consequences that you had not intended (see "The Case of the Angry Children").

Example of a TOD Deed
NAME OF OWNER, as owner, transfers on death to NAME OF BENEFICIA-RY (name of alternative beneficiary(ies), as grantee beneficiary, the following described interest in real estate: (the legal description of the real estate appears here). THIS TRANSFER-ON-DEATH DEED IS REVOCABLE. IT DOES NOT TRANSFER ANY OWNERSHIP UNTIL THE DEATH OF THE OWNER. IT REVOKES ALL PRIOR BENEFICIARY DESIGNATIONS BY THIS OWNER FOR INTEREST IN REAL ESTATE.
   (Include signatures of owners and acknowledgment by notary public)

The Case of the Angry Children

CHARLOTTE, A WIDOW, HAD FOUR CHILDREN, ages nineteen, twenty-two, twenty-six, and twenty-eight. She owned a small house, a car, a savings account, and a checking account. She also had a modest life insurance policy and one $10,000 certificate of deposit.

When she was diagnosed with breast cancer, she wanted to make sure all of her kids would have the right to live in her house and use her funds, but she didn't want to go to an attorney or have anyone else involved in her family business. Of her four children, Charlotte thought Tim, the twenty-six-year-old, was the most businesslike and could be trusted to look after her assets for the benefit of all of her children.

So she went to the bank to ask her trusted bank officer (who had helped her set up her certificate of deposit) just how she could arrange to leave her property. The bank officer advised her to put a TOD, or transfer-on-death, designation on her accounts at the bank and also on her certificate of deposit. He carefully explained that she could avoid the probate process that way and that this was a good option for her.

She went home and discussed all of this with her children. Then Charlotte went back to the bank and put Tim's name on all of her bank accounts as the TOD designee. She also went to a title company and asked them to have their attorneys prepare for her a deed like the TOD deed, and so they prepared for her a joint-and-survivorship deed with her name and Tim's on the deed. She also designated Tim as her beneficiary on her life insurance policy.

Relieved that all would now be well, that Tim would receive all of her assets and distribute them equitably to all of her children, she put the matter completely out of her mind as she turned all of her energies to fighting her devastating disease.

After Charlotte died, all of her assets went to Tim. The car had been sold, so it was not involved. The life insurance, home, certificate of deposit, and savings and checking accounts went to Tim. The entire estate amounted to around $120,000. He distributed $20,000 to each of the other kids and kept the balance for himself. When the others angrily shouted that that was not their mother's intentions, he said it was. He, after all, was the one who had taken care of her, had driven her to her medical appointments, and generally had looked after all of her needs during the last months of her life.

The other three kids went to an attorney to correct the problem, but there was nothing he could do. After all, their mother's actions seemed to make it clear that she fully intended to leave all of her assets to Tim, as evidenced by her written changes on all of her assets. The fact that she verbally expressed her intent that her assets were to be used for all of her children was not admittable evidence in the state where she lived.

Tim kept the assets and lost his family. His siblings never forgave Tim for what they considered his fraud upon them and upon their mother, and they never reconciled.

This case might have been handled differently in some states, but nevertheless, what is reduced to writing certainly has greater weight than what is said orally. And the Statute of Frauds, which is recognized in all of our states, expressly provides that any understanding that deals with real estate must be in writing. In most states, Tim would clearly be the owner of the family home. If they had lived in a different state, his siblings might have had a chance at wresting the other assets away from him, but they would still have had a very difficult time proving their mother's intentions.

In conclusion, although there are five basic ways to avoid probate by co-ownership, recognize that there are often issues involved that are more important than merely avoiding probate. You should consider many facets, such as taxes, control and management of assets during time of disability (which co-ownership does not even address), and finally, serious gift or tax problems for the beneficiaries of these transfers.

Chapter Nine

Trusts

OVER THE PAST SEVERAL YEARS, articles about trusts have appeared with increased frequency in the *New York Times*, the *Chicago Tribune*, the *Los Angeles Times*, *Fortune*, *Money*, *Worth*, and many, many other popular publications. Even small local newspapers, hospital newsletters, churches, and other charitable organizations, including colleges and universities, are providing extensive information to the public about trusts. Estate planning attorneys report a dramatic increase in clients who want trusts drafted for themselves and their families.

Why this overwhelming interest in a legal instrument that has been around for so long? Why are the public and the media so interested in the trust? And why now? After all, the trust concept has been a part of the Anglo-Saxon legal tradition for hundreds of years. Early cases from English law speak of sheep, armaments, and other property items of the Middle Ages left in "trust" for heirs as wealthy warriors joined the Crusades.

Perhaps the reason that trusts are so much on our minds today is that they have finally found a specialized niche in our increasingly complex society that wills cannot serve. The trust is the one special legal document able to embrace the many and diverse possibilities facing all of us in these remarkable times.

Years ago, if you owned a house, you had a deed to transfer it during your lifetime, and you had a last will and testament to transfer the house at the time of your death. Thus, you owned simple assets that you could convey to others, either during your lifetime or at your death, by simple conveyance forms, either by a deed or a will. These modest, uncomplicated legal documents were quite sufficient then, but they are simply not adequate for today's world.

Today, we find ourselves more in the position of small companies. We own real estate, pension plans, insurance policies, and a multitude of other diverse assets; we are no longer merely individuals who own a single asset. Therefore, we need a variety of more complex planning tools to encompass our enormously intricate lifestyles.

Just think for a moment how complex our lives have become. Today, if you are fortunate to have a good job, the employment carries with it many complicated issues: income, income taxes, deferred compensation issues, health coverage, sick leave issues, and disability insurance, to name a few of the complex benefits surrounding our jobs. We have a far different view of ourselves than did our grandparents, who lived whole lives in an agrarian culture free of these concerns.

As we work, we may begin to accumulate a variety of assets: interests in real estate, annuities, collectibles, stock, bonds, precious metals, promissory notes, and inheritances. And each of these issues has an impact on even larger institutional questions, such as the tax consequences—income tax, capital gains tax, and estate taxes, to name only a few.

In addition to the multiple aspects of our financial lives, and in large part due to our growing longevity, our lives now encompass as many as four generations: ourselves, our children, our grandchildren, and our parents. In the past, we lived with perhaps two generations. This linear expansion of families extends our concerns for those we love and our need to do broad estate planning that has the best possibility of including all of these people, as well as each one's separate circumstances. The trust instrument may be the best possible legal document to meet these diverse requirements.

On the other hand, many people are now going to their attorneys and demanding a trust because their neighbor leaned over the backyard fence one sunny afternoon and said, "Boy, I talked to Fred and then my attorney, and I now have a trust, and it's fabulous. And if you don't have one of those, you're crazy."

So off people go to their attorneys and start ordering a trust in the same way they buy a car. Too bad, because a trust, like every other legal document, is only one option among many available to you. And you certainly don't want a trust just because Fred has one or thinks you need one. Furthermore, even if you think you would benefit from having a trust, do you understand the process well enough to feel total comfort in placing your assets in one? Let's examine the nuts and bolts of the process.

What Is a Trust?

IN ITS SIMPLEST FORM, A TRUST is a legal creation established by a written legal document. The document sets forth the manner in which one person gives to another person or institution some or all of his or her property to manage under certain circumstances. I might, for instance, transfer all of my stock into a trust and make myself my own trustee as long as I am competent; I may name my daughters to be my contingent beneficiaries if I become incompetent. In that way, I will manage my own property in my trust as long as I am able to do so. When I'm no longer able, then my children will continue to manage the property and to distribute the income and principal in accordance with the terms of the trust document.

A trust must meet basic legal criteria established in each state. If, for instance, you are a resident of California, that state has specific legal standards that define a trust. Trusts must be written, witnessed, and usually notarized. Like a will, a trust is a creation of the legislative process, which dictates all of the terms that are necessary for a trust's creation.

The person who establishes the trust is the "settlor" or "grantor." The person or entity designated to manage the trust is known as the "trustee." This may be one or more individuals, a company, a trust company, or a banking institution. The assets held in the trust are referred to as the "corpus" of the trust.

If you were named the trustee of a trust, your main job would be to manage its assets in a reasonably prudent manner. You would want to know exactly what you are authorized to do, for how long you are required to act as trustee, and what you are to do with the assets you accumulate.

Because a trustee manages assets for others, it is important that a written trust document specifically set out the scope of authority of both the settlor and the trustee, as well as the rights of those who may receive benefits from the trust, the beneficiaries. Thus, a well-designed trust will specify all the rights and duties of all of the people who may be affected by it.

To give you a general idea of what a trust looks like, look at the trust document of John James Jones, a widower who has two children for whom he wants to provide through his trust, on the following pages.

As you can see, one of the greatest things a trust can do, which no other legal instrument is able to do in quite the same way, is to bridge the gap between life and death. In addition to bridging this gap, the trust also:

➢ permits assets to flow into and out of the trust over a long period of time;

➢ provides management of assets during long or short periods of the settlor's dis-

Revocable Durable Living Trust of John James Jones

TRUST AGREEMENT MADE and executed this 2nd day of January, 2001, between John James Jones, the Settlor, and ABC Bank, the Trustee.

Trust Estate: The Trust owns those assets described in Schedule A, attached hereto, which may be modified to include more assets.

Life Income to Settlor: The Trustee is to pay to the Settlor part or all of the income of the Trust as he may request. In the event the Settlor does not request income to be distributed to him, the Trustee is to pay to the Settlor's children, Alice and Sam, in equal shares, all of the income remaining in the Trust on the last day of each year.

Incapacity of Settlor: In the event the Settlor becomes incapacitated, the Trustee shall pay for the Settlor's benefit the income and so much of the principal as deemed necessary for the care and comfort of the Settlor. Incapacity shall be determined by two physicians to be selected by the Trustee.

Disposition at Settlor's Death: Any Trust assets remaining in Trust at the time of the Settlor's death shall be distributed as follows: Income shall be distributed to my two children in equal shares at the end of each year until each reaches thirty-five years of age, at which time the Trust assets shall be divided equally. Distribution of half of the assets shall be paid to the first of my children reaching the age of thirty-five, with the balance

ability, which may include stroke, illness, accident, or incapacity due to aging or unexpected occurrence;
➤ avoids any probate process;
➤ permits professional management;
➤ allows disinterested nonfamily individuals or institutions to provide professional, objective guidance and distribution;
➤ extends management and control of assets, both corpus and income, far into the future and well beyond the life span of a settlor; and
➤ may assist in tax issues.

Although a trust can do many beneficial things for you, it may not be an easy thing to transfer your assets to this separate entity. You cannot keep your assets in your own name. For a trust to function, it must "own" your assets. This means that

to be distributed when the last of my children reaches the age of thirty-five. In the event of the death of one of my children, his or her children shall receive my child's portion. In the event a child of mine should die without leaving children, then his or her share shall be paid to my surviving child. In the event both of my children die before the Trust funds are distributed, then Trust assets are to be distributed pursuant to the State of Anyplace laws of inheritance.

Trustee Powers: The Trustee has numerous powers of sale, management, and distribution of assets as set forth more fully in Exhibit B.

Settlor's Powers: The Settlor shall control all of the Trust and its assets subject to this Trust and may terminate the Trust at any time.

Accounting by Trustee: The Trustee must file a written accounting with the Settlor and Beneficiaries each year.

Resignation of Trustee: The Trustee may resign at any time and a successor Trustee will be named.

Additional Property: Additional property may be added to the Trust.

Power of Amendment or Revocation: The Settlor may revoke the Trust at any time.

you must actually deed your real estate into your trust. Likewise, all of your certificates of deposit, stock, savings accounts, and other property must literally be titled in the name of your trust and *not* in your individual name.

Some Specific Trust Provisions

THE FOLLOWING INFORMATION IS usually contained in a trust:

➤ The name of the settlor is set forth, as well as the state of residence (as it is this state law that will govern the trust).

➤ The property owned by the trust is specified.

➤ A trustee is named, and this person may be required to sign the trust.

➤ Present and future beneficiaries are named, and the trust document describes how each is to benefit. Monetary shares and times of distribution are specified in clear, concise terms.

➤ Powers of the trustee are set forth precisely.

➤ A spendthrift provision bars beneficiaries from certain acts, such as borrowing against their possible inheritance.

➤ A "saving clause" is included to make sure the trust terminates within state law requirements. This means that all funds are to be distributed out of the trust, and the trustee is discharged from administering the trust.

➤ Bond provisions for the trustee are set out or waived. What does this mean? Most trusts require that the trustee provide a bond for the performance of his or her duties. If the trustee acts negligently or takes funds from the trust, the bond is there to make restitution to the trust for any loss suffered. Sometimes this requirement is waived if there is absolute trust between the parties.

➤ Successor provisions are defined for the named trustee, allowing a successor to the trustee, in case that individual dies. Most trusts include a primary trustee-owner and then a contingent trustee. There may even be a provision for another trustee. Any trustee after the original trustee may be referred to as the successor trustee.

➤ Trustee's fees and accounting requirements are specified.

The Importance of Funding Your Trust

MOST PEOPLE UNDERSTAND the following mechanics of establishing a trust:

➤ You go to an attorney to get a trust drafted.

➤ The trust may be revocable or irrevocable.

➤ Your trust can be included in your will or it can be independent. In other words, you either have a separate legal document as a trust or you have a testamentary trust, which is a trust included within your will that takes effect only when you die. The testamentary trust is an outdated choice at best.

➤ You decide which assets you want to put into the trust, and you sign it.

What few people really understand is that unless you *transfer* assets into a trust, the trust has little, if any, significance. (See "The Case of the Empty Trust," at right.) A trust applies only to assets it owns, so assets to be governed by the trust must be legally transferred into it. This "funds" the trust.

The Case of the Empty Trust

O VER A PERIOD OF MANY YEARS, Ada and Jeff read about trusts, talked to their friends about them, consulted with attorneys about the possibility of setting up trusts, and finally signed up for an estate planning course I taught at a local college.

During the past forty years, this couple had accumulated—through hard work, inheritances from their families, and careful, frugal management—an estate of $1.4 million in assets. They understood that by creating a marital deduction trust, they could save more than $250,000 in estate taxes, and they knew that their children could use that money a lot more than the government could!

Therefore, they had gone to an excellent attorney and had the proper trust drafted for their specific needs. Everything seemed to be in place. They signed everything, discussed their plan with their children, put their trust documents in their safe-deposit box and signed up for my estate planning course on a whim, so they would have something to do on cold winter nights in northern Ohio.

One evening after class we were discussing some specific aspects of trusts. Ada and Jeff confidently informed me that they had the exact kind of trust that we had covered in class that night, and they were excited to learn exactly how marital trusts worked. They went on to say that most of their estate consisted of apple orchards they had inherited from their parents. "Thank goodness we have all of that land in joint-and-survivorship deeds," Ada said, "so if something happens to one of us, the other one will automatically have title to all of that."

Imagine their shock when I told them that they had completely undone their trust by putting all of their property into joint-and-survivorship deeds! That one mistake nearly cost them $250,000. They had not realized that for a trust to work, it must be funded. When they had their trusts prepared and signed, they also should have funded them by putting all of their property into the trust's name. The point of having marital trusts is to fund them with property so that at the death of the first spouse, the trust will control all aspects of distribution of property, which in turn sets up the tax-savings device.

Within a week, Ada and Jeff happily reported that they had funded their trust, which invalidated the old joint-and-survivorship deeds. Now they will enjoy those tax savings that will be so important to their kids to keep the family orchard business going. If you have a trust, make sure your property deeds reflect that fact. This will ensure that your estate planning has the same happy ending as Ada's and Jeff's.

Suppose John James Jones has stock in A Company, B Company, and C Company. Assume stock A is worth $300,000; the stocks of B and C companies have little value. John wants his trust to professionally manage the assets of A Company. In order to achieve that goal, John must fund the trust by actually transferring the stock of A Company into the trust. The legal ownership of the stock is then in the name of the "John James Jones Trust."

What happens to the stock in B and C companies? It remains in the sole name of John James Jones, and at the time of his death, this stock will be transferred according to the terms of his will, through the probate process in effect in his state of residence.

Thus, under this scenario, the A Company stock, having already been placed in trust prior to death, will be controlled by the terms of the trust and not the will. Will the stock be distributed to John James Jones's relatives, or will it be held over a period of years, with only income being distributed to others? This depends upon the terms of the trust. The important thing to remember is to fund the trust. Otherwise, your trust is like an empty closet.

Different Kinds of Trusts

THERE ARE MANY KINDS OF TRUSTS, but by far the most popular trust in the United States today is the living trust. According to the latest statistics, 25 percent of Americans ages sixty-five to seventy-four, and 29 percent of those over the age of seventy-five, have this type of trust. You can revoke or amend a living trust, in whole or in part.

Within the living trust category, however, are many different varieties, each designed to achieve a specific purpose for the estate planner:

➤ **Charitable remainder trust (CRT).** Allows you to make a gift to a charity through a trust that benefits a noncharitable beneficiary (yourself or your children). Offers substantial tax benefits if you are in a high tax bracket and are charitably disposed.

➤ **Crummey trust.** An irrevocable trust established to allow gifting into a trust for the future benefit of children and grandchildren. There are significant tax benefits in this gifting if it qualifies as giving a present interest to the trust for beneficiaries.

Essentially, a Crummey trust is an irrevocable trust into which a person makes a contribution for the ultimate beneficiaries, usually children or grandchildren. When the contribution is made and the trust funded, the trustee gives the beneficiaries the absolute right to withdraw the funds from the trust. Such a right of withdrawal qualifies the gift as a gift of "present interest," which also qualifies it for the gift tax annual exclusion.

The beneficiaries don't withdraw the funds, however. Instead, the funds within the trust are used to pay premiums on life insurance on the trustee owner's life. When the trustee dies, the life insurance proceeds go to the beneficiaries, without passing through the trustee's estate. Thus, all of these funds avoid federal estate taxes.

In a Crummey trust it is not desirable for the person who creates the trust to be the trustee, as that might well defeat the tax benefits possible under the gifting program. Thus, grandparents, who often create these trusts and also provide the funds for them, should not serve as trustees. This is a popular, albeit complicated, trust, so if you are interested in one, you should seek the advice of a qualified attorney who specializes in estate planning.

➤ **Family trust.** A trust set up for the sole benefit of the family. Usually property is transferred into the trust, held in trust, and managed by the trustee over many years for the use of the family, with income to be distributed pursuant to the terms of the trust.

➤ **Generation-skipping trust.** An irrevocable trust that provides income only to the spouse and children of the settlor. The trust terminates when the children die or reach a certain age, at which time the assets of the trust are distributed to the grandchildren.

➤ **Grantor retained annuity trust (GRAT).** A settlor, such as a parent, transfers assets into an irrevocable trust and receives income back from the trust for a period of years (perhaps for a lifetime). When the trust ends at the death of the settlor, the assets remaining are distributed to the named beneficiaries of the trust.

➤ **Life insurance trust.** A trust that is permitted to buy life insurance to protect assets. Today life insurance trusts are being used with greater frequency.

➤ **Marital deduction trust, known as an AB trust.** A special trust that can be used only by spouses to minimize federal estate taxes at the death of the first spouse. Spouses fund the trusts, which are then divided between an A trust, known as the spousal trust, and a B trust, known as the family trust. Division of assets at the death of the first spouse between A and B helps minimize the federal estate tax impact, and several hundred thousands in taxes can be saved if these trusts are properly drafted and funded.

All too often, spouses go to an attorney and have a marital deduction trust drafted, only to find out later that it did not "qualify" under IRS regulations. This usually happens for two reasons. First, the spouses may have failed to actually transfer their assets into the trust. If the assets are to be governed by a trust, the trust must be the legal owner of those assets. If, for instance, you own a piece of real estate, you must actually deed it into the trust. This is also true of all stocks, bonds, bank or investment accounts, and second homes.

The second reason is that the language of the trust may have failed to exactly specify the rights of the surviving spouse. Often spouses do not want certain language put into their trusts, because they feel it is too restrictive or it does not meet their approval for some reason. However, the survivor's legal rights must be set forth specifically in order to satisfy the strict tax regulations. Therefore, if you want a marital deduction trust and can financially benefit from it, make sure you fund the trust, and check with your attorney to ensure that it includes the correct wording to qualify for tax savings.

➢ **Medicaid trust.** Trusts designed to hold assets so the settlor could "keep" property and still qualify for Medicaid benefits. The purpose was to preserve property of parents for their children. These trusts are no longer as effective as in the past, since state and federal laws have been enacted to discourage this practice. The thinking is that you should pay for your care and not be able to transfer your assets to your children to avoid doing that.

➢ **Minors trust.** Trusts created to benefit children eighteen years old and younger. Often grandparents in particular want to establish trusts for their grandchildren. These are good vehicles into which to put assets every year, because you can have a trustee invest the funds, thus providing for the child's education or special needs later in life.

➢ **Qualified personal residence trust (QPRT).** Trusts that hold the title to your home. In the event you become disabled, these trusts provide for a trustee to manage, maintain, or sell the home and to act for your best interest if you are unable to make decisions for yourself. Often the home at your death passes from the trust to your children, thus avoiding probate.

When would you institute such a trust? You would use it only in very specific circumstances. For example, many single people use it, because they don't have anyone as a financial safety net in the event they are disabled. Also, this trust is suitable for those who are disabled or can foresee the day they will need someone else to maintain or perhaps sell their property. This latter group would include those with a progressive or chronic illness.

➤ **Qualified terminable interest in property trust (QTIP).** This trust is often used when there is a second marriage. The spouses contribute funds to a trust and receive the income during their lifetime. The trust assets are distributed to their respective children at the time of the survivor's death, at which time the trust ends.

There is also an irrevocable trust, which is a trust that, once created and funded, cannot be revoked. This means you cannot simply change your mind—you cannot cancel this trust and get back your assets.

Each trust serves a specific purpose and can meet a variety of needs. Only you can decide which one is best for you after careful discussion and review with your professional, legal, financial, and accounting advisers. These are wonderfully useful legal tools, however, and they deserve your attention. Don't think that only the rich need to consider a trust, because it just isn't true. We all need to consider what a trust can do for us, because these are the legal instruments of the future.

Disadvantages of a Trust

THE BIGGEST HURDLE YOU MAY FACE in dealing with a trust in your estate plan is that you simply may not understand it fully. Intrinsically, a trust is not a difficult legal instrument to understand. Often, however, lawyers present to their clients trusts that are pages long and contain lots of legal jargon and many words like "wherefore" and "as hereinafter stated." No one can possibly relate to that kind of legalese except lawyers. Make sure your lawyer explains the provisions of your trust to you in terms you can understand.

Other than not having a complete idea of what the trust document can do and how it functions, one faces the disadvantage of cost. Often it costs more to have a trust drafted than a will. A trust will cost $1,000 and up, depending on its complexity. A will may cost about $35 or more, but seldom does it cost as much as a trust. Over a long period of time, the trust may also be more costly to operate than a will, depending on what the trustee must do and how complex the tasks are as outlined in the trust.

Another disadvantage of a trust is that the trustee, who may be appointed many years after the execution of the trust, may not be attuned to the needs of the ultimate beneficiaries—often children—of the trust. It is also very difficult to remove a trustee should you change your mind about that person's suitability.

Also, few trusts save federal estate tax dollars. The spousal marital deduction trust does have tax-saving potential, but the hard truth is that the great majority of trusts don't save any tax dollars at all.

So why should people even consider having a trust? Because, simply stated, they can do more for the average person with a few assets than any other single legal document, and they may do more than a combination of many legal instruments. If you need to think about how to protect yourself and your assets during your lifetime to provide for asset management during a disability, then a trust is the document of choice. If you want to provide management and continuity of control over your assets after your death, for the ultimate benefit of several generations of your family, again, a trust is the document of choice.

Do You Need a Trust?

HOW DO YOU KNOW IF YOU NEED A TRUST? You need one if you meet six or more of these nine criteria:

1 You need a complex estate plan to cover a disabled family member.
2 You need a plan to cover your possible incapacity during your lifetime.
3 You need a plan that will save substantial estate assets, court costs, and legal fees.
4 You want to avoid the probate process in your state.
5 You want to take advantage of tax savings available to spouses.
6 You are willing to relinquish some, most, or all of the control of your assets during your lifetime, and you are willing to convey some or all of your assets into a trust.
7 You are willing to take the advice of attorneys, accountants, and perhaps institutional advisers, because the benefits of a trust are best realized with the advice of professionals.
8 You own property in several states and want to simplify your estate management.
9 You want absolute privacy in the management and handling of your business affairs.

You need a trust only if one will serve your specific needs. Seek legal, financial, and accounting advice. Then analyze your particular family situation, your tax basis, and your estate holdings. If you are still convinced that you need a trust, have it drafted to meet your particular needs, fund it, and begin to understand its workings during your lifetime. If the trust needs to be modified, do that. This is your trust, and it should make life easier for you and for your family members when and if you are not around to look after them. However, if you are not convinced, after seeking professional advice, that a trust is a substantial advantage for you, then you do not need one.

Whatever you choose, all of your legal and financial tools should be integrated and pulled together so that they form a unified plan. A trust here, a will there, joint-and-survivorship deeds, and a few other plans can wreck havoc at the time of death or disability unless they systematically pull together to strengthen the entire plan.

Chapter Ten

Legal Tools for
Disability Planning

WHAT IF YOU BECOME ILL and cannot manage your assets during your illness? Will your children be able to sign your checks? Make health care decisions for you? Make cash transfers at your local bank? Will your best friend or your neighbor be able to write checks from your account to keep your household bills current until you get back from the hospital? The answers to all of these questions are in doubt unless you have done the proper estate planning to cover these many contingencies.

Let's face it, there are going to be times in your life when you simply will not be able to manage your property interests. You may have surgery, suffer a stroke, or end up in the hospital as a result of a fender bender or more serious accident. Is someone authorized to make health care decisions for you if you cannot articulate what you want? Can someone cover household bills for you if you don't get home right away? And if you haven't given someone else the power to act for you, do you want to do that? Do you want to give someone else legal authority to manage your assets or make health care decisions for you when, and if, you become temporarily or permanently disabled?

People used to think that if they signed some "paper," they could be "put away." Fortunately, we have come a long way from that early ignorance, probably because we realize that, in 99 percent of the cases, whatever we sign, we can change, or, in legal parlance, revoke. Just about everything that we create to manage our affairs can be modified.

What are the legal options for authorizing someone else to manage your health care decisions and your property if you become disabled? There are several legal options, or a combination of them, available for you to consider:

➤ Power of attorney for finances

➤ Power of attorney for health care

➤ Living trusts

➤ Guardianship proceedings

➤ Co-ownership of real estate and bank accounts

The Power of Attorney and the Durable Power of Attorney for Finances

A POWER OF ATTORNEY IS A LEGAL instrument that allows you to appoint others to act for you. You may select one or several individuals to act for you; you may give them many powers to use on your behalf, or you may give them power to do only a single task, such as the ability to write checks on one bank account. You may give them power to make decisions for you of a medical or financial nature.

Every state has different laws that govern powers of attorney, or POAs, as they are commonly called. However, there are basically four kinds of POAs, and you may use one or all of them. These are:

➤ General POA

➤ Durable POA

➤ Springing POA

➤ Limited POA

All of these POAs share one thing in common: they all give you the right to appoint others to act for you. The differences between them are the way they become effective, how broad the powers are that you are giving to others, and exactly how long and under what circumstances the POAs are to stay effective. All of these POAs may be revoked by you as long as you are competent; all may stay in existence for the entirety of your lifetime if that is your desire.

You are the one who can decide what you want to do, whom you want to appoint, and exactly what powers you want to give (or not give) to others under what circumstances, as well as when you want the POA to take effect and for how long.

A general power of attorney is a form through which you, known as the principal, give to another person, called an agent or an attorney-in-fact (and not an attorney-at-law), broad powers to perform certain legal and daily tasks for you. This is

New York Statutory Short-Form Power of Attorney

Know All Men by These Presents, which are intended to constitute a GEN-ERAL POWER OF ATTORNEY: That I (insert name and address of the Principal) do hereby appoint (insert name and address of the Agent) my attorney(s)-in-fact TO ACT in my name, place and stead in any way which I myself could do, if I were personally present, with respect to the following matters to the extent that I am permitted by law to act through an agent:

INITIAL in the opposite box any one or more of the subdivisions as to which the Principal WANTS to give the Agent authority.

(A) real estate transactions;	(.......)
(B) chattel and goods transactions;	(.......)
(C) bond, share and commodity transactions;	(.......)
(D) banking transactions;	(.......)
(E) business operating transactions;	(.......)
(F) insurance transactions;	(.......)
(G) estate transactions;	(.......)
(H) claims and litigation;	(.......)
(I) personal relationships and affairs;	(.......)
(J) benefits from military service;	(.......)
(K) records, reports and statements;	(.......)
(L) full and unqualified authority to my attorney(s)-in-fact to delegate any or all of the foregoing to any person or persons whom my attorney(s)-in-fact shall select;	(.......)
(M) all other matters.	(.......)

In Witness Whereof I have hereunto signed my name and affixed my seal this _____ day of (month), 200__.

_____ (Seal)

Notarized, Witnessed and Filed for Record in accordance with the laws of the State of New York.

effective from the time you sign the POA form. The New York state short-form POA on the previous page is typical of a general power of attorney available in other states. However, note that each state has its own requirements for the language to be included within the form, as well as different requirements for witnessing, notarizing, and filing these POAs in public records.

This type of POA was in use for many years in the United States, but it had serious limitations. For example, if the agent wanted to use the POA to make decisions when the principal became incompetent and could no longer make decisions, the POA could not be used, since it did not contain language that allowed the principal to act in this situation.

Therefore, state legislative bodies across the country devised a more modern and comprehensive document, known as the durable power of attorney. The durable power of attorney is exactly like the general POA but with language added to make sure the agent can act for the principal when and if the principal becomes impaired or incompetent.

For instance, in the New York Short-Form POA, the addition of this clause would make it a durable POA: "This power of attorney shall not be affected by the subsequent disability or incompetence of the principal." These few words are an extremely important addition to POAs, so if you have an old general power of attorney document, be sure to have it brought up-to-date. Otherwise, no one will be able to act for you in times of disability, and the court of your county may have to appoint a legal guardian to act for you—and that does not mean that the court would appoint someone you might have named!

When does a durable POA become effective? It can take effect immediately, or only if you become incapacitated. You have to decide which you want. A POA that is switched on only when you become incompetent is known as a springing POA, which means that it will become active only when third parties, usually physicians, determine that you are incompetent. For this reason, most attorneys today do not recommend a springing POA, as it is too difficult to ascertain at what precise point in time one becomes "incompetent," a rather ambiguous legal standard.

A durable POA that is effective on signing eliminates this issue. It can be used by the agent from that point forward and also allows the agent to act if and when the principal becomes incompetent. The question you need to answer is whether you want to give to others broad powers to act for you in every way or whether you want to give someone the power to act for you only in a very narrow, well-defined way.

A POA is usually a durable POA, meaning the agent can act for you from the date you sign the document through any future disability, but can only act for you in a certain way. You may give your agent the right to do one or a combination of these duties:

➤ Buy and sell real estate and enter into mortgages
➤ Deal with personal property, such as household goods and collectibles
➤ Buy, sell, trade, and manage all investments, including stock, bonds, and bank accounts
➤ Operate any and all businesses
➤ Deal with all tax and insurance matters
➤ Litigate for you or defend any legal actions against you
➤ Take care of social security, pension plans, military service benefits, and similar assets

Or, instead of granting rather broad powers within one of these categories, you may give your agent the power *only* to write checks on a certain account, sell a specific number of shares for you, or any other narrowly defined task.

POA Checklist

THERE ARE MANY THINGS TO CONSIDER before you sign a POA, and each one is important:

➤ Do you trust the person you want to appoint as your agent?
➤ Do you understand the POA form you are signing?
➤ Are you aware that your POA must be recorded in a recorder's office, and thus made public, in some states?
➤ Do you know that your agent will have to keep accurate records of all matters pertaining to your business, and in some cases, that those documents will have to be filed in a court?
➤ Do you wish to provide in your POA for compensation for the agent?
➤ Can you appoint a guardian in your POA in the state in which you live? Do you want to do so?
➤ Do you know how to revoke your POA?

Again, trust is the single most important thing you must consider when you are thinking of naming someone else to be your agent. If you are not totally satisfied with the trustworthiness of your agent, do not sign a POA. You must absolutely trust that person with everything you own, because that is exactly what you are doing with your POA. Remember, your agent may control all of your assets while you are disabled, and it is better never to give another a POA than be sorry later, when it may be too late to find how mistaken you were in being so trusting.

This is why practically every state in the country requires this language at the beginning of a POA: "Notice. Before you sign this document, you should know that the purpose of this power of attorney is to give the person whom you designate as your agent broad power to handle your property, which may include powers to sell or otherwise dispose of some or all of your property, both real and personal, without advance notice to you or approval from you." This language tells you in a forthright way that you must use great care in selecting an honest, reliable person as your agent.

The POA form you use is very important because it contains all of the essential decisions you are making: the name of your agent; the extent of the powers you are granting; the durability of the POA, so that it can be used in the event of your disability or incompetency; and how long you want the POA to exist. Also, it must comply with the laws of the state where you live.

Because it is such an important document, you would be well advised to seek legal counsel before you decide to execute a POA. Today many people get kits and obtain these documents from books and on the Internet. But even if you study and read all about these documents, and even if they appear simple to implement, they are so far-reaching that it is still best to have an attorney advise you on the advantages and disadvantages of each of the POAs. An attorney can also advise you on the safeguards you may wish to consider including in your POA to protect you in the future if your agent is not as trustworthy as you had expected.

Be aware, too, that when and if your agent has to use your POA, state laws usually require that it be filed publicly where you live and/or own property. Although this may seem an invasion of your privacy, it is necessary for your agent to have legal authority to act for you and for all parties who may be dealing with the agent to have legal notice of that authority. That is why the POA must usually be filed in an office of public record.

Also, your agent must keep good records, and in some states, the agent is required to file all those records with a court. This may be burdensome in many cases, but in some instances, it gives added assurance that the agent will not act inappropriately with your assets.

Do you want your agent to be compensated for the services he or she performs on your behalf? This is a personal matter that only you can decide. However, it is usually a good idea to provide at least that the agent will be paid reasonable expenses, such as mileage and related travel expenses when the agent must incur these costs on your behalf. Also, if there are adequate assets, you should consider paying the agent a "reasonable and customary fee of the community" to act as your POA.

In many states, you may also name someone as your guardian, if and when such a necessity should arise. Some states don't permit this; however, if you live in a state that does, it is a very good idea to include the name of a person you would want to serve as your guardian. A court does not have to appoint the person you name in your POA, but it usually will accept your choice. If you become incompetent and you have not previously named a guardian, a court of law will appoint one for you.

It is also important to include these words in your power of attorney: "I may revoke this POA at any time." You want to reserve the right to revoke the POA and to end any and all authority you have granted to your agent if you are no longer satisfied with your decision or the individual's actions. How is a POA revoked? If you are competent, you may destroy the document, but it is far better to revoke the POA in writing through a document that is signed, witnessed, and notarized as required by law. The agent should be informed both orally and in writing that you are revoking the POA previously granted. In all states, a POA ends upon the death of the principal.

Again, if you don't absolutely trust someone, do *not* grant him or her a POA. It may be the biggest mistake you ever make. But if you do have someone you can put your faith in, then by all means make sure that you have a POA so you will have others to help you and make decisions for you when and if you become disabled or incompetent. This will make it unnecessary for a court of law to appoint a guardian, who may be a complete stranger to you, to take care of your financial affairs. A durable power of attorney for finances can be an exceedingly helpful tool in times of need. If possible, you should have one.

The Case of the Disabled Mom

EARLY IN 1999, MRS. JONES, who lived in Ohio, had a serious illness that disabled her for months. She had given her daughters, one living in Virginia and one living in California, her power of attorney for finances years earlier. From the moment Mrs. Jones became disabled, both her daughters could write checks from their mother's checking account to pay the nursing home and home-care bills, take care of the medication expenses, and manage all the essential, day-to-day financial matters such as paying their mother's rent and utility bills. When Mrs. Jones recovered from her disability, she resumed writing her own checks and doing all of her own business.

Without that crucial POA, the daughters could not have used their mother's checking or savings accounts to keep her household bills current; could not have signed the necessary documents at the hospitals to pay bills; could not have done a hundred small things that suddenly became so important.

What happens in a case like this if no power of attorney is in place when a disability develops? No one is authorized to act for another without written authorization. No one can write checks on your account, withdraw funds from savings, or cash your income checks. Only those with some written, legal authority from you can act for you. So, in a case like that of Mrs. Jones, the probate court would have had to appoint a guardian, even for a temporary period of time, to give someone the legal authority necessary to act for one who was so impaired as to be unable to make decisions and perform daily tasks, such as writing checks and paying bills. This certainly would have been unpleasant to all concerned and very sad and embarrassing under the circumstances. The frustration and emotional upset of becoming disabled, compounded by additional expenses, are difficult enough without adding to them worries about how the mortgage will be paid.

Most of us want all of our business and health concerns and obligations taken care of if and when an emergency occurs. If you are going on a trip or if you become ill suddenly and are unable to write checks, you want your finances to be taken care of until you are better. This will occur only if you have put into place a proper power of attorney for financial matters.

You are the person who has to decide whether or not to give another person a power of attorney. You may decide to give it to your children, and most states permit you to give a POA to children "jointly and severally," meaning that one child may act alone or in conjunction with any other child or children named. Listing more than two individuals, including children, on a power of attorney is not recommended, however, because it only creates confusion. For example, in a family of five children, imagine the chaos that might ensue if they were all named to act for their mother in an emergency. If they couldn't all be found, who then has the authority to make life and death decisions? Some patients in this situation have had to be put on ventilators until the confusion is ironed out.

Think long and hard about a POA before you grant this power. Once granted, a

POA is not impossible to revoke, but it may be difficult. Still, a POA for finances is certainly an important tool to include in your estate plan, so don't neglect to think through this important part of the estate planning puzzle.

The Power of Attorney for Health Care

ANOTHER TYPE OF POWER OF ATTORNEY that has become common is a power of attorney for health care. Most states now have enacted legislation to permit the creation of this power of attorney. In this document you give to another person the power to make health care decisions for you on a day-to-day basis when you cannot make those decisions for yourself. The living will and the POA for health care are both known as "advance directives," as they make known your wishes regarding both your day-to-day health care and the care you want, or don't want, when you are in a permanently unconscious state.

Only the POA for health care will be discussed here, in conjunction with the POA for finances. The living will is discussed in Chapter 7, "Wills," although you should also regard it as a disability planning option. Both advance directives are important for you to consider, because as we live longer and medical advances permit life to be extended indefinitely through the use of machinery and medication, having these directives in place can make our wishes clear, and we want to make sure that we authorize others to see that our wishes are carried out.

In 1992, federal law required all hospitals to discuss with each incoming patient at the time of admission the POA for health care. This is a major attempt to determine just who is to be in charge of your health care decisions, who will act for you, and exactly what kind of care you want.

Signing a POA does not release a health care provider, such as a hospital or physician, from any liability. Your care must remain the primary focus of health care providers regardless of the existence of a POA. And in any event, you are not required by the laws in any state to sign a POA, which is and must be a voluntary act. You, and only you, can elect to obtain it—or not. However, if you don't have a POA for health care and an emergency situation arises in which you are not competent or conscious, a physician may have to make a health care decision for you that may result in the use of life-sustaining equipment, such as feeding tubes and a ventilator, choices that you yourself might not want if you were able to make such a decision.

Furthermore, in the absence of a POA, a guardian often must be appointed by a court of law when a health care decision must be made for your care. Often the court will appoint a family member, but that is not always the case, especially when family members are not in agreement regarding your course of treatment. Sometimes the court will appoint a complete stranger to make decisions for you. Better for you to name someone you know than to allow someone you don't know at all to make crucial decisions for you.

In an attempt to educate the public about their health care options, the American Association of Retired Persons (AARP), the American Bar Association Commission on Legal Problems of the Elderly, and the American Medical Association put together a booklet entitled "Shape Your Health Care Future with Health Care Advance Directives." The booklet clearly explains these legal options from both the medical and the legal viewpoints. Also, you may obtain up-to-date, state-by-state information about advance directives, including statutory forms and the booklet, by writing to Legal Counsel for the Elderly (LCE), AARP, P.O. Box 96474, Washington, D.C. 20090-6474.

In the years ahead, you will be hearing more and more about the POA for health care, as all of us have more and more involvement with hospitals, nursing homes, and similar facilities that care for our family members.

Here is the information you should consider when trying to decide if you want to sign a POA for health care:

➢ What is a power of attorney for health care?

➢ Is this a document that I want?

➢ Why is it useful? Do I need it?

➢ Is a POA for health care valid in my state?

➢ If I have a living will, do I need a POA for health care, too?

➢ Am I required to have a POA for health care?

➢ What does a POA look like?

➢ What happens when a POA for health care does not address the situation facing the physician or the agent?

➢ What do I need to consider before creating this advance directive?

➢ How do I actually create a POA for health care?

➢ What if I change my mind after I sign the POA?

➢ What happens if I do not have an advance directive?

➢ What characteristics should my POA agent have?

➢ What else should I know about a health care POA?

What is a POA for health care? It is a document in which you give to others authority and instructions about the nature of the health care you want to receive if you are unable to speak to your health care providers yourself. You keep total control over your health care decisions all of your life for so long as you are well and able. However, this document allows you to take control of your health care when and if you become disabled to the point that you are no longer competent, physically and mentally, to act for yourself.

When does this point occur? Either two physicians can concur that you have become "incompetent," in which case they must enter that decision on your medical chart, or a court acting in a guardianship proceeding can rule that you are incompetent. Each state has its own statutes that define incompetency, but most include words similar to those of Ohio, which states that an incompetent person is one who "by reason of advanced age, mental or physical disability, or infirmity ... is incapable of taking proper care of himself or his property...." Circumstances involved in each situation are unique. More often than not a court will order evaluations, testimony of friends, family, and neighbors, and medical tests to determine the competency of an adult.

Is the POA for health care something that can help me? If for some reason you cannot communicate your wishes (whether permanently or temporarily) to health care providers about the care you want, a POA for health care protects your interests by allowing another previously named person to act for you. The individual with the power of attorney is legally authorized to tell the medical providers exactly what you want—or don't—regarding your health care.

Unless you have already appointed someone, in writing, to act for you, critical decisions may be made for you by others, specifically, health care providers, who may make decisions that would not necessarily be based upon your wishes. For example, you may have religious reasons for refusing a blood transfusion, but if you are unconscious and you need a blood transfusion, a physician is likely to feel morally and legally compelled to give you one to save your life, absent a legal authority telling him to do otherwise.

Is a POA for health care valid in my state of residency? Yes, every state in the country allows people to sign written forms about what health care they want and who can speak for them, when and if they are unable to communicate their wishes for themselves. State laws and forms differ, but the POA for health care is available in every state.

If I have a living will, do I need a POA for health care? In some states, these two documents are combined into one document; in other states, they are separate. Legal planners suggest that a person have both documents to cover any future health contingencies, regardless of how the legal forms are created. The living will covers only a brief period of time at the end of life, when death is imminent. The POA for health

Durable Power of Attorney for Health Care

For Care, Custody, and Medical Treatment Decisions

I, (PRINT OR TYPE YOUR FULL NAME)_____, am of sound mind, and I voluntarily make this designation. I designate_____, residing at_____as my Health Care Agent, Power of Attorney for Health Care and Patient Advocate, with the following power to be exercised in my name and for my benefit, to make decisions regarding care, custody, or medical treatment if I become unable to participate in care, custody and medical treatment decisions. The determination of when I am unable to participate in care, custody and medical treatment decisions shall be made by my attending physician and another physician or licensed psychologist.

[(Optional) If the first individual is unable, unwilling or unavailable to serve as my patient advocate, then I designate my successor Advocate _____ residing at_____ to serve.]

With respect to my care, custody and medical treatment, my advocate shall have the power to make each and every judgment necessary for the proper and adequate care and custody of my person including, but not limited to:

(a) To have access to and control over my personal and medical information;

(b) To employ and discharge physicians, nurses, therapists and any other care providers, and to pay them reasonable compensation with my funds;

(c) To give an informed consent or an informed refusal on my behalf with respect to any medical care; diagnostic, surgical or therapeutic procedure; or other treatment of any type or nature;

(d) To execute waivers, medical authorizations and such other approval as may be

care extends throughout a person's life and covers a wide variety of health care issues, not just those that may arise in an emergency or fatal illness. These issues include decisions about whether or not to operate, which facility is best for someone who needs nursing home or independent living care, the best doctor for the patient, and many others. The POA for health care covers all health care aspects.

Am I required to have a POA for health care? No, not at all. It is your choice. There are no laws requiring you to obtain or sign this form.

What does a POA for health care actually look like? Each state has its own par-

required to permit or authorize care which I may need, or to discontinue care that I am receiving.

My advocate shall be guided in making such decisions by what I have told my advocate about personal preferences regarding such care.

My wishes concerning care are the following: (OPTIONAL).

I authorize my patient advocate to make a decision to withhold or withdraw treatment, which could or would allow me to die. I acknowledge that such a decision could or would allow me to die.

Sign this statement if you wish to give this authority to Named Agent, Power of Attorney for Health Care, Patient Advocate. This Durable Power of Attorney shall not be affected by my disability or incapacity. This Durable Power of Attorney is governed by Michigan law. I may revoke this designation at any time and by communicating in any manner that this designation does not reflect my wishes.

It is my intent that my family, the medical facility, and any doctors, nurses and other medical personnel involved in my care, not be liable for implementing the decisions of my patient advocate or honoring wishes expressed in this designation.

Photostatic copies of this document, after it is signed and witnessed, shall have the same legal force as the original document.

I voluntarily sign this Durable Power of Attorney after careful consideration. I accept its meaning and I accept its consequences.

YOUR SIGNATURE/ADDRESS/CITY, STATE, ZIP CODE (DATE)

Signed, witnessed and notarized pursuant to state law.

ticular form for this document, and you should definitely sign the proper form prescribed by the state where you live. However, most of them look very much like the one printed here, from the State of Michigan.

What happens when a POA for health care does not address the situation facing the physician or the agent? In an emergency situation in which a patient's wishes are not clear, the physician in charge must use his or her discretion to make health care decisions. Under emergency medical circumstances the physician becomes the reluctant decision maker. If no emergency exists but a health care decision is necessary, a guardian must be appointed by a court so that someone is authorized to make a decision in this situation.

What do I need to consider before making an advance directive? First, consider who will make health care decisions for you if you don't appoint someone you know to do so. Are you satisfied to let others, perhaps strangers, make medical decisions for you? If not, do you know whom you want to appoint as your agent to make these decisions for you? Do you want to appoint a successor in case that person is unavailable or ill? What authority do you want to give your agent to make these decisions? How much detail do you want to go into? Are you satisfied to give general authority to your agent, knowing that no document of this nature will ever be able to encompass all of the possible scenarios?

How do I actually create a health care POA? You simply obtain a copy of the POA used in your state and, in front of witnesses and a notary, if required, sign it. These documents are readily available at local hospitals and in attorneys' and doctors' offices. Once you sign a POA for health care, keep a copy of the form for yourself and give a copy to each of the following:

➤ your physician, or if you have more than one, a copy to each physician involved with your care;

➤ your POA health care agent;

➤ several key family members, even if they are not the POA; and

➤ the hospital where you receive your primary care.

What if I change my mind after I sign? A health care POA is revocable. You can revoke it at any time by notifying your agent in writing that you revoke it, but make sure that your physician is aware of this change.

What happens if I do not have an advance directive? A court may appoint a guardian for you if you are disabled in some states. Other states have a publicly appointed surrogate, usually a relative, who is chosen as the decision maker. If, however, family members do not and cannot agree to a course of treatment, then court proceedings, usually in a probate court, will be necessary.

What characteristics should my POA agent have? One who is to serve as your POA for health care should have the following characteristics:

➤ Knows you well

➤ Knows your health care wishes

➤ Agrees with your general health care philosophy

➤ Has a good relationship with your extended family, including your parents and children

➢ Lives relatively close to you in order to be able to act in an emergency
➢ Understands the family dynamics
➢ Advocates for you, regardless of the opinions of others
➢ Is able to act with sensitivity, confidence, and decisiveness
➢ Is a decision maker who can act in an emergency situation
➢ Is a consensus builder if family members should disagree
➢ Has mature judgment and insight into medical issues
➢ Has the firmness to insist upon treatment in accordance with your wishes

Once you decide whom you want to act as your POA for health care, ask that person if he or she is comfortable with the role. Do the same with a contingent person, who may have to act if the primary decision maker is, for some reason, unavailable to serve when needed. Talk candidly with them to make sure they understand your wishes regarding health care issues, particularly those pertaining to the use of life-sustaining equipment.

It is very important to make sure that your primary and contingent POAs for health care are willing to serve for you. Often people go to attorneys and execute a POA by inserting the names of people they think would make good decisions for them, only to find out later that the individuals refused to serve as a POA. In one such situation, an elderly woman was named as her sister's POA for health care. When approached to consent to the amputation of her then-incompetent sister's leg, she declined, saying, "I simply cannot do this to my sister. Someone else will have to do this." The court appointed a disinterested person as the guardian legally authorized to make the necessary health care decision. The amputation was performed—but only after a wait of several weeks.

Keep in mind also that whomever you designate as your POA health care agent will have the legal authority to act for you. This means all other people—including all family members, such as children, parents, brothers, sisters, and other relatives—will not have any authority to make those health care decisions. If they disagree with the agent's decisions, they may attempt to intervene by going to the attending physician to try to change the treatment, and if they are extremely determined, they may go to court to intervene. If, however, you were competent when you executed your POA, then the agent you named will in all likelihood prevail in any contest, either at the hospital or in the court.

What else should I know about a health care POA? State law determines whether the living will or the POA for health care takes precedence in the event of disability. If you are a resident of a state in which these are two separate documents and you have named two different people to act for you, then be sure you seek a legal opinion on the applicable state law on this issue. Naming the same individual for both situations can eliminate this conflict; however, many people feel that they want to name separate individuals in their documents.

Why have more than one individual involved as a POA? Because often one person is good at taking care of one matter while another person is better with other areas. For instance, I might ask my best friend to be my POA for health care, but I would appoint my financial adviser or accountant as my POA for finances. In this way, I might have the best of both worlds. Naming only one person simplifies the management issues. However, this isn't necessarily best, because one may know you and your health care philosophy better, while another may handle your financial matters more efficiently.

In some states you may be able to state your intention to become a donor of (a) any organs or body parts; (b) only those parts or organs you specify, such as lungs, eyes, or heart; or (c) organs or body parts for specific purpose only, such as transplant, therapy, research, or education.

Do-not-resuscitate (DNR) language in a POA for health care varies from state to state. You may insert words to the effect that your agent can summon paramedics and then choose to refuse treatment for you. Or you may give your agent the authority to sign releases from liability that are required by hospitals or physicians to implement your wishes about medical treatment. This includes the authority to request and concur with the writing of a "no-code" (do-not-resuscitate) order by the attending or treating physician. Some states permit this and some do not, due to the many questions and liability issues involved. If you want to include this kind of authority in your document, seek legal advice on what is permissible in your state.

In conclusion, a POA for health care is like "life accident" insurance: if you have a serious automobile wreck, you're going to wish you had bought accident insurance. Likewise, if you get into a health care crisis, you will wish you had set up a POA for health care beforehand. Why get into that situation when all you have to do is go to your local hospital, pick up a form, and sign it? At least you'll know that someone you choose will be making health care decisions for you, rather than someone you don't even know.

The Living Trust

A LIVING TRUST CANNOT GOVERN any health care decisions for you, since only the power of attorney for health care and living wills are designed to do that. However, you may want to consider a living trust as an alternative to a power of attorney for finances.

The POA is one of the most popular legal documents in use today. However, you may think a durable power of attorney is not sufficient to provide hands-on management of your complex assets and payment of your bills. Or you may not have someone to whom you can give power of attorney who has the required skills to continue your business or to look after family matters as well as the other numerous daily financial matters.

To protect your interests in the event of disability, a living trust is simply one more optional legal document you may wish to include in your estate plan. Intended for more complex fiscal management of assets over a longer period of time, the living trust is an excellent tool to consider.

Today more and more people are considering the living trust, because its flexibility and comprehensiveness make it a more sophisticated legal option than a POA for finances. One of its biggest advantages is longevity: a POA ends at the death of the person who created it, but a living trust may endure for generations.

Chapter 9 discusses trusts more extensively, but it's worthwhile to describe the living trust here, because it can be very helpful in disability planning. Generally, a living trust works like this:

➤ A living trust is executed by you as the trustee/grantor. You are your own trustee, and you are the grantor of all of the funds going into the trust.

➤ You convey assets into your trust, known as "funding the trust."

➤ You manage your trust for as long as you are capable.

➤ You state in your trust that you are to receive all of the income from the trust during your lifetime, as well as some or all of the trust assets, at your discretion.

➤ You can also provide that if and when two physicians find you incompetent or unable to make essential financial decisions, your trust will be managed by a person you name as your contingent trustee. This individual will take over the management of the trust and use those assets exclusively for your benefit and care for the duration of your life.

➤ At your death, your assets can be distributed in accordance with your wishes, as specified in your trust or will. Or you may provide that your assets will continue to be held in the trust, with the income to be distributed to a spouse, children, or grandchildren, and the principal assets will be distributed and the trust terminated at some future time.

Like the POA, the limited POA, the joint-and-survivorship deed, and the life estate, the living trust is merely one of a number of planning tools to consider for an integrated estate plan. The great majority of people choose the simpler durable power of attorney for finances. However, the living trust has several advantages over the POA for finances:

➤ First, the trust receives and retains *title* to all assets transferred to the trust, subject to the specific instructions of the grantor. The person who is given a POA does not have title to anything. Although some may think this a good thing, there are statutes requiring your agent to use all of your assets *only* for your benefit. In the event your agent does not do this, or if there is any violation of fiduciary duty, the agent is personally liable for any loss or misuse of your funds. The problem that can unfold when a POA does not have title to assets is that the agent may be unable to act for you when and if needed, since the agent may have no authority to sell assets for your use. This makes things complicated and essentially forces the possible sale to be handled through a legal process, usually a guardianship procedure.

➤ The trust may become *irrevocable* upon the grantor's incapacity, at which time the contingent trustee steps in to manage all assets of the trust in accordance with the trust instrument, thus avoiding probate and providing a smooth transition of asset management.

➤ A POA terminates at the time of death. The assets may be subject to probate procedures, and in general little financial management is possible under the POA.

Although much has been written in recent years about a living trust, it is really a very simple legal instrument that can accomplish many more tasks than other estate planning tools can, and for that reason, it has become more popular. In the future, more people will have living trusts, not because they are wealthy but because this trust can function so well for them in the event of their disability.

You can transfer ownership of your assets into a trust that governs the distribution of those assets at the time of your death. Thus, trust assets are not probate assets *unless* you designate that they should be distributed under your will—which could defeat the non-probate aspect of the trust.

Not only can a trust bypass the probate process, but it can manage assets for you when you are disabled and pay all of the bills of your last illness, your funeral bills, and any special charitable or personal gifts at the time of your death. It can also continue in existence in order to pay income to family members, manage assets, and distribute income in accordance with your wishes. These are characteristics that no power of attorney has, because POAs end at the death of the person who created them. Thus, there are simply more advantages with a living trust than with any other document for disability planning.

Co-Ownership of Real Estate and Bank Accounts

WHAT IF YOU DON'T WANT A POA OF any kind, yet you want some assurance that your property at least will be protected during disability? Would you be well advised to transfer your property to others when, for instance, you are going to the hospital for surgery, or when you have suffered a mild stroke? Are there other options available to you besides the living trust and power of attorney?

Actually, few attorneys would suggest that you put the title of your property in another person's name or co-own it with another during times of temporary or permanent disability. For one thing, if you die, then your heirs and beneficiaries may not receive your property, since you may have given it to another.

However, there are circumstances when you may want to be somewhat creative with your real-property titles and with your bank accounts. Elderly spouses, for instance, with small bank accounts might want to consider such ownership. For example, if a husband and wife have a home together and savings and checking accounts that are modest in value, and one of the spouses suffers a stroke or is in the early stages of Alzheimer's, then joint tenancy with the right of survivorship for the bank accounts, and perhaps for the home as well, is often a good idea, since it has the following advantages:

➤ Each "tenant" has the power to obtain cash from the bank during the disability of the other, up to the entire balance in the account.

➤ At the first co-tenant's death, the entire account automatically becomes the property of the survivor; this is also true of a joint-and-survivorship deed, which passes title from the first-to-die spouse to the surviving spouse without any probate proceedings.

The joint-tenancy concept differs greatly from the POA and the living trust. The basic difference is one of control. With a trust, the owner of the property controls the assets or gives others strict directions for asset management, for certain well-defined purposes stated within the trust document. In joint tenancy, one owner may lose control over all of the assets because the joint tenant, as co-owner, has the legal right to cash all of the accounts. Put another way, during my lifetime, I may have a trust, a durable power of attorney, and a joint-and-survivorship account. My co-owner with the joint-and-survivorship title may withdraw *all* of my funds from that account. Although he may own only half of the account, he has the ability to withdraw all of it, under the laws of most states.

Therefore, even if joint tenancy is not a good tool for property management, it may be helpful in the event of disability; POAs and trusts are far wiser choices if extensive assets are involved. Both property management and disability planning revolve around the issue of whether or not an individual is disabled to the point that he or she can no longer make decisions. Before that time, it is imperative to decide if co-ownership of one or more assets is a good idea or if a more complex trust or POA would be better in such a situation.

Most states also have transfer-on-death (TOD) and payable-on-death (POD) language that is applicable to assets. If, for instance, you want your checking account to become the property of your daughter at the time of your death, you can designate your account as a POD or TOD account. However, although these accounts bypass the probate process, they don't protect those assets during disability. You need to have documents in place so your family or friends can make health care decisions for you and also use your assets to pay bills when you are either temporarily or permanently disabled.

Should you be concerned that your POA agent will use your funds for himself or herself? It can happen, but this is far less common than you might suspect. In 97 percent of POAs, there is absolute trust and proper use of funds. If you're worried about that 3 percent and feel that you do not have anyone who is absolutely trustworthy to act for you, simply do not execute a POA at all. That is your best protection against abuse.

In conclusion, you have several ways to give others the right to manage your property during times of disability: the durable powers of attorney for health care and finances, the living trust, and co-ownership of property. You may use a combination of all of these for different assets, depending on your needs and goals.

But what happens if you fail to plan? Who then will manage your property and make health care decisions for you?

Guardianship Proceedings

IF YOU DO NOT AUTHORIZE SOMEONE else to manage your property or to make health care decisions in the event of disability, state law will do so for you. It will provide how, when, and where your affairs will be managed and who will be appointed guardian or conservator of your estate during your disability to make property decisions and health care decisions for you.

These appointees are not necessarily family members; they may not even be anyone you know. Courts must act swiftly on occasion to appoint someone to make health care decisions, especially in times of crisis when a life-and-death choice must be made. There may not be time to sort through all the people in your family. Courts may be called upon to make an emergency appointment, and that is exactly what they will do. Who is appointed is of less consequence than making sure that someone is appointed to make decisions promptly.

Therefore, it is possible for a stranger to be appointed as your guardian when you are incapacitated. When a court finds you are incompetent or unable to act for yourself, either through illness, age, or otherwise, it appoints a guardian for you. Thereafter, you become what is known in legal language as a "ward of the court"— that is, you are an individual who is under the protection of the court. All decisions from then on will be and must be made by this guardian until you are better and your competency restored.

Just because you have a spouse and five children does not mean that any one of them will be legally authorized to make health care decisions for you or, for that matter, to go to your bank and withdraw funds.

This is particularly true if all members are not in agreement, especially about medical treatment. They have only the legal authority you give them, and if you have given them none, then they have none.

Do you think your best protection is a court-appointed guardian? Here are some questions you may have:

➤ What is a guardianship?
➤ Why would a guardian be appointed for me?
➤ Is there only one kind of guardian?
➤ How long does a guardianship last?
➤ What is the court process?
➤ What can the court-appointed guardian do?
➤ What if I don't want any guardian appointed?

What is a guardianship? A guardianship is a legal proceeding to determine whether a person has the capacity to make decisions for himself or herself. We realize that as we age, we may not have the memory we wish we had, and we are aware that people can have strokes and other health problems that make them impaired. But for the most part, individuals who suffer some disability can, especially with the help of family and friends, continue to function, make good decisions, and live at home.

Even if a person is severely impaired and has difficulty understanding certain things, we allow that person to go about his business on a day-to-day basis. However, when serious concerns arise about health and financial issues, then a guardianship proceeding may become necessary to assure the individual's well-being.

At this point a process is initiated in the proper state court, usually a probate court, to find out whether the person in question lacks the competence necessary to make good decisions.

Why would a guardian be appointed? A guardian is appointed for an adult only if and when he or she becomes incompetent as defined by state law. Incompetence means that the individual involved:

➤ may be living at risk of neglect, abuse, or exploitation;

➤ won't let family or friends assist in making safe decisions;

➤ makes poor decisions, raising serious concerns for his own safety and possibly that of others; or

➤ has no one to help and lacks the basic decision-making skills to obtain food and shelter.

Is there only one kind of guardian? If the court finds that the person needs to become a ward of the court for protective purposes, the court has a number of options. There are several kinds of guardianship options available, and although each state has its own process and definitions, most states provide for the following types of guardians:

➤ Guardian of the person only

➤ Guardian of the estate only

➤ Conservator of the estate

➤ Limited guardianship

A court can appoint one of these or a combination. For example, the usual scenario is for the court to appoint a guardian both of the person and of the estate, otherwise known as a "full guardianship." Also, the appointment may be made on an emergency, temporary, or permanent basis.

Guardian of the Person Only

IF AN INDIVIDUAL IS INCOMPETENT AND cannot make health care decisions, a court might appoint a guardian of the person only. This allows the guardian to authorize medical treatment and to make all decisions of that nature for the benefit and protection of the ward.

Guardian of the Estate Only

IF AN INDIVIDUAL HAS ASSETS AND becomes disabled, someone must be put in charge of collecting assets and paying bills. There is a certain procedure followed in each of the fifty states for appointing a guardian of the estate for such an individual.

Conservator of the Estate

MANY STATES CALL A GUARDIAN THE "conservator" of the estate, and the terms are often used interchangeably. Whatever the terminology, the designation, procedures, authority, and nature of the fiduciary appointed are very specific and are strictly interpreted by each state.

For instance, in Ohio, a conservator may be appointed for you if you yourself apply to the court and request that one be appointed for a certain period of time, such as during surgery or while you are serving in the armed forces. The court will, with your recommendation, appoint a conservator to look after your assets in your absence or disability. Upon your return or recovery, the conservator will file his or her final accounting with the court, the procedure will terminate, and your funds will be returned to you. It is important to understand what your own state requires if you anticipate the need for a guardian or conservator.

Limited Guardianship

TODAY, ALL FIFTY STATES ARE NOW moving in the direction of creating the limited guardianship, which means a special guardianship procedure designed with each individual ward in mind. Fortunately, this is the trend of the future. A potential ward is viewed as his or her own person, and if it appears the ward is unable to live independently, then he or she can be placed only in the "least restrictive environment" in the community.

What does "least restrictive" mean, and why is it so important? Essentially, adults have the right to live independently for as long as they are able and are safe. The turning point occurs when their physical or mental capacity diminishes to the point that they may be a danger to themselves or others. This may include situations like constantly forgetting to turn off the burner on a stove or the water off in a bathtub, or any actions that may cause neighbors to be fearful. In such cases, an individual may need to live in a different environment.

Often, a limited guardianship may be needed. That is, the guardian may need to move the person of diminished mental capacity out of an apartment and place that person somewhere else, such as an assisted-living community. This does not necessarily mean a nursing home, which is considered the most restrictive environment.

In many cases, this is a difficult balancing act for courts. However, courts are required to give a person as much individual freedom as possible while appointing a limited guardian to take care of matters outside of the ward's competence. The limited guardian is responsible only for his or her specific duties. Often the guardian will decide on where the ward is to reside: at home, at a residential placement such as an assisted-living home, or, possibly, in a nursing home.

How long does a guardianship last? A guardian can be appointed only for a certain number of days, months, or years. It depends upon the situation in each case.

What is the court process? No two states have exactly the same procedure. The heart of the process is to protect and preserve the rights of the individual involved, and for that reason, each person is represented by an attorney in the guardianship process.

Not only do states require that the person involved have attorney representation, but the laws also provide that he or she has the absolute right to live in a nonrestrictive environment. Also, laws stipulate that each person's autonomy be protected, so his or her wishes must take precedence over those of family members.

Essentially, good law makes good sense. We want individuals to retain all of their rights for as long as it is possible and feasible. Thus, we strive to maintain even a severely incapacitated person in the environment of choice for as long as possible.

The guardianship procedure is as follows:

➤ An application is filed in the appropriate court requesting that the court appoint a guardian.

➤ Hearing notices are sent to all people concerned.

➤ An attorney is appointed for the potential ward; a physician is appointed to evaluate the mental and physical condition of the person.

➤ A caseworker or social worker may be asked by the court to file a report regarding the necessity of appointing a guardian or giving other advice.

➤ At the hearing evidence is presented to the court to determine whether a guardian is needed.

➤ The court either dismisses the case or appoints a guardian, in which case the court will:

— name the guardian who is to serve;

— define the nature of the particular guardianship; and

— schedule the matter for periodic review.

➤ If a guardian of the estate is appointed, the guardian must file an inventory with the court, be bonded (to assure that he or she will perform the duties honestly), and file an accounting with the court.

➤ If a guardian of the person is appointed, he or she must make sure the ward is cared for properly and make all health care decisions for the ward.

What can the court-appointed guardian do? The guardian can make all of the decisions for the ward, including where the ward will live, what medical treatment to seek, and every other daily decision about the ward. Or the guardian may have the authority to handle only the finances of the ward. Each case is different, and the authority of each guardian is different as well.

Generally, the courts request the guardian make decisions about some or all of these issues:

➤ Deciding where the ward is to live
➤ Refusing or consenting to medical treatment
➤ Agreeing to treatment in a hospital or institution
➤ Possessing or managing real or personal property
➤ Making gifts
➤ Lending or borrowing money

What if I don't want any guardian appointed? If you are incapacitated and don't even know you have a guardian, you may not be concerned about who your guardian is. However, if you are alert and object to the guardianship proceedings, you have the legal right to oppose the appointment of a guardian over yourself and your possessions.

The question you should ask yourself is this: if you should become disabled, are you satisfied to have a court appoint a guardian for you? If not, then you should consider including in your estate plan a power of attorney for health care and a power of attorney for finances.

We know we may at some time become disabled, either temporarily or permanently. In order to make sure that our wishes are carried out, we have to make sure that we give written legal authority to others to give them the ability to act for us. In your estate plan, this planning should have the highest priority. It preserves your rights and your dignity—no small feat.

Part Three

Six Months to a Solid Estate Plan

Chapter Eleven

Seven Steps to a Successful Estate Plan

THERE ARE AS MANY ESTATE PLANS as there are people. Each of us has a particular situation for which we need a special plan. You may have children, elderly parents, or a sick spouse, or you yourself may be ill. You may fear that you won't be able to manage if you become ill, or if other family members become ill or die. Or you may be concerned about the tax consequences if you die or become disabled. You may fear that estate taxes will deprive future generations of your family from receiving an ample inheritance from you.

People make all sorts of mistakes with their estate planning, such as not writing a will or owning life insurance on the wrong family member. But the absolute worst mistake is to procrastinate. As Edward Young wrote in the seventeenth century, "Procrastination is the thief of time." If you want to secure your future, then make a plan. If you want to be certain that your loved ones will be protected in the event of your disability or death, plan. And do it right now, while you still can.

This chapter outlines the seven basic steps to a successful estate plan. Of course, you'll need to modify its exact form, adding and subtracting pieces to fit your needs, but these are the basic building blocks. As you begin the planning process, remember to make copies of documents you will be reviewing so that you can begin to organize your records for the present and the future. In addition, set a realistic time schedule and systematically follow it. By setting small goals along the way, you can succeed little by little, until you have put in place a comprehensive estate plan for yourself and your family.

⎯⎯ Seven Steps to a Successful Estate Plan ⎯⎯

Step 1
Locate and identify all your assets

Step 2
Set your goals and prioritize them

Step 3
Coordinate your financial and estate plans

Step 4
Select your professional advisers

Step 5
Choose individuals to serve as fiduciaries

Step 6
Execute all legal and financial documents

Step 7
Align your assets with your estate plan

STEP 1

Locate and Identify All Your Assets

Time Frame: One Month

THE BASIS OF ALL GOOD ESTATE PLANNING is to define your assets precisely. For example, you should gather the following information:

➤ List each asset you own and when and how much you paid for it. As you list each asset, if you own stocks, bonds, or mutual funds, or if you have a brokerage account or have funds deposited with a bank or credit union, list the name of the account, account number, name of contact person, address, and phone number. For purposes of compiling concise information, assume no one knows anything about your assets. You want to list where each asset can be located, in addition to the source of each asset and the name and address of the person or institution holding it.

➤ Determine how each asset is titled, whether it is in your name as sole owner, co-owner, joint owner, or separate community property owner.

➤ Estimate the value of your proportionate share of the asset to determine your net worth.

➤ Determine whether the particular asset would be probate or non-probate at the time of your death.

➤ If the asset is non-probate, determine who would receive that asset at the time of your death.

It is critical to itemize and evaluate your assets and determine how they are titled and how you want them distributed at the time of your death or disability. Completing this step is half the battle in creating a successful estate plan. To help identify all of your assets, use the following checklist:

➤ Checking accounts
➤ Savings accounts
➤ Credit union accounts
➤ Certificates of deposit
➤ Money market funds
➤ Other cash reserves
➤ Government bonds
➤ Municipal bonds
➤ Corporate bonds
➤ Fixed annuities
➤ Life insurance cash value
➤ U.S. Treasury notes
➤ Intangible property, such as stocks, bonds and mutual funds, and intellectual property, such as patents, copyrights, and creative projects

➤ Personal residence
➤ Vacation homes
➤ Rental properties
➤ Household goods, including furniture, computers, and appliances
➤ Collectibles
➤ Automobiles
➤ Undeveloped land
➤ Miscellaneous assets
➤ Stocks
➤ Mutual funds
➤ Variable annuities
➤ Business interests
➤ Retirement plans
➤ Jewelry
➤ Artwork

We all own a variety of property, and it is important to include not only the obvious items in our property lists but also such intangible property as stocks, bonds, mutual funds, loans, money market funds, notes, accounts receivable, interest in business partnerships, frequent flier miles, and stock options. Also include the intellectual property you may own: patents; designs; copyrights on literary, musical, or artistic compositions; any interest you may own in a business such as McDonalds, Wendy's, or any other franchise; and licenses you may own (those requiring business or government authority), such as a liquor license or a driver's license bureau. Also list any contracts of value you may own, such as a contract you may have to sell your home or business.

Be as thorough and as concise as you can possibly be in the preparation of Step 1, because it is the foundation of your estate plan. Skimping on details can lead to time-consuming problems and incorrect assumptions as the planning process proceeds. You cannot spend too much time on this basic information. The more complete it is, the more complete your final estate plan will be.

Evaluating Your Assets

IT HAS BEEN MY EXPERIENCE THAT WE think our household goods are extremely valuable, when, in fact, they aren't. Conversely, we tend to feel that *we* are not "worth much," when, in fact, we are. Possessions that may mean a lot to you personally may have a modest value when considered from a resale point of view. Real property and stock fluctuate in value with the current market; bonds, annuities, certificates of deposit, and related investments reflect changing interest rates that vary from day to day. In these times, many factors enter into the evaluation of assets. Do the best job you can in assigning a true value to your property, regardless of what that property is.

The true value of your assets forms the basic framework for your estate plan. I cannot emphasize this enough: Get this information wrong, and your estate plan will be wrong. And beyond that, the tax assessed against your estate at death will use these values. That means the IRS may use them to establish cost basis in property, as will a court of law if a dispute arises between beneficiaries.

If, for instance, a parent dies leaving investments and a farm and one of the children wants the farm, the value of all of the estate assets will be very significant to the final distribution of the assets between the children. Courts order appraisals when there is a dispute of this nature—sometimes several different appraisals. Then, based upon those appraisals and the best information available (such as evidence from witnesses such as land developers or comparison figures of property sold in the area), the courts will make a decision on the value of the farm, for instance, so that the investments and farm worth can be added up and the value of all of the property can be equitably divided.

Property has many owners through the years. Every time an owner of property exchanges, sells, buys, or transfers property, particularly at the time of death but often during the individual's lifetime, such an event acts as a "trigger" that an appraisal may be required. When someone dies, nearly every estate is subject to a statutory requirement that all property must be appraised. When the property is reevaluated, this automatically sets off a second "trigger" for income tax and estate tax issues. For these reasons, the value of property and its proper appraisal are critical issues. They affect the value of the estate assets involved, as well as the estate taxes that may be due. The amount of current income taxes may also depend on these issues, and just as importantly, the tax basis of the property is determined, which has a direct impact upon future tax questions.

Valuation of assets involves generally the same techniques for both estate and gift-tax purposes:

Real estate. The IRS indicates that the "fair market value" is the criterion to use for purposes of evaluating real estate. The fair market value is the price that a willing buyer would pay a willing seller for the property, with neither being under a compulsion to buy or to sell and both having reasonable knowledge of relevant facts.

But who can determine what that value is in the absence of such a sale? In the past, courts appointed a friend, neighbor, or group of landowners, such as farmers, to be acting appraisers of land held in estates. Often, a piece of paper with a value scribbled on it was sufficient. However, in 1991, Congress enacted legislation requiring that real estate appraisers be licensed or certified by each state in which they wanted to appraise certain types of "federally related real estate transactions."

From that time, each of the fifty states has initiated specific education experience and examination requirements that a person is required to meet in order to receive a real estate appraiser's license or certification. Since each state has a separate office to handle the certification of real estate appraisers, it is best to locate the Division of Licensing of Real Estate Appraisers by state. Look in the yellow pages of your state capital. Local real estate agents can also give you this information.

Can local real estate agents and others familiar with real estate provide you with an appraisal of your real property? Perhaps, but you may find that such appraisals will not be accepted by courts of law or tax offices. Only appraisals performed by certified appraisers are acceptable in matters of dispute, particularly if there are federal tax returns, audits, or legal questions involved. Other, more informal appraisals may be sufficient to give you a ballpark value, but they may be limited to that role.

One organization that has been around since 1961 is the National Association of Independent Fee Appraisers (NAIFA), which offers courses for appraisers to obtain certification and lists the names, addresses, and phone numbers of certified real estate appraisers. NAIFA's national office can be contacted at 7501 Murdoch Avenue, St. Louis, Missouri 63119; by phone at 314-781-6688; or online at www.go appraisers.com or www.naifa.com. Or contact your local real estate agent to find certified appraisers in your area.

Factors in a Real Estate Appraisal

AN IMPORTANT THING to keep in mind when you are thinking of obtaining an appraisal is that there is not much difference between an appraisal for real estate of a business nature and an appraisal for private residential property. Factors that must be assessed for both are as follows.

➤ Description of property.

➤ Maps and photos of property.

➤ Sketch of floor plan.

➤ Rent roll: that is, the name of each tenant and rent paid, if the property is rental.

➤ Owner's income and expense statement for the property.

➤ Details of neighborhood: location (urban or rural); how built up the area is; whether property values are stable, decreasing, or increasing; whether the area is owner-or tenant-occupied; vacancy rate of apartments in the area; price ranges of single-family homes, apartment buildings, or condos.

➤ Site information: zoning classification; highest and best use of the property in question; list of utilities that service the property; checklist of amenities such as storm sewers, curbs and gutters, sidewalks, and street lights; improvements present or planned; encroachments noted, if obvious.

➤ Descriptions of improvements made to the property; year the property was con-

When all of the information is put together and studied by a competent appraiser (see "Factors in a Real Estate Appraisal," above), the estimated market value can be stated with a high degree of certainty. This does not mean that such an appraisal cannot be challenged; it can. However, in order to dispute it, other appraisals must be done. When there are serious disputes regarding the value of property, it is not unknown to have more than a half-dozen appraisals before a court to determine the true worth of the property. These multiple appraisals usually will reflect the range of values for the property in dispute, which enables the court to ultimately determine a single value.

Automobiles. The fair market value for your automobile is determined by the price a member of the public would pay a retail automobile dealer for an automobile of the same description, make, model, age, and condition. This is

structed; description of the basic construction—brick, masonry, frame; interior walls, floor, ceiling, and roof materials; heating and air-conditioning details; appliances; condition of water heater and other plumbing appliances; comments regarding the physical condition, inadequacies, repairs needed, modernization issues, and general issues.

➤ Cost approach of appraisal: the square feet of space available multiplied by the estimated cost per square foot to build this type of structure using standard costs of construction in the area.

➤ Comparable rental data, if rental property is being appraised: rental figures from other buildings in the area, monthly rent schedules, vacancy rates, and length of the usual rental.

➤ Market approach to appraising property: Appraisers research what similar homes or commercial buildings have sold for in the same area and use that as a basis for determining what the property being appraised is worth. Usually three or four comparable properties are used for comparison purposes.

➤ Income approach to evaluating real property: This is usually done when commercial property is involved. The appraisers take various income figures and expense figures and project the value of the property in question.

not the same as what a used-car dealer would pay you for it.

One of the most popular books used to evaluate cars (available at most bookstores) is the *Kelley Blue Book Used Car Guide: Consumer Edition.* The current guide gives you used-car values covering a span of eight years.

Stock. The fair market value is the value established on the date of death by the market where the stock is traded, such as the New York Stock Exchange. If the stock is a private offering of a company, it is the value on the date of death as officially stated by the company.

Antiques or collectibles. These must be evaluated at "fair market value" and not at what a dealer in used furniture or antiques would pay; the price is what the public would pay. There are many local appraisers of these items available, and you can usually rely on a reputable dealer who has been in the business for a long time.

However, if you have a valuable antique, one worth more than $10,000, it might be well worth your time to contact some of the big antique appraisal firms. One of the finest, and one that has held its place at or near the top of the list, is Christies International, which has been in the business since 1766 (www.christies.com).

Jewelry. The value is the retail value, or what the public would pay. Even an item that's out of style has been valued by the IRS as if the item had been converted into a modern piece.

More often than not, an appraisal done by your local jeweler will serve your purpose. However, occasionally you need a piece of jewelry appraised for insurance, estate, or tax reasons. One of the foremost jewel and multidisciplinary appraisal organizations in the country is the American Society of Appraisers, founded in 1936 and located at 555 Herndon Parkway, Suite 125, Herndon, Virginia 20170, and on the Web at www.appraisers.org.

This organization is an excellent one to contact for information about appraisals in general, and where to find a qualified appraiser in your area. It's also a good place to start when you are looking for an appraiser for unusual assets, because its members appraise many kinds of property.

Business interests. Many factors enter into the evaluation of a business:

➢ the nature and history of the business;
➢ the current condition of the particular industry;
➢ the book value of the stock, if it's a public company;
➢ the demonstrated earning capacity of the business;
➢ the dividend history of the business;
➢ its goodwill, or the customer satisfaction arising from an established, well-run, and well-regarded business, and other similar intangible values;
➢ its sales history and the size of the block of stock involved; and
➢ the market price of stocks in similar publicly traded businesses.

When in doubt about the true value of any of your business property, have your assets professionally appraised only by an appraiser who has been accredited by one of the following four nationally known organizations:

American Society of Appraisers
555 Herndon Parkway, Suite 125
Herndon, Virginia 20170
703-478-2228
www.appraisers.org

Institute of Business Appraisers (IBA)
P.O. Box 17410
Plantation, Florida 33418
954-584-1144
www.instbusapp.org

National Association of Certified Valuation Analysts (NACVA)
1111 E. Brickyard Road, Suite 200
Salt Lake City, Utah 84105
801-486-0600
www.nacva.com

American Institute of Certified Public Accountants (AICPA)
201 Plaza Three
Jersey City, New Jersey 07311-3881
201-938-3000
www.aicpa.org

Each of these organizations offers courses and exams to obtain certification. All of their members have backgrounds in accounting, and many are CPAs, in business, in real estate, or in a combination of these fields. Individuals who obtain certification from these reputable organizations are among the most qualified business appraisers in the United States.

The cost of the appraisal will vary according to the appraiser, the item involved, the value, and the time and expertise required to ascertain the value of the particular business. Get an estimate of the appraisal cost before you enter into an agreement to have the asset appraised.

Many people are casual about finding out what, if anything, their assets are worth. But for purposes of developing an estate plan, it is crucial to have correct appraisals for assets that have substantial value. If you follow the appraisal path, you will know with certainty what value others will put on your assets, and you can then plan accordingly. This information can also be valuable for other reasons. For example, if you know what your business asset is worth "officially," you have a better chance of obtaining loans and credit extensions and getting better tax treatment. For further information, you may want to get the Small Business Resource Guide (IRS Publication 3207) on CD-ROM free from the IRS.

Of equal importance to listing and understanding your assets is listing your liabilities. Here are the major categories for debts and long-term obligations:

➤ Auto loans   ➤ Miscellaneous debts
➤ Bank loans   ➤ Mortgages and home equity loans
➤ Business loans   ➤ Rental property obligations
➤ Credit cards   ➤ Student loans

It is important to list other debts and obligations you may owe as well. What are your monthly expenses? What are your annual insurance premiums? Do you owe a friend or family member any money? Have you signed a promissory note to that effect? What are your estimated annual charitable contributions?

These and similar questions help determine what your cash needs are on a day-to-day basis and what exactly you owe others. From this information, you can begin to formulate a plan to encompass your particular financial situation.

Now that you have a list of both your assets and your liabilities, as well as copies of all of the documents that indicate your ownership, make sure that your original documents are safely tucked away in a safe-deposit box. Furthermore, you should invest in a file cabinet for the copies of all your documents so that you can consolidate them, keep them in order, and consult them at your convenience. You should have a file folder for each asset and liability involved in your estate planning, and you should also have folders for important personal information. Your file system should be set up something like the chart on the following page.

Keep copies of receipts for your assets, if possible, as well as current statements and appraisals. How long should you keep receipts? The IRS requires taxpayers to produce documentation to support their tax returns for a seven-year period. Therefore, for most purposes, keep information for at least that long.

However, when you buy stock, real estate, and similar investments, you are establishing a tax basis for that asset, which has long-range tax ramifications. Therefore, those receipts should be kept forever.

After you organize and compile your financial matters on work sheets, you should look at exactly how the title to each of your assets reads. By that I mean look at the actual deed of your house, your car title, your boat title, and other similar titles, to determine exactly what each says. Is it in your name alone, which means that, when you die, it will be a probate asset, subject to the probate process in your state? Is your name on the deed with that of your spouse or parent? Are there only two names, or does the deed include joint-and-survivorship language, trust language, or life estate language so that your property will avoid probate?

It is at this point that you note, next to each asset on your list, whether it is pro-

ASSETS

Annuities

Business Interests

Cash

Certificates

Checking Accounts

Collectibles

Corporate Bonds

Credit Union Accounts

Government Bonds

Health Insurance

Household Goods

Liability Insurance

Life Insurance

Miscellaneous Assets

Money Market Funds

Municipal Bonds

Mutual Funds

Rental Property

Residence

Retirement Plans

Savings

Stocks

Undeveloped Land

Vacation Home(s)

Vehicles

LIABILITIES

Auto Loans

Bank Loans

Business Loans

Charge Accounts

Mortgages

Other Debts

PERSONAL INFORMATION

Adoption Papers

Birth Certificates

Burial Arrangements (prepaid plots
   or funeral plans, cremation,
   donating organs or whole
   body to an institution, etc.)

Business Contracts

Divorce Papers

Guardian Information

Immigration Papers

Marriage Certificates

Medical History (information for
   each family member)

Military Papers (DD-214)

Passports

Pet Information

PODs

Prenuptial Agreement

Religious Information

Social Security Cards

Statement of Net Worth

Tax Return (most recent)

Trust Documents

Wills

bate or non-probate. If you aren't sure, find out. If you know for an absolute certainty how your property would pass from the present title owner to beneficiaries or others, make a note of that. You need to sort out the particulars of the transfer of property titles from you to others, so that problem areas can be identified and corrected as you work through your final estate planning steps. Say, for example, you want your husband to inherit your share of your home when you die and also to avoid paying taxes on it. But in reviewing your assets, you notice that while the property deed has both of your names on it, it doesn't contain any joint-and-survivorship language. This would prompt you to make an appointment with your lawyer and add the proper wording so that your wishes will be executed properly.

The final task in Step 1 is to prepare a statement of your net worth based on the information you have just compiled. Although financial experts use very complicated formulas to determine net worth, in its simplest form it is merely this: assets minus liabilities equals net worth. Your net worth is a "snapshot" of your finances and is one of the fundamental yardsticks used in financial planning. For this reason, an accurate computation of your own net worth—not that of your parents or of Aunt Harriet, from whom you may receive an inheritance—is important. Unless an inheritance check from Aunt Harriet is already in the mail, do not count on it.

First, look at your list of assets and segregate your income-producing assets from non-income-producing assets and your tangible assets from intangible. Non-income assets are those that produce no income, such as your residence, as opposed to stock and other investments that accrue income. (Your residence may increase in value over the years, but unless you rent part of it to tenants, it does not produce income.) Tangible property is property you can see, such as a house, land, a car, and furniture. Intangible property represents an ownership interest, such as stock, patents, or copyrights.

Once you've finished listing all of your assets, list all of your liabilities. Your net worth statement should reflect your total net worth at a certain point in time, such as the last day of the year or the first day of a month. Since your net worth will change over time, keep the net worth calculations you are working with in a file, so that each year you can update it with ease.

Try to follow a certain logical progression as you work through the calculations of your net worth. If it is helpful, follow this chart to work through the process in a step-by step-manner. The idea is to create a comprehensive list of your assets and liabilities and the value of each so that when you finish, your net worth statement will accurately reflect your true net worth.

How to Calculate Your Personal Net Worth

ASSETS	
Cash	Bonds
Cash value of life insurance	Investments
Certificates of deposit	Mutual fund investments
Checking accounts	Partnership interests
Money market accounts	Stocks
Savings accounts	Other investments
U.S. Treasury bills	**Total $_____**
Total $_____	
	Antiques
Business Ownership	Art
Closely held corporate interest	Automobiles
Stock owned in private companies	Collectibles
Other	Furs and jewelry
Total $_____	Home
	Home furnishings
Employee savings plans,	Personal assets
i.e., 401(k), SEP, ESOP	Vacation home
IRAs and Keogh accounts	Other assets
Pension (present lump-sum value)	**Total $_____**
Retirement funds	**TOTAL ASSETS $_____**
Total $_____	

LIABILITIES	
Alimony	401(k) loans
Automobile loans	Personal loans
Child support	Projected income tax liability
Credit card balances	Student loans
Home equity loans	Other liabilities
Home mortgages	**Total $_____**
Investment loans	**TOTAL LIABILITIES $_____**
Life insurance policy loans	
Total $_____	**NET WORTH $_____**

To give you some perspective on how individuals calculate their net worth, here are five different estate planning scenarios. All of these individuals have a unique set of concerns and family circumstances that have propelled them to calculate their net worth and, eventually, set their estate and financial plans in order.

John James: Single Person with Two Dependents

JOHN, AGE FORTY-FOUR, has been a self-employed mechanic for some fourteen years. He has been the sole support for his two children since his wife died about five years ago, and he has slowly tried to accumulate assets over the past few years so he can buy a bigger house. The bank has asked for his net worth statement as part of the information packet it sends to the mortgage department for evaluation. Here is what John has come up with:

Net Worth: $30,000

ASSETS	
Cash and Equivalents	
Certificate of Deposit	$10,000
Fixed Assets	0
Property Assets	
Residence	$40,000
Vehicle(s)	$10,700
Equity Assets	0
TOTAL ASSETS	**$60,700**
LIABILITIES	
Short-Term Debt	
Auto Loans	$2,200
Long-Term Debt	
Residence: Mortgage	$28,500
TOTAL LIABILITIES	**-30,700**
NET WORTH	**$30,000**

Just before the bank's loan committee was to meet to discuss the details of a possible mortgage loan for John, his tools were stolen from the garage where he worked. They were uninsured. So, instead of trying to purchase a home, John had to concentrate his efforts on buying tools so he could continue to work as a mechanic.

However, John is now beginning to think about getting a will so his children will inherit his house. He will begin his process by making an appointment with a lawyer to discuss the matter. He also wants to ask how the title to his house should be held at the present time. Should he put his children's names on the deed to the house with his own name, he wonders?

Jason Fox and Mary Anastasia: Cohabitants

JASON AND MARY, BOTH IN THEIR mid-thirties, aren't married but have lived together in a community property state for around seven years. They have separated for long periods of time but have reconciled their differences for now. They want to pool their funds and buy a houseboat they can live on permanently, because they've decided this is a fiscally wise thing to do. Although they have had serious differences of opinion about how to spend their combined salaries, they now are both convinced that if they can save some money by living a few years on a boat, they could solve some of the issues that are always driving them apart—all of them of a fiscal nature.

Net Worth: $140,000

ASSETS	
Cash and Equivalents	
Checking	2,300
Savings Account	14,700
Fixed Assets	0
Property Assets	
Residence	150,000
Equity Assets	0
TOTAL ASSETS	**$167,000**
LIABILITIES	
Short-Term Debt	0
Long-Term Debt	
Residence: Mortgage	27,000
TOTAL LIABILITIES	**-27,000**
NET WORTH	**$140,000**

Neither Jason nor Mary has listed on their net worth statement their respective credit card balances, since they don't think they have to. Jason owes more than

$20,000 on his car: $7,800 on one credit card and $14,000 on another card. In addition, he owes on his student loans and is delinquent on the payments.

Mary lists the residence as hers although it is titled in her grandmother's name. Her grandmother is still living and has promised Mary that she will inherit the house. Therefore, Mary thinks she should list the house as belonging to her now, since she maintains it, paints it, and pays the utilities on it, while her grandmother pays only the real estate taxes on the property.

The first question that has to be assessed in this situation is whether the net worth statement Jason and Mary have created accurately reflects their true net worth. To answer that question, it is necessary to decide who must be satisfied with a net worth statement.

In other words, if Jason and Mary have informally agreed that this is the way they want to view their financial situation, that's fine. If they aren't asking for a loan, trying to formulate an estate plan, or seeking financial assistance, what they agree to privately is merely a nonbinding "understanding" without any legal ramifications or obligations. However, once they want to apply for a loan, obtain financial assistance, or in any way apply to a bank, credit union, or other financial institution, they must have a specific, precise net worth statement.

Therefore, all credit card balances must be entered into the net worth statement. What about the house that Mary's grandmother says will be Mary's inheritance? Until such time as the house, or any asset, is actually in Mary's name, she cannot enter it on her net worth statement.

In this case, once the house and the grandmother's mortgage were taken off the net worth statement and all of the credit card charges and student loans were added, the net worth statement clearly indicated that Jason and Mary actually have a negative net worth. Consequently, no financial institution will make a loan to them for any boat.

As they begin to understand their real situation, Mary wonders what will happen when she does inherit her grandmother's house. Will Jason automatically inherit a share of it since they are living together? She is going to make an appointment with an attorney as soon as possible, now that she realizes that Jason's poor spending habits might become a legal problem for her someday.

Julia Anderson: Single Person, Retired

JULIA RECENTLY RETIRED FROM TEACHING at the age of seventy-two and has developed a heart condition. She contacted her attorney to begin putting some estate planning matters in order, and he requested that she try to determine her net worth; list her beneficiaries; name her POA for health care and her POA for finances; and name the individual who would be her agent in her living will. In an attempt to calculate her net worth, she has put together the following information.

Net Worth: $200,000

ASSETS	
Cash and Equivalents	
Checking	1,800
Savings Account	12,200
Certificate of Deposit	10,000
Fixed Assets	
Government Bonds	28,000
Property Assets	
Residence	103,000
Vehicle	20,000
Collectibles	27,500
Undeveloped Land	15,000
Equity Assets	
Mutual Fund	34,000
TOTAL ASSETS	**$251,500**

LIABILITIES	
Short-Term Debt	
Auto Loan	11,000
Long-Term Debt	
Residence: Mortgage	40,500
TOTAL LIABILITIES	**-51,500**
NET WORTH	**$200,000**

One of the most important estate planning questions that Julia should evaluate with her advisers is her health insurance coverage. How much coverage is there under her health care policy? Does it pay 80-20, the standard coverage? Does it have a limit on how much the policy will pay out for an illness? What is her annual income? Does she have enough assets to pay for her medical care if she needs long-term care?

These are the immediate financial and estate planning questions facing her. She knows she must see her attorney and her financial adviser immediately to seek some direction. She wonders if she should sell her house right now while she is still in fair health, investing the funds from the sale so she will have adequate funds for her health care. She is anxious and extremely concerned about her future.

Mary Ann and Patrick Smith: Married Couple with Three Children

MARY ANN AND PATRICK SMITH, BOTH IN their late sixties, have worked hard all their lives in their own business, a small manufacturing plant that specializes in making custom-sized boxes for special industrial needs. All of their children are grown and no longer live at home, but one of their children runs the business for them. They really want to retire and move to Florida, but they don't know how to do this and be fair to all of their children. The son who runs their business wants the entire interest in the business or no interest at all, because he does not want to have to deal with his two younger sisters, neither of whom has a head for business. The sisters already think their parents favor their brother. Dissension surfaces each time the Smiths try to discuss the future with their children. Now they realize they need to see an estate planner to seek professional advice. Where should they turn to find such an expert? And what should they do with their business, to meet both their needs and their children's?

Net Worth: $650,000

ASSETS	
Cash and Equivalents	
Checking	4,500
Savings Account	1,800
Credit Union	450
Certificate of Deposit	10,000
Money Market Fund	10,000
Fixed Assets	
Fixed Annuity	120,000
Property Assets	
Residence	240,000
Boat	23,000
Equity Assets	
Stocks	292,000
Business Interest	180,000
TOTAL ASSETS	**$881,750**

LIABILITIES	
Short-Term Debt	
Charge Accounts	9,900
Bank Loans	13,250
Long-Term Debt	
Residence: Mortgage	88,700
Other Debt	
Business Debt	119,900
TOTAL LIABILITIES	**-231,750**
NET WORTH	**$650,000**

James and Ann Palmer: Married Couple with Two Children, One of Them Disabled

JAMES PALMER, AGE SEVENTY-TWO, inherited an insurance business from his father and uncle when he was in his early thirties. He and his wife, Ann, age sixty-four, have worked together in the business and are still very actively involved in managing it. They have a child who is married and living out of state, and they have a disabled child who lives with them and is in the advanced stages of multiple sclerosis. How, they wonder, should they set up their estate to protect the disabled child and still be fair to the other child? And further, if something happens to them, who will look after and take care of their disabled daughter? They begin to search for the answers, an estate planner, and some help. As they say, "We aren't getting any younger, and we aren't solving our problems by just worrying about them."

Recently the Palmers' accountant informed them that when they die, they may owe federal and state estate taxes of more than $250,000, but that with proper planning they may be able to save all of that money. They are very concerned about this problem, because it will diminish their liquidity, and that may have a significant impact upon their ability to provide assets for their children to meet their needs after the Palmers are no longer alive.

Net Worth: $1,940,000

ASSETS	
Cash and Equivalents	
Checking	18,200
Savings Account	25,800
Certificate of Deposit	90,000

ASSETS *(continued)*	
Money Market Fund	110,000
Fixed Assets	
Corporate Bonds	160,000
Fixed Annuity	237,000
Life Insurance Cash Value	252,000
Property Assets	
Residence	425,000
Boat	25,000
Vacation Home	82,000
Undeveloped Land	450,000
Equity Assets	
Brokerage Accounts	360,000
Mutual Funds	25,000
TOTAL ASSETS	**$2,260,000**

LIABILITIES	
Short-Term Debt	
Charge Accounts	23,000
Bank Loans	37,000
Long-Term Debt	
Residence: Mortgage	93,000
Residence: Second Mortgage	6,000
Vacation Home: Mortgage	61,000
Other Debt	
Personal Note	100,000
TOTAL LIABILITIES	**-320,000**
NET WORTH	**$1,940,000**

IN GENERAL, WHEN YOU ARE SETTING up your estate plan, your personal and financial credibility is important. When you deal with a bank, an attorney, an accountant, or any person or entity about your estate plan, you want them to perceive you as someone who can be relied upon to furnish good, solid, truthful information. The better able you are prepared to verify your net worth, answer a variety of questions, and have information to substantiate your worth, the better advice you are likely to receive.

For example, the Palmers' net worth would be easy to confirm because their figures reflect a realistic snapshot. If, for instance, all of their records of assets, such as their monthly investment records and real estate appraisals, together with copies of their liabilities were collected, their net worth could be easily verified. Such a confirmation would merely consist of obtaining a copy of the Palmers' appraisals, investment holdings, personal note, bank mortgages, loans, and credit card balances.

Mary Anastasia and Jason Fox, on the other hand, don't have their finances nearly as well in hand. Mary doesn't actually own her grandmother's house, so a large chunk of her total assets really aren't there, for the purposes of a bank loan for their houseboat. Even if she listed the house as an asset on a loan application, once the bank checked the title, it would discover that she did not yet own it.

So put your net worth together for your planner, and if necessary, be prepared to provide all of the verification of your worth when the planning begins to take shape. Once you have succeeded in Step 1, the most difficult and the most time-consuming step in this entire estate planning process is behind you.

STEP 2

Set Your Goals and Prioritize Them

Time Frame: Two Weeks

SUPPOSE BY NOW YOU HAVE LOCATED your assets, identified them, and had them evaluated, and you have calculated your net worth. You have done the financial preparation. But numbers are only that: numbers. They don't reveal any pathway to solving your problems. It is at this point that you must focus on your concerns about your future.

Try to spend some time jotting down the issues you are worried about. Is it your health, your future, your financial security, or the financial security of your children, parents, or friends? What problems do you expect your estate plan to help you solve? This is Step 2 in the estate planning process: identifying your estate planning goals and then prioritizing them. Which are the most important goals? The least important? Which one goal do you most want to meet?

Once you have completed your net worth statement, you should review it from a practical financial point of view to determine whether you can do better with your investments. Talk to an accountant who can tell you what tax rates you are now paying to try to determine if you can reinvest your assets more productively.

Cut your losses. Solidify your stock portfolio. Get rid of those "dogs"—not to mention the "strays," the odd bits and pieces of stock that you've accumulated over the years. Inventory your collectibles.

Go to a financial planner if you feel that the whole thing is beyond you. Many people who could manage their own financial affairs with skill elect not to do so. They just don't feel they want to handle the investment of their assets. They go either to a financial planner or to a trust officer at their local bank to let these experts handle their assets. They feel they are at least somewhat protected against loss this way and that professionals have the expertise to take care of their assets in the most productive, profitable manner.

If, however, you are like the majority of people, you don't do anything. You coast along thinking that you should do something, but you're lulled into inaction by your own lack of interest, lack of direction, or both. My advice? Do something. At the very least, confirm with an adviser that what you are currently doing is not to your disadvantage. And think about whether your current financial picture addresses your need to make sure that you and those you love are going to be secure if you become disabled or if you die.

Because events during your lifetime can have far more important ramifications for you than dealing with wealth distribution after your death, be sure to concentrate first and foremost on issues that you may face during your lifetime. Then, deal with the issues that you want to make sure are handled correctly after your death. But begin with your lifetime goals, and work from there.

Goals and Priorities
Lifetime Goals
➤ Health care for myself and my family members
➤ Financial management of assets: maximize what I have now
➤ Payment of debts
➤ Plans in the event of disability
➤ Ability to assist other family members
➤ Assistance for kids' education or businesses
➤ Assistance for parents' well-being

Death Issues
➤ What action should be taken to handle the immediate details of my death?
➤ Who will arrange for my cremation or interment?
➤ Should I make anatomical gifts? Eye bank? Organ bank?
➤ How and to whom do I want to leave my estate?

➤ Do I need a trust?

➤ Can I reduce or eliminate estate taxes?

➤ Should I leave my assets outright to others at the time of my death, or should I try to provide management of those assets for some years in order to assure income production for my heirs?

➤ If my spouse and I die together in a car accident, for example, how do I want to protect my children and those assets that I would want to be used for their care?

➤ Should the children receive my estate when each reaches the age of adulthood (age eighteen), or do I want my assets to go to them only at a later time?

➤ What provision should I make in this situation to name a guardian for my minor children?

➤ Are there special educational, financial, or health needs to be met for one or more of my children?

➤ Do I want to make charitable gifts?

➤ What about my handicapped child?

➤ Who is best suited to make financial decisions and handle my money matters for me when I die?

➤ Is the elimination or reduction of estate taxes of paramount importance to me?

➤ Should I make gifts during my lifetime?

➤ To which charitable and religious organizations do I wish to leave a bequest?

➤ What should I do about future inheritances that I may not live long enough to receive?

➤ What about my parents? What special consideration should I give to their well-being?

➤ When all is said and done, have I forgotten something or someone?

It bears repeating that you need to carefully think through what is important to you. Do you have an elderly parent to protect through planning? Minor children? A disabled spouse? Are you yourself a disabled person? If you are disabled, what should be your goals? Do you have enough health insurance to provide adequate care? What would you think of nursing home care, long or short term? What about intermediate care? And do you have enough financial resources to maintain an apartment or home while you are incapacitated even for a short period of time?

The more informed you are about what you'd want to have happen in such circumstances, the more likely your plans and intentions can be expressed to others so that they, in turn, can carry out your wishes. If you fail to plan, then you will receive a medley of well-intentioned services that may be disorganized and lacking in the kind of assistance that you really need and deserve.

STEP 3

Coordinate Your Financial and Estate Plans

Time Frame: One Month

AS NOTED THROUGHOUT THIS BOOK, the concept of integration is central to the entire estate planning program. It is by bringing together the best thinking from the financial and the legal areas that one can achieve the ultimate estate plan. Integration means incorporating your assets into your estate plan through your legal documents. You do this in such a way that the financial foundation you have built will continue to benefit you both during your lifetime and at the time of your death, when your assets will either be passed on to others through your will or put into trust for future generations.

The best estate plans are those that are very tightly integrated so that your finances and your estate plan are full partners in your life plan. Considered together, your financial and legal plans are the basis of formulating an estate plan that encompasses all of your personal concerns, your financial value, and your legal road map to protect you and your family during your lifetime and then at the time of your death.

Although no two people are alike in their situation, it is helpful to look at other people's planning. What do they worry about? What are their primary goals? What are they going to do to solve their problems? What can you learn from their situation that will help you? Let's revisit the people portrayed in the net worth scenarios to find out what steps they took to achieve their financial and estate planning goals.

John James, age forty-four, two children. **Net worth:** $30,000
   Goals: To protect his children when he dies
            To make sure his house goes to his children

Jason Fox and Mary Anastasia, ages thirty-seven and thirty-five. **Net worth:** negative
   Goals: For Mary to protect herself against financial problems in the event she inherits property

Julia Anderson, age seventy-two. **Net worth:** $200,000
   Goals: To plan her estate so she will be protected if she has long-term health care needs

Mary Ann and Patrick Smith, ages sixty-eight and sixty-nine. **Net worth:** $650,000

Goals: To figure out how to transfer interest in their business to one child and still be fair to their other two children

To retire comfortably to Florida

James and Ann Palmer, ages seventy-two and sixty-four. **Net worth:** $1.94 million

Goals To set up a good estate plan to protect their disabled child and also their other daughter

To diminish or eliminate all estate taxes

John James. John doesn't know it when he goes to see his attorney, but within five years he will suffer a massive heart attack and die instantly, leaving two children, one age nineteen and one age sixteen. Of course, hindsight doesn't often solve problems, but it is helpful to provide insight after the fact. Now let's see what John really did when he went to see his attorney. His attorney gave John the following advice:

➢ get a POA for finances and health care, and a living will;

➢ write a simple will (name guardians for the children), or put your house in a simple trust for a trustee to manage; and

➢ get some life insurance.

Here is what John did:

He wrote a simple will and put his house title into his name with his children as co-owners. He did not name any guardians for his children when he wrote his will, because he had only one sister and did not want to name her their guardian due to her history of substance abuse. He wanted to spend more time thinking about this matter before adding a codicil or addendum to his will to name the guardians.

The problem was that the entire estate plan revolved around planning for the disposal of the house. There were no documents in place to take care of any problems that might arise during his lifetime. When John had his heart attack, he died instantly. Had he remained alive but unconscious, no one would have been authorized to make health care decisions for him. Since no guardian was named in the will, the court appointed a guardian for the minor child—John's sister. There were few funds available to care for the house or this child, so the house was sold, even though it was titled in the names of all three family members. The older child was left with no home and few, if any, assets.

Jason Fox and Mary Anastasia. Mary's attorney gives her the following information. Some states recognize a common-law marriage originated and approved in another state but will not recognize a common-law marriage originating in their state. (Currently, the following states recognize common-law marriages: Alabama, Colorado, District of Columbia, Idaho, Iowa, Kansas, Montana, Oklahoma, Pennsylvania, Rhode Island, South Carolina, and Texas.) The attorney tells Mary he will have to research the matter further if she wants to find out whether her relationship with Jason is considered common-law marriage.

The attorney advises Mary to talk to her grandmother to ask if she will put the house Mary is to receive from her into a trust for her benefit to protect the asset. That way, he says, Mary will be protected if her present relationship becomes fraught with financial difficulty. The attorney believes that Jason's creditors could not attach such a trust to pay for bills that Jason accrued.

What did Mary do? Nothing. Here's the problem: Mary has not yet inherited the house, which was not put into trust for her. She has not married Jason, and she does not know whether, in fact, their relationship is considered a common-law marriage. This means that if Mary does inherit the house from her grandmother, Jason may have a legal interest in it, either by virtue of being her common-law spouse or upon some other legal basis recognized in their state. And if Jason continues to amass bills he can't pay, his creditors will have the opportunity to bring suit against him, obtain a judgment, and attach the property as "his" property. In other words, should Jason's poor financial habits continue, both of them may face ruin and possible bankruptcy.

Julia Anderson. Julia's attorney advises her to get a POA for finances and health care, and a living will; to make a simple will and consider putting the house and perhaps all of her assets into a revocable living trust; and to find out all the details of her medical insurance plan and what it pays for assisted care and for nursing home care and what, if any, monetary limitations the policy imposes. He also suggests that she consider whom she trusts enough to act as her fiduciary if she becomes disabled and whom she should name as trustee and contingent trustee to manage the details of selling her house, if and when it becomes necessary.

Julia decides to give her lifelong friend her POA for health care and to name this person as her agent in her living will. Julia names herself as her own trustee, "to serve for so long as she is competent, until two physicians certify in her medical records that she is no longer competent to make her own medical decisions." She also names her accountant as the contingent trustee. Her attorney drafts a deed for her to sign to transfer her home from her individual name to the Julia Anderson Trust. She signs the deed, which is recorded in the local land record office, thus funding her trust. She has put the wheels in motion for her trustee to manage her property during periods of her disability and also after her death.

What does she do with her mutual funds? She writes to her mutual fund company, asks for the forms necessary to change the ownership of her account, and fills it out to indicate that she wants to transfer ownership of her funds from herself as an individual to herself as trustee. This is a very important step in making sure that as many of her assets as possible are transferred into her trust. That way, when and if she does become disabled, her trustee will be able to act for her and on her behalf with reference to all assets held in her trust. The POA for finances would be empowered to handle all of those assets that are not in the trust but that may need to be liquidated to provide for her care.

To date Julia is managing well with her medical problems. She is anticipating a move to reduce the expenses involved in owning a home. Also, she anticipates that when she needs more medical care, she will be able to transfer to assisted living and then into a nursing care environment. Therefore, she has decided to move into a health care campus that houses all of these options.

Mary Ann and Patrick Smith. The attorney advises the Smiths to "do first things first": get a POA for finances and health care and a living will for each of them; write a simple will to take care of probate assets; and consider a revocable living trust for each of them. He also suggests they update all medical plans and life insurance plans.

Further, the attorney advises the Smiths that being owners of a sole proprietorship limits their estate planning options. They should consider incorporating their business, giving their son the right, through a purchase plan, to buy stock in the company, and also, over time, giving him the option to purchase the stock owned by his parents or sisters. In that way, the child who wants to own the business has the right to purchase it, which in turn gives the other children their fair share of their parents' estate. Setting up life insurance as a means for providing assets for the children is also an option.

The Smiths incorporated their business and made gifts of stock to each of their children. They also established a stock purchase plan for their son so he will eventually own all the stock in the company; the other children will receive their fair share of the value of the company and are completely satisfied. There has been no further dissension in the family since this matter was resolved.

The Smiths also signed a living trust. They are in the process of conveying into their respective trusts assets, such as their second home, which will be easily managed by their trustee in the event of their deaths. They have signed POAs for health care and finances, and they also now have living wills. Their only unresolved problem is how to make provisions for their elderly parents, who are dependent upon them for financial support. They hope to seek advice next on this and begin to make plans for their parents.

James and Ann Palmer. The attorney informs the Palmers that they have two of the most complex estate planning issues possible: planning for a disabled child and planning for tax avoidance. Both areas of the law are difficult to understand and complicated to resolve.

First, however, he tells them to immediately execute POAs for finances and health care decisions and to make living wills, in the event that either or both of them should suffer an unexpected disability. He also advises that they each sign a living will.

Next, in order to avoid estate taxes of $250,000, they should consider a marital deduction trust, which might diminish or eliminate the taxes they might otherwise pay.

In this case, Mr. Smith owns all of the assets in his own name. To receive maximum benefit from the trust (particularly for state estate tax purposes), he would preferably convey to his spouse half of the assets. The wife would hold assets of $750,000 in her name, and he would own $750,000 in his name.

Each spouse would then put the assets into their respective trusts. This means that the majority of their assets would be literally transferred into their trusts.

The marital deduction trust is drafted in such a way that at the death of the first spouse the trust is divided into two separate and distinct trusts: $675,000 of the assets is placed in the B trust, referred to in legal jargon as the "family" or "credit shelter trust." The portion placed in the B trust is equal to the amount of the unified credit or the portion that is exempt from federal estate tax, as determined by federal tax laws. The balance of the funds from the decedent spouse, $75,000, is placed into the A Trust, known as the "marital trust."

The surviving spouse has the absolute right to take the income and the principal from the A trust, even the entire amount of that trust. However, the surviving spouse can take only the *income* from the family trust, for his or her lifetime. However, if the surviving spouse can show that there are serious financial needs, the trustee can release as much of the principal from the family trust as the trustee deems appropriate and necessary.

When the surviving spouse dies, that spouse's estate will approximate

$750,000, and not the full $1.5 million that the spouse might have had if a simple will had given the surviving spouse all of the first spouse's estate. The difference in federal estate tax is the difference between taxing $75,000 (because there is the exemption of $675,000 upon which no tax is due) and taxing $825,000 in assets! A big tax savings.

Planning for a Disabled Child

THE PLANNING NECESSARY FOR A disabled child is one of the most difficult issues a parent ever has to face. If a child is slightly disabled but can still manage resources and is able to hold a job of some kind, perhaps some monthly financial assistance may be sufficient. However, the Palmers' child is cognitively impaired to the point that she is unable to function independently of their daily assistance.

The Palmers decided to set up a marital deduction trust and to work with it until they feel comfortable with it. Since it is revocable and can be modified, even entirely canceled if they are not satisfied with it, they want to try the trust, because it will save them so much money. In addition, after meeting with a financial adviser, they will establish a special-needs trust (see "Six Steps to Planning for a Severely Disabled Child," on the following two pages). They have decided to have their child assessed, although they are not yet open to accepting recommendations, since they feel they are best able to determine the abilities and needs of their child. They will continue to update their letter of intent on a yearly basis, because they do understand how important it is to keep a record for others of their own insights into this special child's abilities and limitations.

STEP 4

Select Your Professional Advisers

Time Frame: One Month

IT IS AT THIS STEP THAT PEOPLE'S minds come to a screeching halt. They've decided what they own and owe. They know what they want to achieve. Now they just need to go to some legal and financial professionals for assistance. But whom do they trust for advice? They don't know, so they do nothing, the worst possible course of conduct. Others simply hire the first attorney or financial planner they talk to. This is like marrying the first person you ever dated. Don't just go to one adviser and expect to be satisfied.

It takes time and effort to find exactly the right professionals for your needs. You

Six Steps to Planning for a Severely Disabled Child

1 **Try to accept the assessment of professionals.** Often parents of impaired children feel their children are better able to manage than the professionals indicate. This is probably because the professionals test the child as if the parents were not in the picture to assist the child—which is the true state of matters when parents become disabled or die. For this reason, the snapshot of children revealed by professional assessments often is closer to the truth than the parents' judgment.

2 **Write a letter of intent.** This is a letter written by parents, family members, and the child, if he or she is able to furnish input. The letter outlines the child's history, current status, and what future hopes the family has for the child. It covers such wide-ranging topics as housing, residential care, education, employment, medical history and care, behavior management, and social activities. This letter will be used as a basis for formulating a legal and financial plan for the child now and also for determining your intentions in the future, should those intentions come into question.

3 **Choose guardians and possibly an advocate for the child.** A guardian is a legal position that carries a wide range of authority to deal with issues from health to housing. An advocate is a nonlegal position that allows the chosen individual to assist the person with disabilities on a daily basis with practical problems.

should actively seek advisers who are on your wavelength—people you can talk to. Since an attorney is arguably the key adviser on your estate plan, you should begin to build your team of advisers by finding a good estate planning attorney.

Selecting a Legal Adviser

ALTHOUGH IT'S BEST NOT TO SEEK legal advice from your family and friends, they are still a great source for leads on potential candidates. Ask them to recommend attorneys who specialize in estate planning. Ask others as well. Try to figure out which law firms seem to get the most recommendations. To whom do lawyers go for their own estate planning? Who represents banks, hospitals, and other public institutions in your community? These are usually good places to begin your search.

4 **Determine the realistic cost of your plan and the resources available.** There are many financial planners available who are experienced in working with families of disabled children. These planners can review a letter of intent and help prepare a detailed financial analysis based on projected costs for the assistance the child may need.

5 **Create a funding plan.** If your child currently receives government benefits, it is important to create a plan that will maintain that eligibility. Bequeathing assets worth more than $2,000 to a disabled individual may eliminate eligibility for many benefits. The regulations are strict, so the most reliable way to leave an inheritance to a disabled child and still preserve eligibility may be through the use of a special-needs trust.

6 **Establish a special-needs trust.** This can be either a testamentary trust, created by will, or a living trust, established while the parents are still living. Most families prefer creating a living trust so they can begin to fund it for the future benefit of their child; they can use the trust funds to pay for current expenses (a good method for tracking expenses), and upon the death of the parent(s), the trust will continue to pay expenses for the child, uninterrupted by court delays.

In addition, check the *Martindale-Hubbell Law Directory,* which is usually located at either your local public library or a law library. This invaluable book not only lists attorneys and law firms but also rates them for excellence and specifies their areas of expertise. This is the resource you can most rely on when it comes to seeking reliable professional advice in the field of estate planning.

Again, it is generally a mistake to pinpoint only one attorney without talking to several, or to depend too much on what others say or think about him or her. To make a sound decision, you should talk to several attorneys, because you will be surprised at the differences between lawyers and how they view you as a client. In the final analysis, trust your instincts and go with a lawyer who has solid credentials, extensive experience in estate planning, and a willingness to listen to you and take time with your concerns. Then, rely on this professional to guide you in obtaining the other professionals you need.

Finding a Financial Adviser

WHAT CAN A FINANCIAL PLANNER do for you? The answer: He or she can assess where you are financially and design a plan to meet your financial goals. A good planner has the background, training, education, and experience to look beyond your financial statement and consider your family, tax, insurance, and investment concerns.

Today, with a volatile stock market, an uncertain job market, and free-wheeling use of credit cards, people are reluctant to spend hard-earned money to pay for the advice of a financial adviser. They often prefer to do their own investing. While this may work for them, most professional estate planners prefer to bring into the planning process a certified financial planner, someone who is qualified, objective, and trained to offer insight and suggestions to improve the client's future financial prospects.

Here are a few tips on finding a good financial adviser:

➤ Do not pick a financial adviser out of the Yellow Pages.

➤ Learn what some of the professional designations mean, such as certified public accountant, certified financial planner, and registered financial consultant. These titles can guide you in determining the adviser's area of expertise and level of experience.

➤ Know exactly what you want a financial planner to help you with.

➤ Determine your risk tolerance level—in other words, how much investment risk you are willing to take to get a higher return. A financial adviser will typically ask you some questions that will reveal your tolerance level.

➤ Ask family, friends, and coworkers for the names of their advisers.

➤ Interview no fewer than three advisers before you select one.

The most important thing you should assess is whether you and your adviser have the same investment philosophy. Make sure the adviser is listening to what you have to say, rather than selling you on his ideas about the market. Ask him questions to try to assess whether you think he will be a reliable adviser. Also, determine at the first interview how your adviser's fees will be paid: based on how many transactions you have, the investment results obtained, or an annual investment fee. What you don't need is a salesperson.

Credentials are important. Make sure the planner you select is licensed by the federal or state government. Ask to see the planner's Form ADV. Your state's securities agency has information on planners, including their Form ADV and CRD records for stockbrokers (North American Securities Administration Association's

Central Registration Depository). Check professional associations, such as the state bar association if the planner is a lawyer, or the state accountancy board if he or she is a certified public accountant (CPA).

The cost to retain the services of a certified financial planner usually runs from $100 an hour to $1,000 and up for a comprehensive financial plan. The cost will depend on the complexity of your needs. Make sure you understand all costs involved before you retain the services of a planner. Even if you aren't going to be charged for the service, you may be charged commissions when you buy or sell stock, a clear incentive for the planner to be aggressive in pushing certain financial instruments.

Here are some organizations you may want to consider. Most of these well-respected organizations offer certification and accreditation programs for members, and most can direct you to one or more advisers in your area.

➤ **Financial Planning Association.** The FPA administers the certified financial planner designation, and its membership includes certified financial planners and others involved in the financial planning process, such as accountants, attorneys, money managers, and so on. The FPA has major offices in Atlanta, Denver, and Washington, D.C. For more information, call 800-322-4237, or learn more about the organization at www.fpanet.org.

➤ **The National Association of Personal Financial Advisors (NAPFA).** NAPFA is a professional association of fee-only planners. Fee-only planners do not accept commissions on the financial products they recommend to you. For more information, call 888-FEE-ONLY; visit the association's Web site, www. napfa.org; or write to NAPFA at 355 West Dundee Road, Suite 200, Buffalo Grove, Illinois 60089.

➤ **The American Institute of Certified Public Accountants.** The AICPA is the professional association for CPAs, and it can help direct you to a CPA in your area. Call the AICPA at 212-596-6200; write to the Institute at 1211 Avenue of the Americas, New York, New York 10036-8775; or visit the AICPA's Web site, www.aicpa.org.

➤ **Society of Financial Service Professionals,** formerly the American Society of Chartered Life Underwriters and Chartered Financial Consultants. This organization administers the Chartered Life Underwriter (CLU) and Chartered Financial Consultant (ChFC) designations. These are financial planning designations with a strong insurance orientation. Write to the American Society at 270 South Bryn Mawr Ave., Bryn Mawr, Pennsylvania 19010-2195; call 610-526-2500; or visit the Society's Web site at www.asclu.org.

STEP 5

Choose Individuals to Serve as Fiduciaries

Time Frame: Two Weeks

NO MATTER HOW MUCH YOU LOVE YOUR family, sometimes it is a good idea to ask a disinterested friend or business associate to serve as a power of attorney or as a fiduciary in your trust or will. Very likely you will know exactly whom among your family and friends you want to ask for assistance, and you will know it almost as soon as you begin to think about it.

In arriving at your decision, remember that the person who will serve as a trustee or fiduciary or who will have your power of attorney must be able to:

➤ take charge of your property when you die or become disabled;

➤ find all of your assets; seek advice about them and handle the daily details of paying bills; keep your assets secure over a period of time; deal with your family and investment and legal advisers; pay taxes; and sell assets if necessary; and

➤ if an estate is involved, make distributions of your property to your beneficiaries.

You may not need someone who has special financial or legal skills, although both may be helpful. But the individuals to whom you are about to entrust your property should be:

➤ honest, organized, conscientious, good at details, and concerned about your family, although they need not be a family member;

➤ willing and able to do the job in an efficient manner without creating any dissension among your family or friends; and

➤ able to deal intelligently with your attorney, accountant, and investment advisers.

If you are selecting someone to serve as your power of attorney for health care, it may not be as important to find someone with specific administrative or financial skills. Instead, you might want the following type of person:

➤ someone you can trust with your health care decisions; someone who knows your deepest thoughts about the type of care you want in critical or terminal situations;

➤ an individual with whom you have discussed your general philosophy about life-sustaining measures and artificial medical intervention;

➤ one who knows your wishes about home care or about nursing home care; and

➤ most importantly, someone who is interested in you and your well-being; someone who will advocate for you and seek the best care for you in the long run.

After you have weighed these considerations, make a list of possible individuals, both family and friends, and spend no less than a week weighing the advantages and disadvantages of involving each person. You and only you can decide whom you want to trust, both during your lifetime and at the time of your death, to carry out your specific plans and wishes.

STEP 6

Execute All Legal and Financial Documents

Time Frame: One Month from Interview to Completion

THE SPECIFIC LEGAL TOOLS THAT YOU'LL use in your plan are determined by you and your professional advisers after much discussion. If you are lucky, and if your data is in order and complete enough to give your counselors a complete picture of your particular situation, they will be able to give, even at the first interview, some preliminary suggestions about options you may wish to consider.

When you have your first interview with your adviser, go prepared with all of the work sheets and checklists you have completed in this book or others. Be succinct, but make sure that you are able to give your basic financial snapshot at that first interview. Also, have clear estate planning goals in mind to discuss. It is good business and completely acceptable in offices of reputable attorneys to discuss legal fees and potential costs at this time. Foolish are the client and the attorney who wade into the deep waters of estate planning together without knowing what the cost might be.

After several discussions with your attorney, you should know the exact outline of your estate plan. Make a list of the documents the attorney will prepare for you and set a completion date for each step. Your work sheet for this stage of the plan could look something like the "Time Schedule for Estate Plan" shown on the following two pages.

Time Schedule for Estate Plan

MONTH	LEGAL DOCUMENTS	FOLLOW-UP ACTION REQUIRED
#1	POA for Health Care Have a primary and secondary POA	Give copy of document to your POA representative. Indicate where the original is kept. Discuss details with your POA representative. See that copies of this document are given to your physician(s), your family, and minister and hospital.
	Living Will	Give copy of document to designated person who will make life and death decisions. Discuss your wishes with that person very clearly. Discuss your plans with your family members.
	POA for Finances Have a primary and secondary POA	Give a copy of the document to designated person, or give the original to that person if the document will be used right now. Talk candidly about where your assets are located, bills you have, and problems that the POA may encounter in managing your finances.
#2	Last Will and Testament	Determine where to keep your will, either in a safety deposit box, a safe at home, or with a friend. Tell your fiduciary/family where your will is located.
#2-5	Keep following through with your tax adviser to determine how to maximize your assets and minimize your taxes. Adviser may assist in refining your estate plan.	Follow-through should consist of coordinating legal and tax advisers' advice.
#2-5	Begin to check on how your assets are titled, including bank accounts, stocks, bonds, real estate deeds, etc.	Request forms for change of ownership. Prepare to change the ownership or title of assets to allow you to integrate assets with plan.

MONTH	LEGAL DOCUMENTS	FOLLOW-UP ACTION REQUIRED
#3-4	Set up and sign any trust(s) documents	Make sure you fund your trust. Seek specific advice regarding exactly what funds to put into your trust; begin to transfer funds into your trust accordingly. An empty trust is not going to help you.
#5	Begin your funding program for your trust; finish the paperwork for changing the ownership on ALL of your assets to make sure that your legal plan and assets are tightly integrated.	Keep good records. Get copies of all ownership documents, especially copies of all of your deeds.
#6	Initiate or continue any gifting program.	Gift according to a plan. Get good advice, and keep careful records of your gifting program. Never gift unless you don't need the resources.
#6	Finish realigning your finances. Go back over your plan to make sure all of your legal documents are signed and filed in a safe place, and that all of your assets have been integrated into your estate plan.	Be satisfied with what you have done. Make an appointment with your adviser(s) to see them 12 to 18 months after you complete this first plan. Continue to review your assets and how they are titled as your circumstances change.

Work with your attorney to devise a timetable you both think is reasonable. You should try to keep yourself on this schedule, and you should call your attorney to make sure that he, too, knows you are expecting to meet the deadlines you have mutually established. Attorneys often get caught up in other emergencies and problems that come to their attention, so you may find that one of your most important roles is to keep your adviser on target with your project. Don't hesitate to do this. Generally, a client who calls and talks over things with the attorney will get a good response much sooner than the client who goes for one interview and then doesn't follow up at all. Keep the lines of communication open.

If you falter, delay, or worse yet, do nothing to complete the plan, your attorney may move on to other people who are serious about their planning, and you may be left in the dust with little to show except good intentions. Do your part to complete your plan. Get all information, addresses, phone numbers, reports, and other data requested by the attorney back to him or her just as soon as possible. So many times this lag from first interview to the compilation of all of the information leads to delays of months and sometimes even years. Don't let this happen to you. Get that information back to your attorney.

The attorney's job is to advise you how best to meet your goals; to draft all the legal documents necessary to achieve your goals; and to execute and bring to conclusion your plan. Together you have great strengths and will achieve a great plan. Don't let yourself or others down by your failure to follow through, because this step is critical to the success of your plan.

STEP 7

Align Your Assets with Your Estate Plan

Time Frame: One Month

AT THIS POINT, YOU SHOULD HAVE discussed the status of all of your assets and liabilities with your professional team. This puts you in a strong position to begin getting your finances into optimal alignment.

It is at this stage, for example, that you retitle assets to designate some as nonprobate assets. Or you may wish to equalize your assets with your spouse or transfer assets for your grandchildren into special accounts.

This is a time-consuming and tedious process. For instance, if you need to retitle your real estate and transfer it into a trust, all of your deeds must be changed, recorded in the legal records where you live, and transferred to the tax rolls. And if there is a trust company or investment company involved, numerous documents may have to be obtained, witnessed, and returned.

Similarly, you will have a great deal of legwork to do if you want to change the title on your stocks or bonds. First, if you have these assets in a street account (an account with a brokerage firm that holds all of your investments in your name but in their brokerage accounts), you must obtain all of the documents necessary to alter the present name on them. This often takes months to achieve.

Each one of your assets may have to be realigned in order to reflect your estate plan goals: to hold your assets in the best manner possible to avoid probate, to assist the next generation, to maximize assets, or to diminish taxes. All of these goals may require the complete reorganization of your assets, but the benefits will

When to Revise Your Estate Plan

IN GENERAL, YOU SHOULD revise your estate plan no less than every other year, or sooner if one of these events occurs:

➤ Marriage
➤ Divorce or separation
➤ The birth or adoption of a child
➤ The death of a family member
➤ The purchase or sale of a major asset (such as a house)
➤ A move to another state, particularly into or out of a community property state
➤ A dramatic change in finances (due to, say, an inheritance or a job loss)
➤ Disability or serious illness
➤ Retirement

come back to you many, many times over the years.

This step is usually the very last one that you will need to complete. Finish this work as rapidly as possible, because it is the final work you have to do. Try to make sure that you stick with it so that your assets and your legal documents are in alignment and your plan achieves the maximum integration. This is, after all, the most important aspect of all, as it smoothly enhances both the legal and financial realms of your life and work and achieves balance for both.

You Have Succeeded

THE TIME AND MONEY YOU HAVE SAVED by creating your estate plan are now yours to enjoy. You can be assured that if you are disabled or die, all of your assets are accessible to only those people you have chosen, and your legal documents are in place to minimize confusion and bureaucracy. You can have peace of mind that you planned now so others won't have to pay later: a perfect ending to the search for the right estate plan for you and yours.

Appendices

Contents

Appendix A

What to Do and What Not to Do When Someone Dies

Do

➤ *Call the funeral director to make proper arrangements* for the interment of the deceased. Take a family member or friend with you to help you remember all of the details. Explain what arrangements you want, understand the range of prices involved, and select what is most appropriate. But sign the contract for services only if you are the person who is legally authorized to make these arrangements; otherwise, you could end up being personally liable to pay for the services you request.

➤ *Ask for several certified death certificates,* as the fiduciary will need them to send to life insurance companies, employers, and stock brokerages. They are also necessary for other legal procedures, such as the transfer of accounts or real property titled as TOD, POD, or joint and survivorship assets. Try to determine as quickly as possible how many death certificates you will need.

➤ *Call your religious counselor* and ask for assistance, guidance, and support.

➤ *Notify family and friends* of the deceased. If you are not sure who should be notified, look in the person's address book and ask close friends. The notice of death will be published in the local newspaper, but it is more meaningful for family and friends to be informed ahead of time, if this is possible.

➤ *Find all of the decedent's important documents.* Try to locate all wills, trusts, insurance papers, and life insurance policies. Make a copy of the person's social security number and safety deposit box numbers. Also, make copies of all stock certificates, certificate of deposits, and U.S. bonds, as well as any other financial data you think could be pertinent. Collect all checking and savings account checkbooks and passbooks. Once you have assembled all of this information, you can begin to prepare a list of the decedent's assets.

➤ *Make a list of those checks* you believe should be written immediately and obtain copies of household bills, medical bills, and tax bills that may need to be paid. You may be unable to write checks or make withdrawals right after the decedent dies, because often those accounts are frozen until the proper party gives the bank or other institution proper tax and legal documents. However, someone should know which bills have priority and that you, or a fiduciary, will be able to write those checks as soon as possible.

➢ *Make an appointment with your attorney* if you are the spouse or fiduciary of the deceased. Find out what will be necessary to settle the estate. Initially you need to determine what process will be necessary to collect the decedent's assets, pay the bills, and make distributions from the estate. You also must determine the court costs, legal fees, and related costs of settling the deceased's business affairs.

➢ *Schedule an appointment with a tax accountant* to determine the status of the decedent's taxes. Was the person current in paying taxes or are income or property taxes due?

➢ *Locate the inheritance tax office* in your area. In most states, this is the office that handles administrative forms necessary to submit to a variety of banks and insurance companies before the assets of the policy benefits can be paid.

➢ *Advise the deceased's employer of the death.* Often it is a good idea to do this both by phone and in writing. Provide the employer with the person's Social Security number and date of death, and ask specifically to receive a written notification from the employer of a list of benefits and insurance, if any, in which the beneficiaries or estate may have a financial interest.

➢ *Notify Medicare of the death* if the person was receiving this benefit. List the full legal name, address, Social Security number, date of death, and cause of death.

➢ *Notify Social Security of the death* if the decedent was receiving this benefit. List the full legal name, address, Social Security number, date of death, and cause of death.

➢ *File a claim with the Social Security Administration* for the survivor's benefit, if applicable. Look for the address of this office under U.S. government offices in your local phone book.

➢ *Notify the Veterans Administration* if the person served in the U.S. military. A spouse or child may be eligible for death or disability benefits.

Do Not

➢ Do not enter into any contracts.
➢ Do not sign any legal documents until you are represented by an attorney.
➢ Do not comment on the wishes of the decedent, as expressed in his or her last will and testament.

➤ Do not advance any funds for the estate unless necessary, and then be sure to keep precise records of all expenditures for tax records and reimbursement later.

➤ Do not allow any use of the person's home or automobile unless you are specially authorized.

➤ Do not make any decisions regarding the deceased or his or her property until such time as a court has appointed you the fiduciary. The exception is if you are the spouse or child of the decedent.

➤ Do not be paralyzed by how overwhelming it seems to settle all of the individual's business affairs. Understandably, you will be grieving throughout this process and sorting through a great many issues, but you will find that you have enough time to accomplish everything. Make sure you get good legal and business advice about exactly how to proceed. Each day you will make progress, little by little, until you accomplish this large, important task.

Appendix B

The Cost of Administering Your Esture

I N DEVELOPING YOUR ESTATE PLAN, you may want to know what an attorney will charge your family to administer your estate, versus the fees for a fiduciary. Legal fees and the fees of the personal representative are usually set by state law or are governed by court supervision and vary widely from state to state. Information about the legal fees in your area is readily available from local bar associations.

Although it is often difficult for an attorney to tell you exactly what his or her fee may be to administer an estate, you should have a clear idea about the range before you or your family decide to retain the person. For every dollar that goes through a state probate process, you will pay attorney fees based in part on complexity, time expended, and the value of the estate involved. Fees may range from 3 to 5 percent of the gross value of the estate. An estate valued at $100,000 in probate assets may incur fees from $3,000 to $5,000.

Probate Expenses

STATE	FIDUCIARY FEE	ATTORNEY FEE
Alabama	2% of receipts and 2% of disbursements. Court considers additional factors.	Reasonable. Will be reviewed by court if a petition is filed.
Alaska	Reasonable customary fee is $10 to $20 per hour.	Reasonable.
Arizona	Reasonable.	Reasonable.
Arkansas	Not to exceed 10% of first $1,000; 5% of next $4,000; and 3% of balance, but more will be authorized if distributees benefit more.	Allowable as 5% of first $5,000; 4% of next $20,000; 3% of next $75,000; 2% of next $300,000; 2% of next $600,000 and 2% of balance.
California	Reasonable.	Reasonable.

STATE	FIDUCIARY FEE	ATTORNEY FEE
Colorado	Reasonable.	Reasonable.
Connecticut	Reasonable. Usually computed as a fixed percentage of the gross estate.	Reasonable.
Delaware	Reasonable.	Reasonable.
D.C.	Reasonable; subject to review.	Reasonable.
Florida	Reasonable.	Reasonable under sliding scale formula based on size of the estate. Additional compensation permitted for extraordinary services rendered for litigation or other complexities.
Georgia	2% on money received plus 2% fee on property delivered in kind. Testator and executor may agree by written contract on executor's compensation, which is binding on all.	Reasonable.
Hawaii	Reasonable.	Reasonable.
Idaho	Reasonable.	Reasonable.
Illinois	Reasonable.	Reasonable.
Indiana	Reasonable.	Reasonable.
Iowa	Fiduciaries and their legal representatives are allowed reasonable fees not to exceed the following percentages upon gross assets per Iowa inheritance tax purposes: 6% on the first $1,000; 4% on the excess up to $5,000; 2% on the excess over $5,000. Additional reasonable compensation permitted upon application for same.	Reasonable.
Kansas	Reasonable.	Reasonable.
Kentucky	May not exceed 5% of value of personal estate plus 5% of income collected, except court may award additional compensation for extraordinary services performed by fiduciary.	Reasonable.
Louisiana	Reasonable.	Reasonable.

STATE	FIDUCIARY FEE	ATTORNEY FEE
Maryland	Appropriate, but not to exceed 9% on property valued at $20,000 and $1,800 plus 3.6% of excess over $20,000.	Reasonable.
Massachusetts	As court may allow by local rules.	Reasonable.
Michigan	Reasonable.	Reasonable.
Minnesota	Reasonable.	Reasonable.
Mississippi	Each court fixes compensation.	Reasonable.
Missouri	Set by statute §473.153; commission on personal property and proceeds of sale of real estate.	Reasonable.
Montana	Reasonable; not to exceed 3% of first $40,000 of value of the estate and 2% of value over $40,000.	Shall not receive more than one and one-half times compensation allow able to personal representative.
Nebraska	Reasonable.	Reasonable.
Nevada	4% of first $15,000; 3% on next $85,000; and 2% on excess over $200,000.	Reasonable.
New Hampshire	Reasonable, pursuant to court approval.	Reasonable.
New Jersey	Reasonable.	Reasonable.
New Mexico	Reasonable.	Reasonable.
New York	5% for first $100,000; 4% for next $200,000; 3% for next $700,000; 2% for next $4,000,000; 2% for all sums over $5,000,000.	Reasonable.
North Carolina	A commission not to exceed 5% of receipts and expenditures.	Reasonable.
North Dakota	Compensation is subject to court review.	Reasonable.
Ohio	4% of first $100,000; 3% on next $300,000; 2% on balance; compensation allowed for extraordinary services.	Reasonable.
Oklahoma	A commission of 5% on first $1,000; 4% on next $5,000; 2% on excess over $6,000. Compensation for extraordinary services.	Reasonable.

STATE	FIDUCIARY FEE	ATTORNEY FEE
Oregon	7% of any sum not exceeding $1,000; 4% of all above $1,000 and not exceeding $10,000; 3% of all above $10,000 and not exceeding $50,000; 2% of all above $50,000; 1% of all not subject to court jurisdiction.	Reasonable.
Pennsylvania	Reasonable.	Reasonable.
Rhode Island	Discretion of court.	Reasonable.
South Carolina	Not to exceed 5% of value of personal property plus sales proceeds of real property plus 5% of income of estate.	Reasonable.
South Dakota	Reasonable.	Reasonable.
Tennessee	Reasonable compensation.	Reasonable.
Texas	5% of all sums received in cash and 5% of all services paid in cash on order of court; not to exceed 5% of the gross estate.	Reasonable.
Utah	Reasonable.	Reasonable.
Vermont	$4 a day and further reasonable compensation.	Reasonable.
Virginia	Reasonable.	Reasonable.
Washington	Reasonable.	Reasonable.
West Virginia	Reasonable expenses and compensation are allowed to personal representative in settling accounts. Corporation usually receives 5% of receipts.	Reasonable.
Wisconsin	Necessary expenses plus commission at the rate of 2% of inventory less mortgages or liens plus net corpus gains or rate agreed upon by personal representative and decedent or persons who receive majority of estate. Additional fees for extraordinary services.	Reasonable.
Wyoming	Fee based on probate estate as follows: on first $1,000, 10%;	Reasonable.

STATE	FIDUCIARY FEE	ATTORNEY FEE
Wyoming (cont'd)	from $1,000 to $5,000, 5%; between $5,000 and $20,000, 3%; for amounts over $20,000, 2%.	Reasonable.

Sources: *Martindale-Hubbell Law Digest, 2000;* www.lexislawpublishing.com; www.law.cornell.edu.

In most states the compensation to the personal representative—who is responsible for guiding the estate proceedings through the state and federal probate process and the complicated morass of rules and regulations—is required to be "reasonable." This simply means what is equitable and fair under the circumstances of each estate proceeding. After all, some estates are very simple to administer, and others are extremely time-consuming, difficult, and frustrating.

Criteria to determine reasonable compensation include the following:

➤ How much time and labor is necessary
➤ The novelty and difficulty of settling the estate
➤ The skill required to perform the service properly
➤ The likelihood that the acceptance of duties will preclude other employment by the fiduciary
➤ The fee customarily charged in the locality
➤ The nature and value of the assets of the estate, and the amount of income earned by the estate, the responsibilities and potential liabilities assumed by the person
➤ The time limitations imposed by the circumstances
➤ The experience, reputation, diligence, and ability of the person performing the services

What if the will specifies the compensation to be paid to the personal representative? What if the decedent entered into a contract with the representative on the compensation for his duties? In many states the personal representative may renounce—and in other states, must renounce—the contract before qualifying as a personal representative, so that the fiduciary to be appointed will have no financial interest in the outcome of the proceedings. In fact, some states do not allow the appointment of fiduciaries who have made contracts for compensation, fearing that the compensation issues could overshadow the duties involved.

If there is no will and an intestate proceeding is required, the personal representative may receive, as a reasonable fee, commissions upon the amount of personal property accounted for by the personal representative, excluding personal

property not defined as assets, as follows:
- ➢ on the first $1,000, at the rate of 5 percent;
- ➢ on all sums over $1,000 and not exceeding $5,000, 4 percent; and
- ➢ on all sums over $5,000, at the rate of 2.5 percent.

How is real estate handled? Often it is treated as if it were personal property; if it is sold during the estate proceedings, then the representative may receive as a fee a percentage of the sale price.

The exact compensation paid to a personal representative and the attorney who may be retained to assist the representative vary from state to state, but in all cases they are computed according to the case law, statutes, and custom of each individual state. If you are involved in any estate proceeding, you should have a firm understanding of the compensation involved early on. If you don't know, find out.

Appendix C

Web Sites for Estate Planning

Advance Directives and Living Will Sites

www.aarp.com: This is the Web site of the American Association of Retired Persons. It contains a great deal of information on elder law and estate planning issues.

www.abanet.org: This is the Web site of the American Bar Association Commission on Legal Problems of the Elderly. It offers excellent material on advance directives.

Community Property Sites

www.calcpa.org: This is the Web site of the California Society of CPAs; it offers information about community property issues.

www.ca-probate.com: Information and links about community property and estate planning in California.

www.findlaw.com/california: Links to community property information.

Estate Planning Sites

www.dtonline.com: Offers an excellent introduction to estate planning. This is the Web site of Deloitte and Touche, one of the largest accounting firms in the United States.

www.estateattorney.com: Provides ongoing information on wills, estate tax, trusts, probate, Medicaid, and elder law.

www.estateplanforyou.com: American Academy of Estate Planning Attorneys' site.

www.estateplanning.com: Information and links to estate planning material.

www.estateplanninglinks.com: This site has multiple links to other Web sites for information about estate planning, IRAs, valuation, life and long-term care insurance, elder law, probate and living trusts, and retirement planning.

www.nnepa.com: This is the Web site of the National Network of Estate Planning

Attorneys. It's primarily for attorney members, but there's also a good deal of information on estate planning for the layperson.

www.ll.georgetown.edu: This is the E. B. Williams Law Library of Georgetown University. You can use this site to search for legal information and links.

www.lawfind.com: A search tool to find legal information on the Web.

www.moneycentral.msn.com: Information about general estate planning.

www.mtpalermo.com: A site to read before you consult an attorney about estate planning. Good solid info with links to other sites.

www.mycounsel.com: An easy-to-use site that focuses on a variety of legal issues, including estate planning.

www.lifenet.com: This site offers calculators for a variety of different estate and financial planning considerations.

www.nafep.com: Site of the National Association of Financial and Estate Planners, with easy-to-understand info.

www.nolo.com: An easy read on estate planning topics.

www.prudential.com: Contains an estate plan work sheet.

www.savewealth.com: This site offers financial news plus estate planning strategies and other related resources.

www.schwab.com: Estate tax and probate calculator planning guide.

www.seniors-site.com: This site features a series of articles on wills, estate tax, trusts, probate, Medicaid, and elder law.

www.seniorlaw.com: Search engine for information about elder law, Medicare, trusts, wills, and estate planning.

www.uslaw.com: General information about estate planning.

Financial Sites

www.annuityscout.com: An interesting site for info about annuities.

www.bankrate.com: At this site, you can compute the return on your investments with one of its many calculators.

www.cashflowzone.com: Information and tools for cash-flow issues.

www.financialplan.about.com: General financial planning site.

www.kiplinger.com: Contains good basic information about insurance.

www.moneycalculators.com: Check out this site, a collection of business and finance calculators, for its net worth calculators.

www.prudential.com: Features an estate plan work sheet.

www.quicken.com: Good all-around site to read about Keogh plans; a great explanation and planner to compare the traditional IRA with a Roth. You can launch the planner program and print the results.

www.smartmoney.com: This site offers solid general investing information.

www.thestreet.com: Another excellent investing site.

www.vanguard.com: This is the Web site of one of the largest mutual fund providers. It offers excellent information on investing and retirement planning.

www.wallstreetcity.com: General investing information.

Probate Process Sites

www.law.cornell.edu/uniform/probate.html: In-depth information about probate, including the Uniform Probate Code and the steps involved in the process.

www.priweb.com/internetlawlib/1.htm: Links to primary source material, such as the Internal Revenue Code and state statutes.

www.usalawcentral.com: Offers good legal information, both general and specific, about joint-and-survivorship status.

Titling Assets

www.premack.com: This is the Texas Elder Law Archive, and it provides readable information about life estates and other estate planning topics.

Trusts

www.friran.com: Describes itself as the "legal survival Web site." Among the many other legal topics, it covers elder law and estate planning, and often has articles on trusts.

www.mbscott.com/intrust.html: This is the site of an estate planning attorney; it offers some good background on trusts.

Glossary

Abatement. The legal process that occurs when assets left by a decedent are insufficient to pay the debts and expenses of administration as well as the legacies and devisees (recipients of real estate gifts from the will). Distributions to beneficiaries are reduced in proportion to the funds available.

Abstract of Title. An abbreviated memorandum of the history and legal status of a specific parcel of real property, including a listing of mortgages, taxes, and other liens, together with the names of past owners.

Accession. The right a legal owner has to the increase in value of an asset.

Accumulated Trust. A trust that receives the interest only from funds invested elsewhere.

Acknowledgment. A formal statement at the end of a legal document that "acknowledges" that the person signing the same is doing so of his or her own free will.

Ademption. A situation that occurs when a specific item of property that the decedent gifted by will is no longer in existence at the time of death.

Adjusted Basis. A tax term that refers to the basic cost of an asset plus or minus certain allowable gain or loss computations.

Administration. The process whereby the decedent's estate is administered or settled by collection of assets, payment of debts, and distribution of assets within the probate procedure established by the decedent's state of residence.

Administrative Expenses. Those expenses incurred, usually through the probate process, (1) to administer the estate of a decedent: attorney fees, court costs, and appraiser fees; or (2) to administer a trust.

Administrative Powers. The specific authority given to the fiduciary under a will or by statute to settle a decedent's estate, such as the power to sell real estate without an order of a court.

Administrator. A person appointed to settle intestate estates, which are those in which a person dies without leaving a will.

Adopted Child. A child who has been adopted by an adult(s) who is not his biological parent.

Adoption. A legal procedure created by each state to permit nonrelated adult(s) to become legal parent(s) to a child or an adult who is not a biological child.

Affidavit. A written statement made under oath (usually before a notary) that declares the truth of certain facts contained in a legal document.

Alimony. A payment, usually court-ordered, for one spouse to pay another spouse; it may also be a division of real and personal property defined as alimony by court order.

Alternate Date of Valuation. A date other than the actual date of death that may be used to evaluate estate assets to determine the amount of taxes due.

Appreciated Property. Property that has increased in value.

Augmented Estate. An estate that has been added to or has increased in value after the person's death.

Beneficiary. A person or institution who inherits assets under a will, trust, or insurance policy.

Bequest. A gift of personal property (not real estate) under a decedent's will.

Breach. A person's failure to perform a duty required by a contract.

Charitable Gift. A monetary gift made to a religious, charitable, educational, scientific, medical, or similar organization that has tax-exempt status.

Charitable Lead Trust. A trust used to maximize the donor's tax benefit for gifts made to charitable institutions. (See Charitable Remainder Trust.)

Charitable Remainder Trust. A trust designed to accept gifts from a person who receives income during his or her lifetime, with the principal of the trust payable to charity, which gives the donor maximized tax benefits.

Child. Any person less than eighteen years old.

Class Gift. A gift made to a certain group of individuals, such as nieces, nephews, cousins, aunts, uncles.

Clifford Trust. A trust used for a certain term of years to provide distribution in the future for a set purpose, usually to pay for a college education; often created by grandparents to provide a college education for grandchildren.

Codicil. An addition, amendment, or modification to a will, which must be in writing, signed, witnessed, and notarized in the same manner required by state law for a Last Will and Testament.

Community Property. Property classified in certain states as owned by spouses in certain portions, regardless of how the title to the asset reads. A car titled to a wife may, in such states, be classified as spousal property shared by the husband. (See Separate Property; Transmuted Property.)

Community Property State. A state that has legislation to define the nature of each asset owned by an individual that dictates how that property will be classified and distributed under certain circumstances, such as death or divorce.

Co-ownership of Property. When two or more people own property as co-owners, each owns an undivided interest in the property.

Corpus. The assets held by a trust.

Custodial Account. An account under control of a custodian (an adult) for the benefit of another (usually a child).

Death Taxes. Those taxes imposed by states and the federal government upon the estate of a deceased person.

Debtor. A person or entity who owes another cash, goods, or services.

Decedent. A person who has died.

Decedent's Estate. The assets and debts of an individual who has died.

Deed. A legal document that conveys a real estate interest to another.

Deferred Compensation. Earned compensation that is invested in a plan for withdrawal at a later time.

Descendant. An individual who is related by blood to a deceased person.

Devise. A gift of real estate in a will.

Disclaimer. A legal document that declines a gift from a will, trust, or other contract, such as an insurance policy.

Disinherit. A property owner refuses to acknowledge or gift property to a biological relative, such as a parent refusing to gift property to a child.

Distribution in Kind. Property distributed in a probate procedure. "In kind" means that the specific item referred to in a will is distributed, as opposed to the value of the item.

Divorce. A legal termination of the marriage contract between spouses.

Document. Any writing with legally binding significance.

Domicile. A place where one intends to live permanently.

Donor. One who makes a gift to another, usually through a will or trust.

Durable Power of Attorney. A person gives to another certain "power(s)" to manage property in the event of disability for as long as the disability remains.

Election to Take Against the Will. A legal right granted by certain states, only to a spouse, to elect to receive a set statutory share of the deceased spouse's estate rather than follow the decedent's will.

Employee Retirement Income Security Act (ERISA). Enacted by Congress in 1974 to safeguard the soundness of retirement plans for employee protection.

Employee Stock Ownership Plan (ESOP). A plan whereby stock in a corporation is transferred to the employees of a company.

ERISA. (See Employee Retirement Income Security Act.)

ESOP. (See Employee Stock Ownership Plan.)

Estate. All of the property one owns.

Estate Assets. Those assets owned by a person at the time of death.

Estate Planning. The process integrating financial and legal planning for life and death, to provide maximum benefit to an individual during lifetime and to his or her family and friends at the time of death.

Estate Taxes. Taxes imposed by a government entity—state or federal—upon those assets owned by a person at the time of death.

Executor. The person named in a will to administer the decedent's will.

Fees. The amount charged by an attorney, financial adviser, or trustee for services rendered, based upon work performed, time expended, and complexity.

Fiduciary. One who owes a legal duty to another, such as an administrator or trustee.

Funeral Arrangements. Plans made to either bury or cremate the body of a person who has died.

Future Property Interest. An interest in existing property that will vest in the future.

Gift. A transfer of property from one to another without compensation.

Gift Tax. A tax imposed by the IRS upon a gift over a certain sum per year.

Grantor. One who owns and conveys land to another.

Grantor Retained Income Trust (GRIT). A trust in which the owner, known as the grantor, keeps the income of the trust, although the principal may belong to another.

Guardian. One who is legally appointed to care for another person and often to make all financial decisions.

Guardian of the Estate. One who is appointed (usually by a court of law) to safeguard, manage, and invest the financial assets of another.

Guardian of the Minor. The natural guardian of a minor is usually a parent, unless a court appoints a disinterested person in that capacity.

Guardian of the Person. One who is appointed (usually by a court of law) to make all health care decisions for another.

Guardian of the Property. One who is appointed (usually by a court of law) to safeguard and protect the property of another.

Heirs at Law. Those individuals designated by state law who are lineal descendants of a deceased person, who will inherit if there is no will.

Individual Retirement Account (IRA). A retirement account for individuals who do not qualify for certain other plans, it often offers tax advantages.

Inheritance. Property distributed to heirs and beneficiaries after death.

Inheritance Tax. Tax levied upon the value of property received from a decedent.

Insurance. An agreement whereby a company, such as an insurance company, provides funds in return for the payment of premiums to insure against the loss of life or property.

Insurance Trust. A trust that is funded by insurance and not by stock, bonds, or real estate.

Inter Vivos Trust. (See Living Trust.)

Intestate. A person who dies without leaving a will.

Irrevocable Trust. Once it is established, this trust may be modified as provided by the trust instrument involved, but it cannot be revoked.

Issue. A legal term that may mean either (1) the point of law disputed in litigation or (2) the lineal descendants of a decedent.

Joint-and-Survivorship. An account, stock, or deed that is co-owned by the named parties jointly, in which the respective interest of each at death passes automatically to the survivor(s).

Joint Bank Account. A bank account in the name of two or more individuals, each of whom has the power to withdraw all of the funds in the account, regardless of who contributed the funds.

Joint Ownership of Property. (See Joint Tenancy.)

Joint Tenancy. Co-ownership (usually of land) by two or more individuals; each co-owner has certain legal rights during his lifetime, and at death, a survivorship right may be involved, depending upon state law.

Keogh Plan. A pension plan (commonly known as the HR-10 Plan) established for a self-employed individual as a retirement fund that has certain tax benefits.

Lapsed Legacies. A gift made to another in a will that expires (or lapses) for some legal reason so that the gift does not take place. A lapsed gift goes into the residue of an estate and is distributed according to the residual terms of the will.

Last Will and Testament. A legal document created by an individual who owns property to distribute that property at the time of death; commonly called a will.

Legacy. A gift of personal property made according to a decedent's will.

Life Estate. An interest in land that lasts only during the lifetime of the person who owns the life interest.

Life Expectancy. How long one is predicted to live. Actuaries determine longevity for life insurance companies to determine the cost of premiums for life insurance policies.

Life Insurance. An insurance contract on the life of an individual that pays a set sum upon the death of that person to a person named in the policy as the beneficiary.

Life Interest. An interest in real property that lasts only for the lifetime of the individual who receives the interest.

Lineal Descendants. Blood relatives of a decedent.

Liquid Assets. The cash assets of an individual or a business.

Liquidity of the Estate. The cash on hand in an estate proceeding from which to pay bills, fees, taxes, and distributions to beneficiaries. An estate is very liquid if it contains checking, savings, and related accounts with few, if any, bills.

Living Revocable Trust. A living trust can be revoked at any time by the individual who created it during his/her lifetime. After the death of that individual, however, the trust becomes revocable or irrevocable according to its terms.

Living Trust. A trust funded during the lifetime of the person establishing it. Known in legal terminology as an "inter vivos trust."

Living Will. A legal document, permitted by some states, that permits one to give to another the power to determine the use of life-sustaining medical equipment under certain circumstances.

Marital Agreement. An agreement made between a husband and wife during their marriage. Some states do not permit spouses to enter into these contracts; other states have specific statutes permitting the contract under certain circumstances.

Marital Deduction. A tax term used by the IRS to connote a deduction permitted to married couples.

Marital Deduction Trust. A trust created by a husband and wife (which may be a living trust or a testamentary trust) drafted in such a way as to maximize tax savings upon the deaths of the parties to the trust.

Marital Living Trust. A trust created by a husband and wife during their lifetimes to maximize savings and provide management of their assets and/or estates.

Marital Property. A term having great significance in community property states. Generally, in those states it means the property accumulated by the spouses during the marriage. It is designated as belonging to both parties, as opposed to belonging exclusively to one or the other of them.

Medicaid. A government assistance program for nursing home and medical care, administered by each state for the benefit of qualified adults.

Medicare. A government assistance program for hospital and medical care administered by the Social Security Administration for the benefit of qualified individuals.

Minor. An individual who is not an adult as defined by law in each state. Most states provide that a minor is a person who is under the age of eighteen.

Mortgage. A legal document (usually accompanied by a promissory note) that is recorded as an official lien against the real estate upon which the mortgage attaches.

Mutual Wills. Some states permit a husband and wife to execute one common will that both sign, making it the will for each. In other states, this practice is not permitted. Common practice today is for each person to execute his or her own separate will.

Net Taxable Estate. Tax terminology for the total sum of a decedent's assets against which an estate tax may be levied.

Next of Kin. (1) Those individuals closest in blood to an individual or (2) those entitled to inherit from a deceased person by the laws of intestate succession as defined by each state.

Nuncupative Will. An oral will. (See Oral Will.)

Oral Will. An oral statement made by an individual during a last illness, with the intent of disposing of his property after death. Oral wills seldom hold up in court.

Organ Donation. Human organs donated to another at the time of death.

Payable-on-Death (POD) Account. An account, usually in a bank, in which the owner can designate who is to receive the account when he or she dies.

Personal Property. Items that are movable, such as a pen, a table, or a car, as distinguished from real property (land), which is a permanently fixed asset.

Personal Representative. One who represents the estate of another. May also apply to an attorney who is representing a person.

Pour-Over Trust. A provision in a trust that provides that the trust's assets "pour over" into a will or another trust.

Power of Appointment. The power existing in a will or trust to appoint an individual or institution, such as a bank, to perform certain acts.

Power of Attorney. A legal document that gives another person the right to make decisions for you.

Power of Attorney for Health Care. A legal document that gives another person the legal authority to make health care decisions for you, including the right to decide life-and-death issues pertaining to life-sustaining equipment.

Powers. A broad general term used in a variety of legal instruments to refer to the specific rights one has been given, as defined by language in a will, a trust, or a power of attorney document.

Prenuptial Agreement. A contract entered into by a man and woman prior to marriage to determine primarily the distribution of their respective assets in the event of divorce or death.

Presumption of Death. A statutory determination of who died first when two spouses die simultaneously. Most states have a statute providing that in circumstances when it is not possible to determine who predeceased the other, for legal purposes each is presumed to have died "before the other."

Probate Assets. Assets defined by state law that are subject to a probate court or administrative process.

Probate Court. The court that deals with the settlement of a decedent's estate.

Probate Fees. Court costs, attorney fees, administrative fees, and related expenses that are charged in a probate estate proceeding.

Probate Process. The procedure, which varies by state, required by law to collect assets of a decedent's estate, pay bills and taxes, settle disputes, and distribute the estate.

Q-Tip Trust. Known in legal terminology as a "qualified terminable interest property" trust, this is a trust created for spouses and devised to meet IRS standards, which allow the principal assets of such a trust to qualify for inclusion in computations of the marital deduction at the time of death.

Qualified Terminal Interest Property Trust. (See Q-Tip Trust.)

Real Estate. Land, as opposed to personal property, which consists of movable objects. Real estate is referred to in legal terminology as "real property."

Real Property. Land and that property permanently affixed to the land, such as a house or other permanent structure.

Residual Bequest. The gift left to a beneficiary in the will of a decedent after other prior gifts have been made.

Residual Property. The property a beneficiary receives according to the residual clause in a decedent's will.

Residuary Beneficiary. A beneficiary who receives the "residue" of an estate according to a decedent's will, usually after others have received special or specific gifts designated by the will.

Retirement Plan. A specific plan to take effect at the time of an employee's retirement from work. Such plans usually have tax advantages to permit an employer to receive a tax deduction for contributing to the plan and to permit the employee to delay tax recognition of income earned until it is received in the future.

Revocable Living Trust. A trust established and in operation during your lifetime, as opposed to a testamentary trust, which is established at the time of death.

Roth IRA. An individual retirement account that permits qualified contributions to a defined plan for tax advantages. All interest earned on monies within the Roth is accrued tax free.

Separate Property. Property held separately by a husband or a wife in community property states to distinguish it from a community property asset.

Settlor. A trust term that describes the person who is establishing a trust by placing property "in trust" for another. A settlor may also be called a donor of the trust.

Spendthrift Clause. A clause, usually in a trust, providing that a beneficiary of the trust cannot transfer or encumber the assets of such a trust. This ensures that a beneficiary who is not financially responsible will be protected against himself.

Spray Trust. A trust whose principal assets will be distributed or "sprayed" to beneficiaries as they attain a certain age.

Springing Durable Power of Attorney. Many states have this legal document, which is a power of attorney (usually for financial matters) that "springs" into effect if and when a specified event occurs in the future.

Sprinkling Provision. A trust term designating how the assets of the trust are to be distributed, or "sprinkled," to its beneficiaries.

Statutory Will. The will each state creates for you if you have not created your own.

Successor Trustee. An individual or institution designated in a trust document to assume the job of trustee if the primary trustee is unable or unwilling to serve in that capacity.

Survivorship Account. Usually a bank account titled to two or more individuals that provides that the account will pass to the "survivor(s)" when one of the titled owners dies.

Survivorship Deed. A deed titled to two or more individuals that provides that the real property described in the deed will pass to the "survivor(s)" when one of the titled owners dies.

Tax. That sum of money due and owing to the state or federal government or both upon property, income, and an estate.

Taxable Estate. That portion of an estate against which a tax is applied to determine the amount of taxes due and payable. For federal estate tax purposes, it is the gross estate less allowable estate deductions, credits, and charitable gifts.

Tenancy in Common. An interest in land held by two or more people in which each is entitled to the use and possession of the whole.

Testamentary Trust. A trust created in a person's will that is funded and goes into effect after the person's death.

Testate. An individual who died leaving a will.

Testator. One who makes a will.

Transmuted Property. Property that has been altered or "transmuted" by the actions of the parties.

Trust. A legal document created for a certain purpose in which you (known as the settlor, grantor, or donor) transfer assets into a trust to be managed by a trustee for the benefit of yourself or another (known as the beneficiary of the trust).

Trust Corpus. The assets of the trust.

Trustee. That individual designated in a trust to manage the trust.

Trustee Powers. Rights set forth in a trust that specify what authority the trustee is to have. These powers may be broad or limited.

Trust for Minor. A trust established for the benefit of a minor.

Trust Property. The assets owned by the trust, also referred to as the "corpus" of the trust.

Will. A legally binding document created by the owner of property that specifies how the property is to be distributed at the time of death.

Will Contest. A legal proceeding seeking to invalidate a will.

I n d e x

ABOUT BLOOMBERG

Bloomberg L.P., founded in 1981, is a global information services, news, and media company. Headquartered in New York, the company has nine sales offices, two data centers, and 79 news bureaus worldwide.

Bloomberg, serving customers in 100 countries around the world, holds a unique position within the financial services industry by providing an unparalleled range of features in a single package known as the BLOOMBERG PROFESSIONAL™ service. By addressing the demand for investment performance and efficiency through an exceptional combination of information, analytic, electronic trading, and Straight Through Processing tools, Bloomberg has built a worldwide customer base of corporations, issuers, financial intermediaries, and institutional investors.

BLOOMBERG NEWS℠, founded in 1990, provides stories and columns on business, general news, politics, and sports to leading newspapers and magazines throughout the world. BLOOMBERG TELEVISION®, a 24-hour business and financial news network, is produced and distributed globally in seven different languages. BLOOMBERG RADIO™ is an international radio network anchored by flagship station BLOOMBERG® WBBR 1130 in New York.

In addition to the BLOOMBERG PRESS® line of books, Bloomberg publishes *BLOOMBERG® MARKETS, BLOOMBERG PERSONAL FINANCE™*, and *BLOOMBERG® WEALTH MANAGER.* To learn more about Bloomberg, call a sales representative at:

Frankfurt:	49-69-92041-200	São Paulo:	5511-3048-4530
Hong Kong:	85-2-2977-6600	Singapore:	65-212-1200
London:	44-20-7330-7500	Sydney:	61-2-9777-8601
New York:	1-212-318-2200	Tokyo:	81-3-3201-8950
San Francisco:	1-415-912-2980		

FOR IN-DEPTH MARKET INFORMATION AND NEWS, visit BLOOMBERG.COM®, which draws from the news and power of the BLOOMBERG PROFESSIONAL™ service and Bloomberg's host of media products to provide high-quality news and information in multiple languages on stocks, bonds, currencies, and commodities, at **www.bloomberg.com.**

ABOUT THE AUTHOR

STEPHEN BELLAMY

The Honorable Jane B. Lucal has had a long and diverse legal career. She has served as Judge of the Common Pleas Court, Probate Division, for Erie County, Ohio, since 1985. Judge Lucal served as an assistant prosecuting attorney and later as a private law practitioner in Ohio. Early in her career she also worked as an attorney for the Interstate Commerce Commission in Washington, D.C.

As a probate judge, Jane B. Lucal has presided over hundreds of cases in the probate court, both simple and complex, in which she has seen both good and bad estate plans. As a practicing attorney, she has drafted documents from simple wills to complex trusts for multifamily generational estates. She appeared on a recent *Dateline* segment discussing a controversial adoption case over which she presided.

Judge Lucal has published articles in many professional publications, including *The National Law Journal*, the *Ohio Probate Newsletter*, the *Ohio Northern University Law Review*, and the *Computer Users Legal Reporter*. She currently teaches, writes, and lectures about various aspects of estate planning.